Queer exceptions

Manchester University Press

theatre
theory • practice
• performance •

series editors
MARIA M. DELGADO
MAGGIE B. GALE
PETER LICHTENFELS

advisory board
Michael Billington, Sandra Hebron, Mark Ravenhill, Janelle Reinelt,
Peter Sellars, Joanne Tompkins

This series will offer a space for those people who practise theatre to have a dialogue with those who think and write about it.

The series has a flexible format that refocuses the analysis and documentation of performance. It provides, presents and represents material which is written by those who make or create performance history, and offers access to theatre documents, different methodologies and approaches to the art of making theatre.

The books in the series are aimed at students, scholars, practitioners and theatre-visiting readers. They encourage reassessments of periods, companies and figures in twentieth-century and twenty-first-century theatre history, and provoke and take up discussions of cultural strategies and legacies that recognise the heterogeneity of performance studies.

also available

Queer exceptions

Solo performance in neoliberal times

STEPHEN GREER

Manchester University Press

Published by Manchester University Press
Altrincham Street, Manchester M1 7JA
www.manchesteruniversitypress.co.uk

British Library Cataloguing- in- Publication Data
A catalogue record for this book is available from the British Library

ISBN 978 1 5261 1369 6 hardback
ISBN 978 1 5261 1370 2 paperback

First published 2019

The publisher has no responsibility for the persistence or accuracy of URLs for any external or third- party internet websites referred to in this book, and does not guarantee that any content on such websites is, or will remain, accurate or appropriate.

Typeset by Out of House Publishing

CONTENTS

FIGURES

ACKNOWLEDGEMENTS

This book was conceived, researched and written in Glasgow and London over a period of three busy years. It would not have been possible without the support and generosity of friends, colleagues and theatre-makers who have shared their time, energy and insights with me.

For the conversations about comedy, writing and giving me a place to stay in London, thanks to Dave and Danielle; for giving me a home in Chicago and bringing a show to Glasgow, thanks to Dan and Casey; for Sunday morning coffee, thanks to Harry and Jon; for being funny, generous and brilliant friends, thanks to Idil and Neil.

I would also like to extend thanks to friends and colleagues who took the time to read and offer thoughts on draft chapters or give feedback on conference and seminar papers leading to this book – in particular, Dee Heddon, Carl Lavery, Liz Tomlin, Margaret Ames and Gareth Evans. I am also very grateful to the artists, performers and theatre-makers who agreed to interviews during the course of this project, notably Rachel Mars, Ron Athey, Scottee and FK Alexander. A large part of the development of this book owes to conversations and debates with students, starting with those who took the original 'Queer Exceptions' course at the University of Glasgow in 2014. For the questions, trust and sheer hard work: many, many thanks. I am also grateful to the photographers who have kindly given me permission to reproduce their work here.

Short sections of this book appear elsewhere in print. Parts of chapter 1 were first published as 'What Money Can't Buy: The Economies of Adrian Howells' in Deirdre Heddon and Dominic Johnson (eds), *It's All Allowed: The Performances of Adrian Howells* (London: Intellect, 2016). Discussion of the vacuum cleaner in chapter 6 appears in extended form as 'Between Care and Self-care: Dramaturgies of Mindfulness in the Work of the Vacuum Cleaner', *Scottish Journal of Performance* 5: 1 (2018).

Introduction

In the opening moments of *Our Carnal Hearts* (2016) – a show about envy, competition and 'the ugly bits of ourselves we would never usually admit' – theatre-maker Rachel Mars offers up a ritual invocation to 'millionaires and billionaires and executives and Wall Street' before leading the audience in collective rendition of Spandau Ballet's pop hit *Gold* (1983). Performed by Mars, accompanied by singers Rhiannon Armstrong, Louise Mothersole, Orla O'Flanagan and Rachel Weston, the show straddles church service, group therapy session and ritual intervention in staging a darkly comic satire of capitalism's celebration of avarice as well as our own personal practices of self-congratulatory individualism. With the audience positioned to confront itself across the four sides of the stage, *Our Carnal Hearts* invites recognition of envy as a communal affect which turns us against our neighbour. In one narrative thread, Mars tells the parable of a fairy who knocks on your door and offers to grant any wish with the catch that

> Your best friend, your colleague, your associate, your team mate, your rival, that person you know who is like you, but better, they get double of what you wish for. And you say [pause] cut out one of my eyes. (Mars 2016)

Jabbing at a culture that requires us to always want more while labouring to conceal the signs of our greed, the show provokes us to acknowledge our complicit and even pleasurable attachment to that which may be socially or personally destructive. Standing in the middle of the room, Mars is our surrogate and scapegoat: the representative of a community of which she is not quite a part.

This book is a study of solo performance that explores the contentious relationship between identity, individuality and the singular subject in neoliberal times. Drawing together works from the overlapping fields of theatre, performance, cabaret, live art and stand-up comedy, it sets out to trace the cultural significance of exceptional, threshold subjects who are neither wholly excluded nor fully assimilated, and instead occupy a suspended relation to the social and political sphere. Focusing on critical readings of performance in the UK and from across Europe, each chapter is structured by a different figure – the entrepreneur, the martyr, the pariah, the misfit, the stranger, the killjoy and the optimist. Presented as critical analogies for describing how cultural and political values are concentrated or dispersed, each figure offers a different heuristic for understanding contemporary debates concerning individuality and subjectivity while allowing diverse examples of performance to be brought into conversation with each other and the socio-cultural moment of their production. This approach does not assume that performance and its effects are inherently radical or progressive, but chooses instead to argue that it is solo performance's potential compatibility with neoliberal structures and values which might most usefully provide for a powerful critique of neoliberalism's gaps, inconsistencies and contradictions. As its title suggests, this book also has queer ambitions: while drawing on a broad range of critical and conceptual sources from across the fields of performance studies, sociology, political science and philosophy, it owes its existence to a field of queer and feminist enquiry characterised by an attempt to open up 'what counts as a life worth living' (Ahmed 2006: 178). Arguing against neoliberalism's forms of compulsory individuation, it presents a case for how solo performance manifests our precarious, constitutive and sometimes unsettling exposure and accountability to one another. It is through that exposure that other worlds – 'worlds of transformative politics and possibilities' (Muñoz 1999: 195) – are made possible.

Scoping solo performance

This project adopts a deliberately catholic approach to the study of solo performance in its inclusion of works from a broad range of forms, traditions and contexts, albeit focusing on a period of production and reception that spans the last decade. Though including a significant number of queer artists, it is not primarily a study of LGBTQIA (lesbian, gay, bisexual, trans, queer, intersex and allies) performance and its critical enquiry takes it beyond the territories of sexuality and gender most intimate to queer studies in order to think more broadly about the contemporary conditions of exception. Many of the works explored here are performed by their creator – what Michael Kirby (1979) once defined as the genre of 'autoperformance' – but a significant number involve performers presenting work developed with or by others. All of these works reflect Peggy Shaw's observation that 'I am a solo artist and, by virtue of that, a collaborator' (2011: 39) as each involves the creative labour of more than one person. Several notionally 'solo' works examined here have more than one performer, not least in the case of one-to-one performances which require an audience-participant to play an active role. I have also deliberately included a small number of group works which have emerged from – or led to – the creation of single performer works where they might inform an understanding of how an artist's practice has developed, and where a work's staging of a singular, exceptional subject might inform this book's overarching study of neoliberalism. While a number of the works encountered in this book have been published as scripts, I have accessed many through documentation in the form of photographs, scores and films shot in HD for archive or broadcast alongside piecemeal clips captured on mobile phones and uploaded without permission to YouTube, as well as published reviews and less formal responses posted to blogs and social media. I also draw on artists' own accounts of their practice, whether articulated through press releases and marketing, or through interviews with journalists and academics as in the form of Dominic Johnson's invaluable oral history of performance art, *The Art of Living* (2015). In moving between these sources alongside my own first-hand experiences as an audience member, I attempt to capture some sense of the contingent materiality of performance, its circulation and its reception.

These choices serve several interlocking goals, the first of which is to reflect a diversity of form and convention in current practice within the UK and Western Europe, and contextualise that work in a broader field of cultural production and artistic endeavour. Many elements of the artists' work discussed here straddle live performance, film, visual and sculptural arts to be shown in theatres, galleries and other public spaces. 'Mixing' performance across perceived genres also allows me to trace a genealogy of practice that extends between established and emergent artists, and to do so in a way that respects how practice has evolved over the last decade or so without the 'new' simply replacing the 'old'. The second is to inform a consciously critical approach to matters of form and genre that resists the compartmentalisation of practice and allows diverse examples of, say, stand-up and live art to mutually inform understanding of each other. While it is possible to identify formal characteristics that might distinguish work in one field (say, Neil Bartlett's monologues) from practice in another (La Ribot's performance installations), I follow Michael Peterson's observation that meaningful difference between forms of solo performance 'more often lies in the material circumstances of production and the cultural uses to which these forms are put' (1997: 22). In this respect, I am less interested in preserving a strict definition of solo performance as the work of a solitary performer than exploring what the varied manifestations of solo practice might have to say about this particular cultural moment – one in which the twentieth-century's liberal projects of recognition and inclusion seem in increasingly profound tension with the logic of neoliberalism at the start of the twenty-first.

To that end, I privilege a critique which contextualises examples of solo performance in respect of cultural debates which surround their production and reception, and the pragmatic circumstances which mean – as Sean Bruno and Luke Dixon's recent guide to creating solo performance observes – solo performances 'are usually less expensive to mount and can offer greater returns than non-solo shows' (2015: 15). Nonetheless, this project takes it roots in acknowledgement of the close relationship of solo performance to questions of identity, individuality and autobiography, and the entanglement of those associations with a cultural tradition that 'recapitulate[s] philosophical and theological explanations of genius' (Frieden 1985: 18). In this frame, an attachment to the idea of the exceptional artist coheres to a belief in the unique qualities of solo performance – an understanding that 'more than any other form of live performance, the solo show expects and demands the active involvement of the people in the audience' (Bonney 2000: xiii) or, more expansively, the notion that

> the solo can be seen as the quintessential form of performance. The audience's relation to the soloist is undivided, gratifying the performer's deepest desires not only to be seen but to be the centre of attention. The solo is a means of presenting the self to others, generally in terms of a display of virtuosity designed to elicit the spectator's admiration and awe. (Carroll 1979: 51)

If solo performance is part of an extended tradition of rhetorical forms which 'represent and accomplish individuality' (Frieden 1985: 20), it is nonetheless one in which the notion of the individual has undergone continuous (and in the twenty-first century, *rapid*) change.

Eddie Paterson's study *The Contemporary American Monologue* (2015), for example, traces the emergence of a late nineteenth- and early twentieth-century 'modern' sensibility characterised by 'an increasingly solitary self, preoccupied with an inner world' (2015: 24) alongside the longer standing tradition of the soliloquy as a performance mode by which a character expresses some authentic, interior aspect of himself to himself. For Paterson, it is the work of Bertolt Brecht, Samuel Beckett and Harold Pinter which from the mid-twentieth century onwards challenges the status of the monologue as expressing psychological truth, either by inducing a critical distance between a performer and the character which they portray, or by questioning the assumed narrative authority of the monologue through speech which is shown to be ambiguous, unreliable and fragmented (see Paterson 2015: 30–7).[1] Retained, though, is the sense in which solo performance is associated with the figure of the auteur: Paterson's engaging study is focused on major artists – Spalding Gray, Laurie Anderson, Anna Deavere Smith and Karen Finley – whose status as singular performers may overshadow the broader networks of collaborative endeavour through which their reputations as soloists have been established. Part of the problem, perhaps, is the degree to which the tradition of the monologue – emerging from a history which imagines its origins in the work of Alfred Tennyson and Robert Browning (see Byron 2003) – always, already has in mind an author.

While praising solo performance as a format 'seemingly infused with the infectious raw energy of spontaneous storytelling', Jo Bonney's introduction to the solo performance anthology *Extreme Exposure* (2000) notes that the semblance of spontaneity is the product of skilful performance 'with the support of offstage collaborators such as directors, co-writers, designers, composers and technicians' (Bonney 2000: xiii). Mirroring Paterson's history of the singular self, Bonney locates the rise of solo performance in the shift from a nineteenth-century emphasis on community to the twentieth century's emphasis on the individual, passing through 'the hedonism of the twenties, the radical individualism and activism of the sixties and the so-called "me decade" of the eighties' (2000: xiv) before the 1990s finally made room for previously marginalised voices. Speaking to this point, Deirdre Heddon's *Autobiography and Performance*

---

1 For a parallel history of the monologue from the ancient Greeks through Shakespeare to modernists such as Ibsen and Strindberg, see Geis (1993).

(2008) identifies the significance of solo autobiographical performance within and arising out of the second-wave feminist movement as a means 'to reveal otherwise invisible lives, to resist marginalisation and objectification and to become, instead, speaking subjects with self-agency' (2008: 3). While alert to essentialising claims on 'authentic' experience and the reiteration of normative narratives within autobiographical performance, Heddon traces a tradition in which members of marginalised communities have sought to 'challenge, contest and problematize dominant representations and assumptions about those subjects' (2008: 20). This development is further significant for its broadening of the kinds of artists involved in making and presenting work – that is, for its diversification of both professional and amateur spheres of cultural production.

The centrality of such practices to LGBTQIA art and activism – and their allegiance to the political logic of 'coming out' as a mode of individual and collective transformation – is apparent in queer theorist José Esteban Muñoz's affirmation of 'the spectacle of one queer standing onstage alone … bent on the project of opening up a world of queer language, lyricism, perceptions, dreams, visions, aesthetics, and politics' (1999: 1). For Muñoz, the queer soloist offers a singular perspective of 'being queer at this particular moment' that is capable of taking on 'ever multiplying significance' which exceeds the bounds of any individual signifying event. The introduction to *O Solo Homo: The New Queer Performance* (1998) – a significant collection of primarily North-American performance texts co-edited by Holly Hughes and David Román – goes one step further, offering that 'I don't think it's too much of a stretch to suggest that all of us who are queer can loosely be described as solo performers insofar as we have had to fashion an identity around our gender and sexuality' (Hughes and Román 1998: 6–7). In these and other accounts, solo performance's relative low cost, accessibility unfettered by industry gatekeepers, and willingness to treat the personal as the political locates it within a 'tradition of "witnessing," a project of revising history, educating others about one's personal experience, and mobilizing them to political or social action' (Sandahl 2003: 29) that is of particular significance to marginalised communities. This dynamic may be readily apparent in Jo Clifford and Chris Goode's recent play *Eve* (2017) in which Clifford appears alone on stage in front of projected photographs of her childhood at an all-boys boarding school and, later, as a young man in love with the woman who would become her wife. Refusing 'a story of unhappiness and betrayal and being a victim of it all' (Clifford and Goode 2017: 7) from its opening lines, the work is structured by moments in which Clifford's compassion for her younger self – 'dear John' – offers a trans biography structured by something other than the disavowal of a former name. On the night of its final performance at the Citizen's Theatre in Glasgow in September 2017, Clifford took the closing moment of applause to call our attention to the inherently political nature of our gathering as an audience – and to call for solidarity with Brazilian trans performer Renata Carvalho whose production of Clifford's earlier work *The Gospel According to Jesus, Queen of Heaven* (2008) had been threatened with violence.

While several of the works explored in this book elaborate this tradition and its claim on the congruity of social and theatrical performativity, I am also interested in how recent practice may problematise the affirmation of solo performance as inherently or unreservedly empowering for politicised subjects. Observing that the primary focus of autobiographical works made by LGBTQIA artists has remained relatively stable since the 1980s, performance scholar and trans performer Lazlo Pearlman interrogates the now received wisdom that performative acts of confession are 'key to advancing liveable identities, not only for and as artists but also for and as representatives of identity groups as a whole' (Pearlman 2015: 88). Reading such acts via Michel Foucault as potential expressions of an internalised disciplinary power which 'creates, controls and regulates the limits of identities', Pearlman's practice has deployed 'truth traps' in which seemingly genuine autobiographical details lead the audience 'down a false path toward "understanding" my non-heteronormative identity' (Pearlman 2015: 89–90). In making use of 'the material but not the identity' of his body, Pearlman's work articulates an understanding of how the affirmative potential of self-narration may be constrained by the pressure to produce oneself as an intelligible subject in full mastery of one's social identity and existence. Such a privileging of transparency and self-assertion in the performance of 'coming out' is problematic insofar as it lends itself to an understanding of 'the effects of structural inequality as the personal failure of those who suffer from it' (Clare 2017: 19).

Without insisting upon a paranoid reading that finds solo performance always compromised, I am conscious of the ways in which the special value accorded to solo work may operate to reflect and sustain social hierarchies of different kinds, and serve to sustain a broader economy of professional arts practice which offers disproportionate opportunities to white, male-presenting and able-bodied performers. As Peterson argues in *Straight White Male: Performance Art Monologues* (1997), the circumstances of the soloist have been occupied with greatest frequency by white men even though monologue performance has been practised 'as well, as complexly and as (in)famously' (Peterson 1997: 6) by women and by men of colour. Centred on readings of the work of Spalding Gray and Eric Bogosian, Peterson's critique points to the particular coincidence of 'a performance form that privileges personality, individual creative energy, and singular performance presence', the array of identity privileges 'that accrue to whiteness, maleness and heterosexuality' and the high value placed on monologic genius within 'modern Western conceptions of artistic quality' (1997: 46). While aspects of this study reflect the dominance of white and male-identifying performers with the Anglo-European performance scene, and the relative dearth of opportunities for queer, trans and minority ethnic practitioners as well as those from working-class backgrounds, my choice of case studies is nonetheless intended to broaden recognition of the diversity of contemporary artists – both established and emergent – who are engaged in creating and performing solo works.

This selection also reflects the programming practices of the new and experimental performance festivals described in chapter 1, and ongoing attempts by a new generation of creative producers, programmers and practitioners to address long-standing issues of diversity and access in the arts as well as the political efficacy of performance in its relationship to institutional arts structures.[2] One feature of this trend may resemble what Joanna Krakowska has described in the context of contemporary Polish theatre as a form of 'auto-theatre' in which

> authors speak from the stage in their own names, from the self about the self, referring to their own experiences, studying personal limitations, revealing weaknesses, exploring situations in their works, defining and questioning their identities, revealing the back-stage processes, interpersonal relations, economic conditions and ideological unrest in theatre itself. (2016: 24)

As I will explore at several different points across this study, such work engages reflexively with the conditions of its production to deliberate – as in Ivana Müller's *60 Minutes of Opportunism* (see chapter 7) – on how the patterns of labour particular to artistic activity might generate a critique of neoliberal conditions that reaches beyond the theatrical sphere.

Finally, if the critical trajectory of this study means that it does not attempt a general survey of the field of contemporary solo performance, it remains cognizant of the exercise in power marked by including some artists' work while excluding others. Most of the work described here

2 See, for example, Toni Lewis and Demi Nandhra's 'A Seat At The Table' (2017) retreat, in association with the Live Art Development Agency, intended to explore historical and contemporary relationships of race, culture and identity through participants' relationships as peers and colleagues working in the arts industry.

is English-language, and my access to it has turned on its appearance within UK-based festivals (or related documentation) produced over a fairly tight window of research activity following 2014. Though this study repeatedly returns to the conditions of queer lives, it is consciously and critically partial in its terms of reference – and largely avoids the use of more expansive acronyms such as LGBTQIA to avoid giving the impression of a cultural moment which is more inclusive, diverse and egalitarian than exists in actuality. In this regard, the title of chapter 6 – the misfit, a term drawn from the work of disability scholar Rosemarie Garland-Thomson – calls deliberate attention to ableist suppositions which persist within liberal cultural spaces. This strategy is double-edged: on the one hand, it allows me to focus more explicitly on the privileged terms by which some but not all queer lives are legitimised; on the other, it may serve to push discussion of bisexual, trans, intersex and asexual experiences, as well as those of minority ethnic lives, further into the margins. In this sense, the authority of the broader argument offered here may be as meaningfully structured by what it omits as by what space and time – alongside my own editorial choices – permit me to include.

Individuality and neoliberalism

Solo performance's relationship to issues of identity and selfhood – explored at greater length in the following chapters – marks its potential compatibility with many of the forms of governmentality which characterise contemporary neoliberalism. David Harvey observes that 'any political movement that holds individual freedoms to be sacrosanct is vulnerable to incorporation into the neoliberal fold' (2005: 41) and the claim on solo performance as a venue for the affirmation of previously unheard lives and experiences may describe a particularly invidious form of susceptibility – not least when, as Matthew Causey and Fintan Walsh argue in the introduction to their study of neoliberal subjectivity, 'capitalism sees in the fracturing of identity a wonderfully lucrative commercial project, to the extent that it does not simply respond to identitarian distinctiveness, but actively cultivates it for its own purposes' (Causey and Walsh 2013: 2). While often conceived as a primarily economic logic that has overseen 'the financialization of everything' (Harvey 2005: 33), this study approaches neoliberalism as a field of cultural production preoccupied with individualism and individuation, rooted in a conceptualisation of freedom as the right to participate in market exchange but extending far beyond it to involve an array of practices and expectations concerning biographical self-fashioning and 'responsible' life management.[3] In this respect, neoliberalism can be understood as the development of the liberal tradition of the 'possessive individual' that is apparent – as political theorist Sharon Krause observes – across the work of philosophers John Locke, Immanuel Kant and John Stuart Mill as a discourse in which the individual is understood 'at least in principle, to be the master of her domain' (Krause 2015: 2).

Echoing the terms of Elin Diamond, Denise Varney and Candice Amich's recent edited collection *Performance, Feminism and Affect in Neoliberal Times* (2017), this book turns to solo performance as part of the 'social stitching' of the forces which comprise neoliberalism as well as their potential unravelling, as a means of historicising neoliberalism, and as evidence that the 'world has not become homogeneous; neither are neoliberal regimes everywhere dominant or stable' (2017: 4). This perspective is informed by the work of sociologists Ulrich Beck and Elisabeth Beck-Gernsheim who distinguish between the free market 'egoism of Thatcherism' (Beck and Beck-Gernsheim 2002: 202) and the concept of individualisation: a process by which neoliberalism 'requires individuals to become entrepreneurs in their own lives, making choices within a highly volatile world and taking individual responsibility for their failures' (Bockman 2013: 15). Faced with the diminishing relevance or power of institutions that in previous generations offered stable roles or rules for dealing with risk and opportunity, individuality shifts from being something determined by birth into a particular set of social preconditions (such as class and religion) to become

> a choice among possibilities, *homo optionis*. Life, death, gender, corporeality, identity, religion, marriage, parenthood, social ties – all are becoming decidable down to the small print; once fragmented into options, everything must be decided. (Beck and Beck-Gernsheim 2002: 5)

Here, the imperative 'must' indicates that an emphasis on decision-making is not the same thing as a celebration of free will or agency. Individualisation is instead characterised by the expectation that people conduct themselves as responsible, productive and self-actualising individuals, and do so through the orderly stage-management of their life stories.

---

3 See, variously, Bauman (2001), Guthman and Dupuis (2006), Brown and Baker (2012) and Barker (2014).

Crucially, this expectation is not confined to one's own intimate biography but involves the bonds and networks surrounding it, with the consequence that individuals are required to seek out and devise biographical solutions for systemic crises even as risks and contradictions go on being socially produced. This idea is developed in the work of sociologist Zygmunt Bauman who coins the term 'subsidiarization' to describe how neoliberalism's increased imperative on individuals to develop and maintain political choices has not been accompanied by the social resources or political mechanisms 'which would allow choices to be effectively made and realized' (Dawson 2013: 57). Bauman distinguishes between individuality *de facto* and individuality *de jure* to describe the difference between those who can 'afford' individuality, and those who lack the resources to fulfil this duty but are still expected to conduct themselves as though they can – while maintaining that

> we are all individuals now; not by choice, though, but by necessity ... self-identification, self-management and self-association, and above all self-sufficiency in performance of all these three tasks, are our duty whether or not we command the resources which the performance of the new duty demands. (Bauman 2001: 111)

An exploration of this double-bind recurs across this study where I explore how an occupation of involuntary terms for being may nonetheless allow a form of critical resistance. Though neoliberalism is undoubtedly the dominant political and cultural logic of our time, it is not so utterly hegemonic as to preclude alternatives, and this study proceeds from recognition that neoliberalism is an incomplete regime fraught with 'contradiction and partiality and subject to limitation' (Kingfisher and Maskovsky 2008: 115).

Theorising exceptionality

While adopting a queer scavenger methodology in combining perspectives and insights from potentially disparate fields of enquiry in the attempt to 'collect and produce information on subjects who have been deliberately or accidentally excluded from traditional studies of human behaviour' (Halberstam 1998: 10), this book's initial understanding of exceptionality is drawn from the work of philosophers Giorgio Agamben and Roberto Esposito. As I will trace briefly below, what these theorists share in common is an attempt to describe 'the paradoxical dynamic of the political inscription of life: a paradox by which the "excluded" reinscribes itself systematically in the "included," and the "outside" … breaks in and disrupts the "inside"' (Giorgi and Pinkus 2008: 100). Though the work of these theorists has come to occupy a less central place in my thinking as this project has developed, my starting point remains Agamben's exploration of exceptionality as a break from the general rule that does not operate absolutely without reference to the rule. It is, rather, the presupposition of the rule 'in the form of its suspension' (Agamben 1998: 21). Rejecting narratives in which exception is understood as either an emergency measure anticipated by the law or the expression of unrestrained sovereignty (see Humphreys 2006: 678), Agamben proposes that

> The state of exception is neither external or internal to the juridical order, and the problem of defining it concerns precisely a threshold, or a zone of indifference, where inside and outside do not exclude each other but rather blur with each other. (2005: 23)

The challenging nature of this logic may be more clearly articulated in Agamben's earlier discussion of 'homo sacer', drawn from Ancient Roman law as the paradigmatic figure of exception who 'can be killed but yet not sacrificed' (1998: 8).

In Agamben's words,

> the most proper characteristic of the exception is that what is excluded in it is not, on account of being excluded, absolutely without relation to the rule. On the contrary, what is excluded in the exception maintains itself in relation to the rule in the form of the rule's suspension. *The rule applies to the exception in no longer applying, in withdrawing from it.* (1998: 17–18, original emphasis)

This concept of exclusive inclusion has served to describe 'how certain subjects undergo a suspension of their ontological status as subjects when states of emergency are invoked' (Butler 2004: 67): most notably, non-citizen 'enemy combatants' detained without trial at Guantanamo Bay, displaced persons living in refugee camps or confined to concentration camps, and 'illegal' immigrants held in detention zones at airports and other border sites. Agamben's account, though, does not offer a hierarchy of victimhood and the larger claim of his work is that the state of exception has become the paradigm of contemporary political life to the extent that we are all 'virtually homines sacri' (Agamben 1998: 115). While certain aspects of this study address the extremity of bare life which *homo sacer* represents, my intention is to develop from Agamben's work an account of marginalisation 'that goes beyond the binary distinctions to be had in dichotomies such as inside/outside, centre/margins, inclusion/exclusion' (Downey 2009: 109) in order to better understand the significance of threshold subjectivities characterised not by their exclusion from the legal, political or social sphere but by their suspended relation to its terms.

This ambition is served by insights drawn from Esposito's trilogy of works concerning political community – *Bios* (2008), *Communitas* (2010) and *Immunitas* (2011) – which dispute the popular conception of community as a place of 'mutual, intersubjective "recognition" in which individuals are reflected in each other so as to confirm their initial identity' (Esposito 2010: 7). Noting the etymological origins of community in the term 'munus', understood as a form of obligatory gift, Esposito theorises that the 'subjects of community are united by an "obligation," in the sense that we say "I owe *you* something," but not "you owe *me* something"' (Esposito 2010: 6). This constitutive debt arises from our status as finite subjects continually exposed to what we are not: the exterior 'nothing' which constitutes the 'outside' of our being. Consequently, Esposito argues that community

> isn't a mode of being, much less a 'making' of the individual subject. It isn't the subject's expansion or multiplication but its exposure to what interrupts the closing and turns it inside out: a dizziness, a syncope, a spasm in the continuity of the subject. (Esposito 2010: 7)

Against this account of community as the 'outside' which threatens our coherence as properly individual subjects, Esposito offers the biopolitical metaphor of immunisation as that which 'brings us back within ourselves by cutting off all contact with the outside' (Lemm 2013: 4) to protect us from the demands of undifferentiated community.

While Esposito finds that immunity is necessary to the preservation of both individual and collective life – allowing individual bodies to resist infection, and members of a body politic to develop collective mechanisms of protection from external threats – he cautions that any immune system that is 'exclusive and exclusionary toward all other human and environmental alterities' (Esposito 2013: 86) will come to threaten the very life that it seeks to protect once its operation crosses a certain threshold. This dynamic takes the form of an 'autoimmune crisis' wherein structures or policies notionally intended to preserve a particular way of life – whether in the form of austerity economics or the 'war on terror' – serve to force life 'into a sort of cage where not only our freedom gets lost but also the very meaning of our existence' (Esposito

2013: 85). In response, Esposito calls for a reconceptualisation of community and immunity that places them in reciprocal relation. In this conceptual frame, immunity is posed not as a barrier of separation but a filter of relations: a potential mode of continuous exchange 'between an internalised outside and an externalised inside' (Esposito 2011: 174). As I will argue most directly in discussion of Martin O'Brien's work in chapter 6, this metaphor is valuable to a queer critique of exceptionality for its deconstruction of the oppositional logics of common/proper, inside/outside and exposed/immune on which neoliberal thought (in its attachment to notions of autonomous personhood) heavily depends.

The figural

As indicated above, this book deploys a figural logic to organise its case studies and structure its argument. This approach echoes those undertaken by queer and feminist scholars such as Lee Edelman, whose critique of reproductive futurity turns on the figure of the child, and Sara Ahmed whose ground-breaking work on the figures of the killjoy and the stranger directly informs several of the following chapters. In this respect, it joins a longer-standing critical tradition in which Michel Foucault's studies of the figures of the patient, delinquent and homosexual animate a historiographical analysis of knowledge, power and subjectivity.[4] First explored in his lectures of 1978 and 1979 at the Collège de France, Foucault's concept of governmentality emerges from a figural discourse to describe how practices of governing others relate to the practices of governing the self, whereby the 'docile bodies' required of modern political and economic institutions are produced by 'arranging things so that people, following only their own self-interest, will do as they ought' (Scott 1995: 202–3). Concerned with the 'conduct of conduct' rather than the exercise of direct force, governmentality describes how processes of subjection signify 'the process of becoming subordinated by power as well as the process of becoming a subject' (Butler 1997a: 2). While Foucault's work may be read to conclude that there is no possibility of subversive subjectivity, his account asserts that power is not simply monolithic but

---

4 See Foucault's *The Birth of the Clinic: An Archaeology of Medical Perception* (1973), *Discipline and Punish: The Birth of the Prison* (1995) and *The History of Sexuality: Vol 1. The Will to Knowledge* (1978).

always opposed by other forms of power. Moreover, the operation of power is also always reversible, in the sense that mechanisms of power used by one group to control another may be re-appropriated and turned against their original ends (Heller 1996: 101).

In this context, subjectivity – and the relation between subjectification and subjugation – emerges as the terrain in and through which the operation of power may be examined and challenged. This book emphasises the figure over the subject, though, to draw attention to the ways in which ideology 'bodies forth' subjectivities of different kinds: to figure is to invoke an embodied human form, and to pay critical attention to the ways in which such a form becomes intelligible *as* human. Given so, while many of the figures named in this study invoke readily identifiable, established cultural tropes – the entrepreneur, the martyr, the pariah and the stranger – these titles are not intended to assert their historical permanence or appeal to any universal truth about subjectivity encoded in their form. They are, instead, intended to serve as a critique of the ways in which contemporary neoliberalism imagines and produces subjectivity, and organises a diverse array of sometimes contradictory imperatives as naturalised, inevitable forms of being. As such, this book reads figurative representation as involving allegorical and metonymic forms of association that are expressive of historically and culturally located values and processes, whereby the logic of analogy (in which one object is given to stand for another) describes how power relations of different kinds are concentrated or dispersed. This thinking acknowledges the normative quality of 'figuring' in the sense of a practice which represents something's readily intelligible or typical form, and thereby serves as an example which 'transforms singularities into members of a class, whose meaning is defined by a common property (the condition of belonging)' (Agamben 1993: 9).

At the same time, it asserts that to engage in figural thinking is to deliberately deviate from the orthodox syntactical relations of words and ideas, and challenge that which is 'most normal' or 'obvious'. To figure is to test and play with the domain of the sensible in pursuit of that which exceeds its regular bounds: to work with figural representations is to invoke and challenge what Pierre Bourdieu understands as doxa, 'an adherence to relations of order which, because they structure inseparably both the real world and the thought world, are accepted as self-evident' (Bourdieu 1984: 471). Such a practice is not only deconstructive but generative, serving the attempt to better apprehend marginalised lives which are not recognised by recognition itself by calling attention to the limits of existing regimes for social intelligibility. This latter claim is informed by the work of Jean-François Lyotard, who differentiates between the discursive – that which belongs to the order of signs and linguistics – and the figural 'which is a libidinal event irreducible to language' (Pavis 2003: 87). For Lyotard, the figural is not the opposite of language, but rather 'a semiotic regime where the ontological distinction between linguistic and plastic representation breaks down' (Rodowick 2001: 2). Serving to deconstruct the opposition of word and image, the 'scandal of the figure is that it is both inside and outside of discourse' (Rodowick 2001: 9) in having the status of that which 'is only approachable within the boundaries of discourse while always remaining outside its grasp' (Gaillard 2013: 234).

Characterised by the febrile mobilities of desire, the figural marks the body's resistance to discourse while – recalling Foucault's analysis – describing how resistance always take place within or in relationship to the domain of ideology rather than through reference to some imagined outside space. On these terms, we might draw parallels between the figural and the logic of Agamben's state of exception insofar as the figural occupies a suspended relationship to the authority of discourse – named within it, but exceeding (or perhaps failing) its remit. Yet where the Agambian state of exception is always, already punitive, the status of the figural as that which linguistic space 'cannot incorporate without being shaken, an exteriority it cannot interiorize as signification' (Lyotard 2011: 7) marks the possibility of generative resistance to hegemonic conditions. Though the figural may be translated into a linguistic signified and thereby enter discourse, this 'by no means exhausts their meaning and function' (Pavis 2003: 87). It is this untranslatability – a queer excess that does not directly oppose because it operates without reference to a linguistic norm – which 'shows that alternatives to established forms of discourse – not only language and critical philosophy but also visual methods – are possible' (Bamford 2012: 21).

Queer exceptions

This book's chapters are written as part of a larger critique but intended to be accessible as essays on their own terms. While a conceptual framework drawn from Agamben and Esposito is laced through the study as a whole, each figure invokes and examines a different set of dynamics concerning solo performance, subjectivity and neoliberalism while pointing towards the ways in which exceptional subjects might manifest different modalities of resistance, or alternative ways of being. In attempting to take up 'the positions and perspectives of sexual minorities in order to reread the social world' (Phelan 2000: 438), this book also challenges a reading of queerness as primarily oppositional to instead explore the complex conditions of *complicity* which characterise the neoliberal experience.[5] Each chapter begins with a short introduction that locates its titular figure in its corresponding cultural tradition or conceptual context before moving to discuss instances of performance. The grouping of performers under each figural title is not intended as an act of formal classification but an attempt to describe particular emphases within the discursive field through which exception finds it forms. In plainer language, the figures overlap: works by David Hoyle discussed in chapter 3 under the banner of the pariah might also be viewed through the lens of the killjoy in chapter 4; Ron Athey's practice – considered in discussion of the martyr in chapter 2 – might also be understood in relation to the questions of bodily propriety which animate my exploration of the misfit in chapter 6. Structured by analogy, movement between chapters invites – or perhaps requires – a sideways step to re-examine a familiar set of problems from a new perspective. Chapter 1 offers a material context for the book as a whole by exploring the figure of the creative entrepreneur in relation to the economies of contemporary performance production, and argues for the significance of arts festivals as spaces in which neoliberal logics find their most acute expression for the creators of solo performance. After scoping the rapid proliferation of new and experimental performance festivals over the past two decades, I focus on the ecology of the Edinburgh festivals to examine how the uneven distribution of artistic labour and financial risk that characterises the Fringe Festival mainstream has been countered by alternative models of organisation and collaboration.

Mindful of neoliberalism's preference for subjects who are willing and able to exploit their own well-being, chapter 2 turns to performance through the figure of the martyr to explore works in which the staging of endurance implicates its audience as witnesses to the function and necessity of public suffering. Focusing on the aura of 'involuntariness' that surrounds the martyr figure which allows them to be claimed as representatives for contrasting (if not directly opposed) causes, I explore

---

5 For further discussion of the inflection between 'studying queers' and a study that begins from the knowledge and practices of sexual minorities, see 'The Refusal of Sexual Difference: Queering Sociology' in Seidman (1997).

the highly selective terms on which such subjects are allowed – or called upon – to stand as surrogates for others or speak for themselves. By moving between performances by live artists Ron Athey, Kira O'Reilly and Franko B, and performance makers Eddie Ladd, Adrian Howells and Scottee, I consider the relationship between self-injury, exhaustion and confession as technologies of the self, and the possibilities for ritual presentations of the self to be occupied to ends other than those of normative or disciplinary redemption. Building on that account, chapter 3 examines performance through the lens of Hannah Arendt's notion of the 'conscious pariah' as an outcast who is aware of his own place in history, and sceptical of the promise of equality offered by assimilation. Framed by what Heather Love describes as a tendency to 'rescue' injured queer lives from the past, I explore Neil Bartlett's AIDS-era work *A Vision of Love Revealed in Sleep* alongside more recent works by Marc Rees and Seiriol Davies as performances concerning subjects whose refusal of recuperation frustrates progressive narratives of recovery and inclusion. I then turn to Jon Brittain and Matt Tedford's *Margaret Thatcher Queen of Soho* and the work of performance artist David Hoyle to examine how pariah identifications offer a new perspective by which to understand the politics of 'wounded attachment' – what Wendy Brown (1995) describes as the structuring of politicised identity through an investment in its own subjugation, and in which social progress is unthinkable apart from a history of hurt.

In continuing to trace where the conditions of complicity within neoliberalism might yet provide a basis for critique, chapter 4 draws on Sara Ahmed's discussion of the feminist killjoy to read stand-up and cabaret works by performers Bridget Christie, Ursula Martinez and Adrienne Truscott which anticipate and invoke antifeminist sentiment in order to subvert its force. Mindful that the trope of the killjoy persists whether or not the killjoy is actually present, I explore how La Ribot's live art 'distinguished pieces' series might frustrate a demand for sociable happiness by deploying the body against the conceit of an already constituted, sovereign subject. From this perspective, I reframe the killjoy as a scapegoat through a reading of Cristian Ceresoli's *La Merda / The Shit* and Gary Owen's *Iphigenia in Splott* as dramatic monologues in which the killjoy's disturbing public affects force a reconsideration of the terms on which togetherness is constructed and sustained, and in which marginalised or politicised subjects are required to participate in the terms of their own exclusion. This examination of highly conditional citizenship is further explored in chapter 5, which animates the figure of the stranger to read a range of works made in response to contemporary border regimes. Drawing from the work of Georg Simmel alongside more recent scholarship by Bauman and Ahmed, I read Kay Adshead's *The Bogus Woman*, Zodwa Nyoni's *Nine Lives* and Oreet Ashery's *Staying: Dream, Bin, Soft Stud and Other Stories* – each made in relation to the UK's asylum system – as works in which compulsory testimony calls into question the believability of the one who is bound to speak, and where recognition turns on one's ability to resemble or perform what is already being looked for: the 'right' kind of refugee. In arguing that the contemporary stranger acts a space of projection for liberal fantasies of difference, I turn to consider Nassim Soleimanpour's *White Rabbit, Red Rabbit* – written when he was unable to leave his home country of Iran – and Yugoslavian-born artist Tanja Ostojić's sequence of border works concerning the 'immediate outside' of the European Union to address how the stranger is not merely 'any' body, but one whose misrecognition is a constitutive condition of their inclusion.

In chapter 6, I develop a critique of neoliberalism's bodily norms through the figure of the misfit – a term drawn from the work of disability scholar Rosemary Garland-Thomson – and through performance works concerning illness, disability and impairment. Adopting 'propriety' as a term for thinking about the intersection of various norms concerning bodily autonomy and responsibility, I discuss how performances by Rita Marcalo, Brian Lobel and Robert Softley invite fresh understanding of the assumed relationship between agency and autonomy, and of how social judgements about both are shaped by norms for sexuality and gender. The claim on the misfit as a figure capable of interrupting those norms is further explored through works by Bobby Baker, Katherine Araniello and the vacuum cleaner (artist James Leadbitter) whose interventions in public spaces draw critical attention to neoliberalism's configuration of the relationship between care and self-care as a demand for personal responsibility. In pursuit of alternative relationalities, I examine the practice of live artist Martin O'Brien as elaborating forms of interpersonal contact characterised by contagion and exposure rather than sovereign immunity, and in which the performative rendition of disgust brings to light social judgements about the assumed integrity of autonomous bodies.

The final chapter of the book offers a reparative turn to the figure of the optimist in examining a range of works which describe the difficult and uncertain relationship between the present, futurity and the possibility of change. Reading against accounts of utopia in performance offered by Jill Dolan and José Esteban Muñoz, I consider Deborah Pearson's *The Future Show*, Ivana Müller's *60 Minutes of Opportunism* and

Duncan Macmillan's *Every Brilliant Thing* to argue for an understanding of optimism as a form of radical present-tenseness which might resist paranoid, neoliberal demands for a well-ordered future. In understanding that such an attentiveness to the here and now might be characterised by vulnerability rather than autonomous sovereignty, I explore three further works by performance artists FK Alexander, Rosana Cade and Nando Messias to propose how forms of subordination that are a constitutive condition of subjecthood might be mobilised to address those which are socially contingent, and open to change. In a brief conclusion, I then explore some of the common characteristics of solo performance encountered in this book and outline what a politics of queer exception might make possible next.

1

Locating solo performance

Hannah Gadsby's critically acclaimed show *Nanette* (2017) may or may not be her last work as a stand-up comedian. Toured internationally since its premiere at the Melbourne International Comedy Festival, the show presents a swansong to comedy in which Gadsby revisits material from earlier acts – most notably, jokes about her experiences of homophobia – to refuse the comedian's obligation to deliver cathartic relief to an audience confronted with difficult topics. 'I have a responsibility to make you laugh', she offers at one point, 'But I'm not in the mood'. In part, the show is structured as a masterclass in the convention of creating tension in order to diffuse it with a punchline. In the latter part of the hour, though, Gadsby deliberately abandons the pay-off in order to deconstruct comedy's potentially 'abusive' relationship to its audience, and to call attention to the human cost of gender violence. Gadsby has had enough and, we are told, she is walking away from comedy: whatever balm was offered by performance in the past now threatens to make living with her life experiences more difficult. Perhaps ironically, *Nanette* has been a considerable commercial success: touring to sell-out performances at the Edinburgh Festival Fringe and for a month at the Soho Theatre, London, attracting multiple awards including the Helpmann Award for Best Comedy Performer, and recently recorded live at the Sydney Opera House for release on the streaming service Netflix. Though *Nanette* might challenge the demand for self-exploitation in stand-up, it also reflects Gadsby's self-description as a comedian who likes 'to take a story of woe from my actual factual life and make it hilarious' (Gadsby 2017). If *Nanette* ultimately defers laughter for a critique of anger, it may do so in active recognition of a complicity which exists between an audience and industry's appetite for a particular kind of comedy, and Gadsby's willingness – if not desire – to create it.

This introductory chapter examines contemporary arts festivals as spaces which provide the most intense examples of the neoliberal economies within which solo performance is produced and consumed, and in which dynamics of self-exploitation are informed by the intersection of creative and economic imperatives. In doing so, I first locate the work of the contemporary solo performer in relation to the figure of the solitary, entrepreneurial arts worker. Though theatre-makers involved in the creation of solo performance are not necessarily solo workers – and are more frequently engaged in collective or collaborative labour with a range of others in different creative and administrative roles – the paradigm of individualised entrepreneurship nonetheless dominates the larger context in which contemporary performance is commissioned, produced and presented. Both product and driver of post-industrial economies, that field is defined by forms of immaterial and affective labour: work centred on the production of information, services, entertainment and culture rather than material goods. Accounts of affective labour as a form of postmodern immaterial labour developed through the work of Maurizio Lazzarato, Antonio Negri and Michael Hardt have emphasised the intangible quality of its products, even as the act of producing them 'remains corporeal and intellectual' (Hardt and Negri 2009: 132). Seeking to avoid 'misrecognizing the ontological immateriality of performance, its ephemerality and disappearance' with an inherent resistance of commodification, Bojana Cvejić and Ana Vujanović have argued for the need to treat performance as 'a material artefact, being a product and commodity of the institutional market of the performing arts' (in Puar 2012: 175). In turn, Gabriele Klein and Bojana Kunst's introduction to 'On Labour and Performance' (a special issue of *Performance Research*) argues that any claim about the capacity of performance to 'directly challenge the practices of value-circulation and production of subjectivity in contemporary capitalism' (2012: 2) requires the critical contemplation of the proximity between performance and contemporary modes of labour.

In response, this chapter explores the material and organisational circumstances in which solo work is made to offer a structural analysis of the demand for artists to self-exploit as entrepreneurial individuals motivated by risk and characterised by a willingness to subsidise their own labour. While I will argue throughout this volume that the experience of contemporary neoliberalism is characterised by our complicity in its operation, this chapter's particular examination of performance labour acknowledges the alluring and problematic belief that the arts play a pioneering role in the critique of capitalism (Abbing 2014) and the oftentimes romanticised 'aesthetics of self-invention' (Waldrep 2004) which surrounds popular conceptions of the artist. First tracing the key terms of entrepreneurialism in the arts – an aspect of what I will explore in later chapters as liberalism's 'excessive freighting' of the individual with self-making agency (Brown 2006: 17) – I then focus on contemporary arts festivals as environments in which the pressures on the creators of solo performance to conduct themselves as entrepreneurs are felt most acutely, and where the ambivalent relationship between opportunity and exploitation is most sharply expressed. Widely construed within globalisation as 'entrepreneurial displays, as image creators capable of attracting significant flows of increasingly mobile capital, people and services' (Quinn 2005: 931), festivals are spaces in which solo performance finds its broader audience, and in which experimental forms and practices enter the mainstream. Moreover, they are spaces in which broader commercial imperatives and professional logics find their focus, with the comparatively low cost and high mobility of much solo work rendering it particularly compatible with the financial and logistical constraints of festival contexts (and, consequently, to the venue-based networks of touring which conjoin them). Nonetheless, and while festivals reflect the dominant conditions of the cultural marketplace in which performance is produced, they also indicate the ways in which neoliberal economies of value have been challenged and in which alternatives have been pursued.

The creative entrepreneur

Following the Blair Labour government's mapping of the 'creative industries' at the end of the 1990s – a methodology since adopted around the world as the basis for economic planning and development – the cultural entrepreneur has emerged as the figurehead of a new creative workforce that is 'meant to be young, multiskilled, flexible, psychologically resilient, independent, single and unattached to a particular location' (Ellmeier 2003: 3) and whose employment is characterised by atypical forms of labour defined by 'flexibility, mobility, project work, short-term contracts and voluntary or very low-paid activities' (Ellmeier 2003: 10). As political theorist Greig de Peuter observes, the freelance, contract and self-employed nature of employment in the arts, media and cultural industries has led to the depiction of arts workers 'as paradigmatic figures of 21st century capitalism' (2014: 264) whose compatibility with the conditions of the creative economy is manifest in the qualities of habituated self-reliance, adaptability and a willingness to self-exploit in the name of getting ahead. For cultural theorist Angela McRobbie, the imperative to 'be creative' is also a 'potent and highly appealing mode of new governmentality … whose main effect is to do away with the idea of welfare rights in work by means of eclipsing normal employment altogether' (2016: 14) wherein creative workers have served to 'test out the water of working life without welfare or with substantially reduced welfare' (2016: 58). Creative workers, in other words, are intended to model a broader shift to a post-industrial 'liquid' employment market in which insecurity, uncertainty and temporariness in the conditions of one's labour are intended to service the greater and more efficient exchange of capital, freed from the dead hand of government regulation.

At the same time, the figure of the creative entrepreneur has been celebrated by Richard Florida (2002) and other proponents of the 'creative classes' as enabling forms of affirmative self-realisation through modes of 'non-alienated labour' in which capacities for self-expression and experimentation are 'facilitated and liberated by development of one's career within an expanding marketplace for creative work' (Brouillette 2009: 142). This narrative of self-authored fulfilment may be exemplified in Charles Leadbeater and Kate Oakley's *The Independents: Britain's New Cultural Entrepreneur* (1999), a study produced by the New Labour-aligned think-tank Demos which figures the model entrepreneurial worker as having few material, social or financial commitments and whose 'main assets' are 'creativity, skill, ingenuity and imagination' (1999: 11). For Leadbeater and Oakley, cultural entrepreneurs believe in 'small is beautiful' and make a virtue of running 'small, under-capitalised and quite fragile companies' (1999: 26), while productively blurring the distinctions between production and consumption, and between work and leisure. Making it as an independent requires that prospective entrepreneurs take control of their creative destiny by surrendering themselves to the whims of the market. While 'timing is critical' because technology 'is moving so fast it's easy to be either too early or too late', they are warned against having a plan ('it will come unstuck because it's too inflexible') and advised instead to 'have an intuition and a feel for where the market is headed which can adapt and change with the consumers' (Leadbeater and Oakley 1999: 28). Success, in short, turns on almost preternatural capacity to anticipate and respond to change, and a willingness to embrace if not actively pursue the conditions of social and economic precarity by strategically undervaluing one's labour in the hope of a return which is always projected further into the future.

Crucial to this affirmation of entrepreneurialism 'is the belief that one has chosen his or her own living and working situations and that these can be arranged relatively freely and autonomously' (Lorey 2009: 187), presented in the figural form of the romanticised creative whose satisfaction with the conditions of their labour evokes the 'dubious yet enduring notion that self-expressive work offers "nonmonetary rewards" ... which counteract the sting of low earnings' (de Peuter 2014: 271). This narrative requires that artists and other culture workers embrace precarious and informal working as virtuous 'flexibility' and, moreover, as evidence of their compatibility with (and hence suitability for) contemporary funding regimes. Jen Harvie's extended discussion of the figure of the 'artrepreneur' and the rise of creative economy policy discourse in *Fair Play* (2013), for example, opens with the observation that public and private funding regimes

> regularly exhort artists to model creative entrepreneurialism, marked by independence and the ability to take initiative, take risks, self-start, think laterally, problem solve, innovate ideas and practices, be productive, effect impact and realize or at least stimulate financial profits. (2013: 62)

In this frame, entrepreneurialism is both the engine and end-goal of a policy intended to further reduce the need for institutional support by producing workers who do not need to turn to the state or private enterprise in order to 'self-start'.

For Harvie, an emphasis on entrepreneurialism is not inherently problematic and may indeed carry benefits, with greater business acumen and financial independence allowing artists to retain greater artistic control over their work without ceding it to others, and with multiple forms of employment allowing artists to develop 'multiple artistically complementary talents and modes of expression' across a range of fields including film and media production, education and arts administration (Harvie 2013: 75) while gaining temporary access to rehearsal spaces and other technical and administrative resources. As a form of post-Fordist labour, work as an artrepreneur may indeed endow considerable flexibility to one's working patterns, affording greater choice in potential projects and collaborators while also rewarding flexible forms of specialisation. Characterised by economies of scope (that is, efficiencies of variety rather than volume), such work may also provide considerable opportunities for personal and career development, with a mix of employment and self-employment allowing one to reflect and explore different facets of one's interests and abilities. In the absence of a 'job for life', a portfolio career allows individual workers to continually explore new experiences and opportunities. The difficulty with this narrative – and as Harvie herself infers – is the degree to which it frames structural conditions as choices (with the supposed freedom to 'cross-subsidise' one's own practice somewhat perversely framed as an affirmation of artistic practice rather than offering evidence of the underpayment of creative labour) and with a perpetual requirement to continually re-invent oneself understood as an advantage rather than a stressful burden which might interfere with one's ability to make work.

The self-employed artist

Though arts and cultural policy discourses continue to emphasise the benefits (and even necessity) of entrepreneurialism, there is widening institutional recognition of the particular challenges faced by those working in the arts. While part of the steep rise in the number of workers who are self-employed – and on whom economic growth depends – creative freelancers are rarely consulted on the policies that affect them, or have not been considered when policy was originally designed, such as higher education policy or the need for freelance visas (Easton and Cauldwell-French 2017: 4). Creative Scotland's *Arts Strategy 2016/7* is notable for its explicit acknowledgement of how

> [b]eing an artist, and working in the arts, is not always an easy choice. Many artists and cultural producers work as freelancers, are self-employed and juggle more than one job. This can result in challenging working patterns and unpredictable and uneven rates of pay despite the fact that many in the sector are highly trained, educated to degree, and often to postgraduate and Masters, level. Others are self-taught and learn in more informal but equally important ways … However, there is no guarantee of ever earning a stable salary. Artists often work for very little or for free. They devote long periods of unpaid time for the artistic research, fundraising and professional development necessary in order for them to progress their work. They are not recognised as 'job-less', even though they may be 'income-less' … Disabled

artists often find themselves unable to earn as doing so could mean losing their benefits. (Creative Scotland 2016: 15)

These structural conditions stand at the centre of artists' practice, where self-employment as an artist demands a continuous negotiation of pay and conditions, and an uncertain commitment that extends beyond the terms of any one contract or project.

As I have explored elsewhere in the life and career of theatre-maker Adrian Howells – whose work is considered in chapter 2 – artists who notionally work for themselves will be obliged to sign many contracts with others, and manage and administer their labour so that it might become intelligible as work (Greer 2016). Howells' personal financial papers – held at the Scottish Theatre Archive – record how each instance of his employment during the peak of his career demanded a separate contract setting out the terms of his labour: teaching on a particular course for a university, mentoring another artist, a commission to produce a new work or an engagement to perform an existing one. Howells is repeatedly reminded in the formal terms of his contracts that as a self-employed worker he is personally liable for his own payment of tax and national insurance and, in the case of at least one university employer, required to prove his eligibility in accordance with the Asylum and Immigration Act 1996 to work in the UK. These terms do not appear as bespoke conditions, unique to Howells' work, but rather as the standard terms of arts industry practice even though his work – frequently centred on one-to-one exchanges, as in the intimate ceremony of *Footwashing for the Sole* (2008) – brought with it particular demands for his own individually embodied labour, not least of which was the expectation that he should offer additional performances for the same fee so as to make the work more financially viable for programmers (Greer 2016: 267).

While dominated by short-term contracts, Howells' practice was enabled by a number of long-term associations – most notably a three-year Creative Fellowship funded by the Arts and Humanities Research Council (AHRC) in the department of Theatre Studies at the University of Glasgow from 2006 to 2009 (and thereafter an Honorary Research Fellow – an unpaid position) and his role as The Arches artist-in-residence from 2011. Though the development of these longer-term relationships may mark the mitigation of precarity, they do not describe security – pointing instead towards the affective labour required in cultivating professional networks of support (whose resilience may, in turn, be precariously dependent on research or Arts Council funding, and the caprice of local governance). The broader picture of professional participation and occupational development in the arts hinted at within Howell's archive is the significance of social class, with working-class performers significantly underrepresented within the profession as a whole. Those from working-class origins who do enter the profession do not have access to the same economic, cultural and social capital as those from privileged backgrounds, wherein familial economic resources may provide performers from middle-class backgrounds 'insulation from much of the precariousness of the labour market, particularly the need to seek alternative work to support one-self between acting roles' (Friedman, O'Brien and Laurison 2016: 1000). In Katy Baird's *Workshy* (2016) – a show about work and the things we do for money – it is clear that training and working as an artist will likely involve other kinds of labour: Baird details working for fast food restaurants, chain pubs and a sex website in the attempt to pay for university study.

Though the model of the artist as entrepreneur may be imagined as open to all who chose to embrace it, the risks and challenges which accompany that mode of working are not evenly distributed. For queer performance artist and theatre-maker Scottee, developing and maintaining multiple simultaneous projects and forms of work across a range of settings – encompassing solo performances, directorial projects and the creation of bespoke workshops for organisations and others artists – is a financial necessity: 'In its simplest form, if I don't earn a living, I have to find another job' (Scottee 2016, interview with the author). At the same time, developing his career without formal training in performance means that Scottee has 'learnt on the job' with his varied works serving as his 'university practice where I'm working things out in a public forum ... I do a lot because I'm trying to learn things and work things out'. The progress of Scottee's practice over the past decade has been shaped by the tactical appropriation of opportunity alongside the development of self-generated projects. Making work for mainstream arts venues and festivals – often for primarily white, middle-class audiences – allows him to 'keep his company going' and make work in a broader range of contexts for different, more diverse and working-class audiences: a site-specific work like *The Door*, installed in a shop on a high street in Hull, 'that makes people say "nothing like this ever happens here"' (Scottee 2016, interview with the author). This dynamic is also informed by race, with a white-dominated arts sector manifesting sometimes plainly racist beliefs. As Selina Thompson examines in her durational work *Race Cards* (2014) – in which she painstakingly writes more than a thousand questions about race and presents them to an audience for answers – the ideas that 'black audiences make white audiences feel uncomfortable', 'black audiences only support black work so aren't worth investing in' and 'the fact of the matter is, most BAME [Black and Minority Ethnic] artists make terrible work' (Thompson 2016: 191) may persist in what we might imagine to be liberal, progressive arts spaces. Beyond the detail of Scottee and Thompson's own professional experiences, research produced by Arts Council England indicates that 'those most actively involved in arts and culture tend to be from the most privileged parts of society; engagement is heavily influenced by levels of education, socio-economic background and where people live' and that 'Black, minority ethnic and disabled audiences continue to be under represented' (Arts Council England 2016: 22). As the Andrew Lloyd Webber Foundation's *Centre Stage: The Pipeline of BAME Talent* (2016) report observed, the professional theatre sector remains 'hideously white'.

The proliferation of unpaid internships – often for work that was previously paid, and in venues as established and well-funded as London's Globe Theatre – has further inhibited widening participation amongst those without family or other support, and thus contributed to the perpetuation of existing employment and participation demographics (see Arts Council England 2009). Though crowd-funding has been valorised for its purported role in democratising access to capital (MIT Sloan 2014) and increasingly embraced by funding bodies for its growth potential, Scottee's experiences suggest how such alternatives to existing funding regimes may serve to exacerbate the neoliberal dynamics within contemporary artists' working conditions. For *Liam Gallagher is My Grandad* (2014) – in which Scottee attempted to turn his grandfather into an internationally renowned artist known for work tackling ageism – Scottee raised £5,960 using Wefund.com from 220 donors. Though he exceeded his original goal of £5,800, Scottee estimates that the project demanded around 1,000 hours of unpaid work. It also involved a significant burden of emotional labour:

> For all of the time that crowdfunding project was open, I doubted myself constantly, my grandad's ability to be any artist, my ideas, my worth, my 'following' or audience, I doubted my friends and my family because they weren't giving enough money or quick enough. It was just me, my mental health and a computer. (Scottee in ArtsAdminUK 2014)

If entrepreneurialism grants autonomy, it might also serve to isolate and, in the case of crowd-funding, require artists to assess their personal, social and professional contacts through the primary lens of monetary value, with that value understood in turn as an expression of an artist's own worth. This dynamic may be characteristic of neoliberalism's logic of individual responsibility as applied to the creative sphere, where 'the individual only has him or herself to blame if the next script, film, book or show is not up to scratch' (McRobbie 2011: 84) and where a failing in the work is understood as a failing in the worker.

Despite the emphasis placed on individual culpability for success or failure, arts practices circulate within a scene of constraint described by cultural norms for artistic expression, and at a historical moment when relatively small groups of people can wield significant social and political pressure. While the reforms of the Theatres Act (1968) ended direct censorship of the British stage, Aleks Sierz has observed that 'the will to censor remains alive and well' (2001: 226) – whether in the form of commercial censorship or the actions of self-appointed moral guardians. When playwright Jo Clifford's *The Gospel According to Jesus, Queen of Heaven* (2008) was staged at the Tron Theatre during Glasgow's Glasgay! festival in 2009, the work was picketed by fundamentalist Christians who objected to Clifford's rendition of Jesus as a transwoman even though they had not seen the show or read its script. Performed by Clifford as a sermon structured by the re-telling of biblical parables (with the prodigal son becoming the prodigal daughter), the play insists on the queerness of Christ and the necessity of compassion. When *Queen of Heaven* re-appeared during the Edinburgh Fringe in 2012, it did so after being rejected by the concurrent Festival of Spirituality and Peace whose organisers judged the work to be 'too risky'. Elsewhere in Europe, theatre-makers face similar if not sharper challenges from socially conservative religious groups and political parties: in Poland, for example, works accused of undermining 'national values' aligned with majority-Catholic beliefs have been threatened with protests and the withdrawal of public funding.[1] Through later involvement with Creative Scotland's 'Made In Scotland' scheme, Clifford and producer Annabel Cooper were able to remount *Queen of Heaven* at Summerhall during the 2015 Fringe, where it was invited to Brazil – the country with the highest rate of transgender murders in the world – by one of the programmers of the International Theatre Festival of Belo Horizonte. While the work has since been staged during Queer Contact in Manchester and Outburst Arts Festival in Belfast, the play was only possible in the first instance because Clifford – a prolific playwright of over eighty works for stage and radio – was able to self-finance the work beyond an initial grant

---

1 See, for example, attempts by the ruling Law and Justice Party's culture minister Piotr Gliński to ban a production of Elfriede Jelinek's *Der Tod und das Mädchen* at the state-funded Polski theatre, and the cancellation of Rodrigo Gonzales' *Golgota Picnic* during the Malta Festival in Poznań following threatened protests from Catholic groups, both in 2015.

from Glasgay! and because 'the majority of those who contributed their time and skill to the production did so on a voluntary basis' (Clifford 2012: 21).

Pay and transparency

Though commercial sponsorship plays an increasingly significant role in the funding of galleries, museums and venues across Europe, it takes a more indirect role in the working practices of solo artists in the UK whose economies are dominated by funding distributed by national, governmental cultural agencies through a network of venues, companies and charities, and only in smaller proportions to individuals as 'sole trader' businesses. This income is frequently supplemented with other work – as suggested above in discussion of Howells' career, through teaching, mentorship roles, production work on other creative projects and occasional private commissions. This ecology contributes to a state of continual negotiation between different revenue sources, and between that which is necessary (to pay rent and keep a production company solvent) and that which might also serve the development of an artist's practice and the creation of new works. In a 2013 blog titled 'You Show Me Yours', theatre-maker and performance artist Bryony Kimmings offered an extended account of the economics and realities of making work for the touring circuit: the labour of weighing up 'the jobs I love doing with the ones I have to do just for the cash', the 'never-ending haggle' of negotiating with venues over the fee for her work and the continual requests to work for free, or at extremely low wages (Kimmings 2013). In calculating the one-night cost for the touring production of the multiple-award winning show *Credible Likeable Superstar Rolemodel* (2013) – performed by Kimmings alongside her nine-year-old niece Taylor – following its success at the Edinburgh Festival Fringe, Kimmings observed that her requested fee from venues did not include rehearsal fees, overheads or her own writer's fee, or the cost of days spent in the studio honing the show to tour again. Despite this, Kimmings described the routine expectation that she should – as a self-employed artist without regular funding – take on the same kinds of financial risk as regularly funded venues through box-office splits, or seek further Arts Council funding to support the tour. This demand is particularly insulting because Kimmings prides herself on her ability to be 'a good business woman' who knows 'income cannot come from one client or customer … I will ask the Arts Council for the money I want to ask for … not be told by a venue' (Kimmings 2013).

While employment conditions and rates of pay in parts of the commercial and subsidised entertainment industry are determined by negotiations led by Equity, BECTU and other trade union groups (in Germany, the GDBA and in France, the Syndicat Français des Artistes Interprètes), these agreements are applied inconsistently across the sector and far less frequently in the work of independent artists and producers. Though Arts Council England and other funding bodies asks that grant holders cost their activities in line with minimum rates identified by relevant professional bodies (and advise applicants not to lower their own fee/wage in order to decrease overall project costs), the predominance of self-employment in the production of contemporary solo work means that negotiations over pay and conditions frequently falls to the level of the individual practitioner, who may or may not then be responsible as the employer of others. In a broad range of online responses to Kimmings' original post (see ArtsAdmin 2013) artists, venues and independent producers frequently raised the issue of transparency in artists' pay and conditions, with Andy Field – theatre-maker and co-director of Forest Fringe, discussed below – suggesting that artists might develop an online space in which to declare how much they have been able to charge for their work, venue by venue, in the UK and internationally. Proposed alongside a campaign to encourage venues to declare as a percentage how much of their annual income goes directly to artists, this measure was not intended to 'shame' venues or festivals but rather discover 'simple ways in which to gauge the fairness and consistency of the way in which venues are dealing with artists' (Field 2013).

Though the sector as a whole remains opaque – with artists' contracts having the social status of private correspondence if not containing formal provisions barring disclosure of their terms – a small number of arts organisations now disclose the financial details of the typical deals which they offer to artists. London's Ovalhouse venue has previously published a report describing its total budget for supporting artists in the development of new work alongside an estimation of the further value of 'in-kind' support (e.g. access to rehearsal spaces, technical, production and marketing assistance) that may be made available (Ovalhouse 2014). In addition to an up-front financial contribution – ranging from £0–500 for work-in-progress showings to up to £15,000 for a full commission – artists working with Ovalhouse may receive between 40 and 60 per cent of box office income, though the nature of the deal varies from artist to artist. As to extend collaborations geared to producing work, the venue selects a number of artists to receive a bursary of £500 intended to leverage applications for further funding, alongside access to subsidised tickets.

While committed to nurturing long-term relationships with artists – and to offering a range of advice and support from initial idea to touring production, Ovalhouse is unable to accept unsolicited scripts 'which do not have a director or producer, or a production budget attached. This is because we do not have a literary department or the resources to take scripts to production' (Ovalhouse 2016).

In detailing its own range of production and support agreements offered to artists, London's Battersea Arts Centre has described the challenge of acting as a development house while being unable

> to benefit from selling the tickets for the successful shows you have helped develop. But equally, what about the artists who have often created this work on little or no wages? … it is those artists that provide theatre in London with a huge hidden subsidy that people don't see or understand. Another subsidy is provided by the staff in grassroots venues who work long hours and often for low pay. (Battersea Arts Centre 2013)

While offering a range of different models of support – including box-office splits, an artist's fee in exchange for 100 per cent of box office income, support for scratch work and occasional direct commissions or co-productions – the venue's team is

> very aware that when artists are looking for a gig it is sometimes too easy to take a bad deal because you want the gig. Very few of BAC's deals offer a scenario where there is enough money for everything. So one of the things we are working on as a team is to try and ensure artists take time to reflect on whether they can afford to work with us. (Battersea Arts Centre 2013)

Evident in the Battersea Arts Centre's account of its pursuit of an ethical practice is a sense of how a calculus that weighs up financial, professional and artistic incentives also involves the gauging of an 'opportunity cost' – that is, an artist's assessment of whether they can afford to turn down a chance to present work (even when it loses them money) because of the perceived value of exposure or future employment that might consequently be lost.

Arts festivals

While venues continue to play a significant role in commissioning and programming solo work, and in fostering the development of solo artists, contemporary arts festivals are territories which crystallise the larger macro-economic and macro-cultural context in which venues operate – and not least because venues are increasingly involved in curating their own festival events. Rapidly proliferating since the late 1980s – with over half of all currently active festivals in the UK launched since 1990 – theatre and performance festivals across Europe constitute a year-round programme of cultural production of which solo work constitutes a majority of the performances staged. These events are part of a wider development of post-war European culture in which – as the EU-sponsored 'Europe for Festivals, Festivals for Europe' project narrates – 'festivals have spread across Europe just as monasteries and cathedrals did in the Middle Ages' (European Festivals Association 2015). Tasked with 'communicating something meaningful about identity, community, locality and belonging', the contemporary arts festival has become a significant site for 'representing, encountering, incorporating and researching aspects of cultural difference' and a means for its participants to 'negotiate and secure individual and collective meaning and belonging' (Bennett, Taylor and Woodward 2014: 1–2). At the same time, festivals are celebrated as the powerhouses of a modern creative economy and for modelling forms of entrepreneurial culture work. In the words of British Arts Festivals Association's 'Festivals Mean Business' advocacy document, 'festivals are an essential part of the UK's cultural ecology and economy. They act as a focus for innovation where artistic risk can flourish, pushing boundaries, challenging convention and creating life affirming experiences' (2008: 2) while also serving as exemplary models of 'sustainable' business. That purported sustainability, though, rests on the widespread and heavy use of volunteer labour (Finkel 2009: 15) and, as explored below, the willingness of individual artist entrepreneurs to engage in unpaid or low-paid work, and risk significant personal debts.

Despite cuts to public arts funding across Europe following the financial crisis of 2007–8, the second decade of the new millennium has seen the launch of a number of new festivals dedicated to solo performance across Europe and elsewhere around the world. Since 2010, multi-arts venue Contact in Manchester, UK, has held its own solo performance festival, Flying Solo – notable for an annual open-call contest to commission new work – that is programmed alongside its Contacting The World and Queer Contact festival events, the latter of which also heavily features solo work. Since 2013, Denmark's Stand Alone Festival has invoked the Danish word 'enestående' – meaning outstanding or to stand alone in a positive sense – to market itself as 'the only one of its kind in Europe' (Aarhus2017 2016), aligned in 2017 with a cultural programme marking Aarhus's year as European Capital of Culture. More recently again in 2015, formerly UK-based director Martin Lewton and producer Andrew McKinnon have launched ¡BARCELONA SOLO! as a new festival of solo performance based in Sitges (a coastal town southwest of Barcelona known for its sizeable gay community) that showcases a range of Spanish and international work in association with the Institute of the Arts Barcelona. Programmed through an open submission process, the festival organisers express an interest in work which reflects the location of the festival through Catalan or LGBT themes. Elsewhere in Central and Eastern Europe, solo performance festivals are frequently billed as mono-performance or mono-drama events (distinguished from monologues in showcasing works in which a single performer plays multiple parts) and include St. Petersburg's Monocle festival (since 1997), Germany's biennial THESPIS festival (1999), Luxembourg's Fundamental (2010) and Cyprus's International Monodrama Platform (2015) – as well as the world's oldest monodrama festival, Wrostja, organised in Wrocław, Poland, since 1966.

While the majority of these events are supported by public funding, the rise of corporate sponsorship and private investment informs their availability to potentially exploitative commercial logics.[2] First held in 2010, New York's United Solo Theatre Festival is currently the largest festival dedicated to solo performance with over 120 productions in its 2016 programme. The festival's offering encompasses an expansive list of genres ('storytelling, puppetry, dance, multimedia, documentary, musical, improv, stand-up, poetry, magic, performance art, tragedy or comedy') though is dominated by storytelling, drama and comedy and by work from New York and US-based performers. Since 2013, the festival has also produced a smaller European showcase – United Solo Europe – which presents an annual programme of work in Warsaw, Poland, and includes a small number of works from the US edition alongside a series of workshops open to the general public. Programmed through an open-call application process, performers selected for the festival must pay a non-refundable $695 'participation fee' and receive 25 per cent of box office net sales from each performance, though acceptance to the festival guarantees only one performance in an up-to-sixty-five-seat venue with further slots only offered on the basis of strong, early ticket sales. As top-priced tickets are set at $40, participants who are not offered multiple slots cannot recover the expense of the participation fee and the cost of the production itself, and the emphasis on pre-sales favours artists who

---

2 For broader discussion, see Philips and Whannel (2013).

have existing public profiles, who are presenting work which has already been critically well-received elsewhere, or can afford to engage in media and publicity activities. As such, the primary benefits of taking part are framed as the 'opportunity to reach out to the industry' and 'receive media attention through previews, profiles, and reviews' while also being considered for inclusion in the United Solo showcase in Europe, 'as well as for script publication and Festival awards' (United Solo 2016).

New performance festivals

These and other events specialising in solo performance circulate within a larger ecology of international theatre and performing arts festivals. Since the early 1990s, long-standing post-war theatre festivals such as Berlin's Theatertreffen (since 1964), the Belgrade International Theatre Festival (1967) and the Dublin Theatre Festival (1957) have been joined by a significant number of events emphasising new and experimental work, including the Netherland's Noorderzan Performing Arts Festival Groningen (1990), Brussels' Kustenfestival des Arts (1995), the Slovenian Mladi Levi Festival (1998) and Alkantara Festival in Lisbon, Portugal (2006) alongside the biennials Homo Novus in Latvia (2003), Baltoscandal in Estonia (2008) and Ireland's LIVE COLLISION (2013). In the UK, the first two decades of the new millennium have seen a range of new small and mid-scale festivals dedicated to live art, experimental and queer performance that include SPILL (since 2007), Forest Fringe (2007), Manipulate (2008), SICK! Festival (2008), Shout (2009), BE Festival (2010), Tempting Failure (2011) alongside Glasgow's BUZZCUT (2012) and Take Me Somewhere (2017). These festivals join larger and longer-established events such as the Manchester International Festival (since 2007), Fierce Festival (1998), LIFT Festival (formerly London International Festival of Theatre, 1981), the Edinburgh International Festival (EIF) and the Edinburgh Festival Fringe to form a network of national and international presentation and development. Programmed by small groups or individual artistic directors through a mix of open calls, direct programming and, less frequently, commissions of original work, live art and experimental performance events in the UK have built on the legacy of the National Review of Live Art (NRLA), directed by Nikki Millican from the mid-1980s onwards to become an internationally significant event of almost legendary status. Originated in 1979 as an event called the Performance Platform at Nottingham's Midland Group arts centre and staged in London and Glasgow since the 1990s – though most frequently in Glasgow – the NRLA's programme sustained an avowedly international programme of cross-platform, experimental arts practices and sometimes marathon durational works until its sudden cancellation in late 2010.[3]

Of particular significance to this ecology is the work of Lois Keidan, former director of Live Arts at London's Institute of Contemporary Arts, whose personal and institutional support of artists and creative producers as co-founder and director of the Live Art Development Agency (LADA) has informed and animated critical debate through public events and the publication of a range of works incorporating documentation, artists' writings and scholarly criticism.[4] While distinguished by particular themes (e.g. SICK! Festival's interest in work at the intersection of health and the arts) and the sensibilities of individual festival directors (e.g. Robert Pacitti's curatorship of SPILL), the work of BUZZCUT, Tempting Failure and many others reflects Keidan's framing of Live Art as

> a cultural strategy to include experimental processes and experiential practices that might otherwise be excluded from established curatorial, cultural and critical frameworks. Live Art is a framing device for a catalogue of approaches to the possibilities of liveness by artists who chose to work across, in between, and at the edges of more traditional artistic forms. (Live Art Development Agency 2005)

If 'mixed-arts' festivals across the UK have tended towards a stable if not predictable and even homogeneous range of fixed genres (see Finkel 2009), then live art and new performance festivals have emerged (or, given their heritage, persisted) to position themselves as the vanguard of experimentation and innovation in both form and content, and in resistance of market-driven neoliberal logics of 'value for money'.

Supported by a range of funding sources including elements of commercial sponsorship in the form of donations (of equipment and services, or resources in kind in the form of access to venues and rehearsal spaces), these events rely heavily on Arts Council, local government and charitable income. Across a range of commissioning and programming practices – including co-productions with venues and independent production houses – the most commonly offered deal is a fixed artist's fee

---

3 See Heddon *et al.* (2010).
4 Key works published by LADA include Keidan and Brine (2011), Keidan and Mitchell (2012), Johnson (2013) and Heddon and Johnson (2016).

for a pre-agreed number of performances of a given capacity, alongside expenses to cover travel and accommodation claimed back after
the event. While a small number of tightly programmed international
festivals such as the EIF and Festival d'Avignon are able to cover all
administration and production costs associated with a performance, the
logic of small, fringe and mid-scale festivals more commonly necessitates
that participating artists mediate an anticipated gap between the financial
return of taking part and the potential value of 'exposure' to audiences,
programmers and commissioners, alongside the benefit of access to a
peer community of performers. In this context, artist-led collectives –
often centred on artists who are also independent producers – have taken
on increasing significance. Curated by Nick Alexander, Rosana Cade
and Karl Taylor, Glasgow's BUZZCUT emerged following the cancellation of the NRLA in 2010 as an attempt to foster support for new and
experimental work which remains attentive to the wider context in which
artists are expected to subsidise their own labour, and in which live art
practices are perceived to be an inaccessible, niche or elite performance
form. Supported at various stages with funding from Creative Scotland,
the Jerwood Charitable Foundation, the British Council and the Goethe
Institut, BUZZCUT's model turns on transparency in the terms of the
deal that it extends to artists who appear at the festival – an offer which
has included travel expenses to the festival, accommodation with a local
resident during the event and a daily meal, documentation of the performance work, technical support and a financial contribution to each
artist's costs.

Emphasising the possibilities of the festival as an accessible,
community-oriented environment, BUZZCUT forgoes all ticket sales in
favour of a 'pay what you can' collection after each performance and a
system of voluntary contributions from the public in support of the event
as a whole. While charging set prices for tickets would insure a level of
needed box-office return, this would

> exclude some people from attending, as they wouldn't be able to afford the
> ticket cost … Also, £10 isn't necessarily a fixed cost. £10 has different value
> to different people. To some it is easily disposed of cash, to others it is their
> food budget for the whole weekend. So the idea of a fixed cost is an illusion.
> (BUZZCUT and LADA 2016)

LADA's own statement on 'pay what you can' – offered alongside
BUZZCUT's at the 2016 festival quoted above – concurred that most cultural offerings are still prohibitively expensive and perpetuate exclusion,
and acknowledged that 'pay what you can' was a way of getting around

the question of the 'value' of an artistic experience and the barrier of cost of innovative and experimental art. Nonetheless,

> [j]ust as someone is paying for there to be cheap clothes in Primark (the children making them pay rather than the cheapskates buying them) someone has to pick up the tab for pay-what-you-can. Ideally this would be funders or sponsors, but more often than not it's artists if their financial arrangements are based on box office takings. Or it's the promoters having to work for free or cut corners in other aspects of their programmes. (BUZZCUT and LADA 2016)

BUZZCUT's model, in other words, may have as much to do with how artistic and performance labour may be valued by its audiences as by artists themselves. Located at the Pearce Institute in Govan – a former ship-building district with high levels of unemployment – that valuation is part of a broader concern for the festival's place in its adopted community, and the possible conversations which might take place around art and place.

If festivals manifest different value systems of support, community and artistic development, their recent history also describes the fragility of the ecology on which contemporary performance depends. As noted above, BUZZCUT's launch followed the collapse of NRLA in 2010 amidst allegations of financial misconduct which led to the sudden cancellation of the following year's planned events. Host to the NRLA from the late 1980s onwards, Glasgow's internationally reputed venue The Arches was itself forced to close following a licensing dispute in 2015, leading to the cancellation of its two high-profile performance festivals: Arches Live, a mini-festival of new, experimental and risk-taking live performance that emphasised new or emergent artists, and the multi-week BEHAVIOUR, characterised by a mix of award-winning Scottish and international performance, most often at the boundaries of theatre, dance and live art. While The Arches was praised by policy-makers and funding bodies for its mixed-economy financial model in which income from live music, world-class club nights, private commercial hires and a restaurant bar subsidised its performance programme, it was the venue's dependency on these revenue streams which led to its closure when pressure from Police Scotland relating to drugs-related incidents forced the withdrawal of a late alcohol licence. Elsewhere in the UK, Manchester's upscale international Queer Up North festival – known for a mixed programme of popular and experimental work – closed its doors entirely in 2011 after nearly twenty years when the sudden announcement of a funding cut worth £30,000 to a grant from Manchester City Council was compounded by the reduction of a long-running sponsorship package by a further £10,000 which led planned co-producer Manchester Pride to withdraw from the collaboration on the grounds that it was no longer financially viable (ArtsProfessional 2011).

The Edinburgh Festival Fringe

The complex relationships between curated, juried and open entry festival programming practices, between commercial and public funding structures, between 'free' and 'paid' access, and between possibilities for creative innovation and the demand for individuated entrepreneurialism may be exemplified by the economy of the Edinburgh Festival Fringe. Once the unofficial alternative to the EIF, the Festival Fringe is now the largest arts festival in the world, growing from fifty-seven participating groups in 1969 to 3,314 shows across 313 venues in 2015. In recent years, the origin story of the Fringe Society as dedicated to an 'open-access arts event that accommodates anyone with a story to tell and a venue willing to host them' has developed as an explicit marketing strategy encapsulated by the 2015 slogan 'defying the norm since 1947' which lays claim to more than a half-century of transgressive creativity. Framed in contrast to the EIF's elite offering, the Fringe Society's website presents the festival as open to all:

> Unlike many other festivals our constitution celebrates the fact that the Society shall do no vetting of the Fringe programme. That means we have no artistic director and that the programme is shaped by the very initiative and vision of performers willing to showcase their work here. (Edinburgh Festival Fringe Society 2016a)

This emphasis on entrepreneurial instinct – here figured as 'initiative', 'vision' and 'willing' – elides the reality of what journalist and critic Mark Fisher more accurately describes as a festival in which 'anyone who can afford it is free to perform' (Fisher 2012: 11). Though the Fringe exists as a space of diverse arts practice and experimentation, it is also one riven with opportunities for (self) exploitation – a dynamic to which I return below.

While the Fringe Society does not programme the Fringe – leaving such decisions to individual venues – it nonetheless engages in a range of curatorial practices: at a simple level, by identifying the categories of performance which appear in the official programme and setting the fee and advertising rates for appearing within it, by enforcing perceived cultural standards for good taste by reserving the right to edit any images or text submitted for inclusion that they judge 'to be inappropriate in any way', and by censoring 'potentially offensive' words with asterisks so that the publication as a whole will remain 'family friendly' (Edinburgh Festival Fringe Society 2016b: 1). The standing of the Fringe as an industry trade show also carries its own conservative dynamics, with pressure for artists to produce new work year on year according to a fixed calendar in order to appear before bookers during 'theatre's transfer window' (Wicker 2016) and so secure work opportunities for the season ahead. There may also be expectations for artists to produce work which sustains their personal reputation, and makes their practice both attractive and intelligible to potential programmers: Scottee has described the development of his award-winning show *The Worst of Scottee* (2013), discussed in chapter 2, as a response to industry expectations that he should make a solo show so everyone would know what he was 'about'.

In the competitive mainstream of the Fringe, even a comparatively modest solo show will face significant production costs – including but not limited to fees for venue hire, marketing and accommodation, even as the far larger costs of staging work with multiple cast members makes solo work appear more financially viable. These conditions include the requirement for a guarantee against ticket sales to be paid before the festival begins, and additional charges beyond venue hire for technical support, inclusion in a venue's publicity materials and use of their promotional street team. The prospect of debt has been institutionalised to the extent that the Fringe Society's own sample budgets all anticipate that artists and companies will lose money. Based on costs for venue hire, production, publicity and insurance as well as accommodation for the duration of the festival and a likely income based on 30 per cent of ticket sales, the Society's recent guide to staging a show at the Fringe anticipates a debt of a show on the commercial fringe ranging from £3,900 to £14,700 (Edinburgh Festival Fringe Society 2017). These budgets also exclude wages or salaries, meaning that the Fringe Society's cost estimates assume that participating artists will work for free. As a whole, advice for artists on the Fringe centres on 'how to limit your loss' (Fisher 2012: 251) even as other parts of the festival's economy – venues, publicists, equipment hire companies, food and convenience stores, landlords etc. – are paid in full. As comedian Stewart Lee observes, 'The Fringe, the biggest, best and most diverse arts festival in the entire world, is almost entirely underwritten by participants, most of whom go home thousands of pounds in debt' (Lee 2012).

For Charlie Wood – co-owner, director and programmer of the
Underbelly venues – these conditions mean that there are three reasons
to take a show to the Fringe: to have fun (which means deciding whether
you want to take a cheap or expensive working holiday), to make money
(though fierce competition means that even 'one man and a microphone
… can lose £5,000 or £10,000') or, alternatively

> because you hope your show will get bought and find a future life. It happens
> every year, which is why people keep coming back, not because it's a myth. It
> does genuinely happen, but be aware that it only happens to a very small per-
> centage of the overall number of shows. (Wood quoted in Fisher 2012: 252)

The development of Phoebe Waller-Bridge's Fringe First winning comic
monologue *Fleabag* (2013) from a short sketch to an original Fringe show
through extended runs around the UK to become a six-part series on the
BBC (promoted from BBC3 to BBC2 and eventually sold to the subscrip-
tion service Amazon Prime) may exemplify this latter route – though the
future life of successful work more often takes the form of national and
international tours, as in the case of Cristian Ceresoli's *La Merda* (see
chapter 4) or Matt Tedford and Jon Brittain's *Margaret Thatcher Queen of
Soho* (see chapter 3). Nonetheless, Wood's seemingly pragmatic advice –
and the advice of others like him – elides the role of the Fringe's larger
venues in producing, perpetuating and amplifying a market in which the
cost of commercial failure is largely absorbed by performers, in which
competition for audiences is increasingly between shows programmed at
the same venue, and in which well-established venues and organisations
have sought to protect their overall market share from smaller, emergent groups. In 2017, ticket sales at the 'Big Four' venue groups – the
Pleasance, Underbelly, Assembly and Gilded Balloon – are estimated to
comprise more than 50 per cent of all sales at the Fringe (Chortle 2017).

The fringe of the Fringe

If the Edinburgh Festival Fringe has become increasing commercialised
since the late 1990s – for the *Guardian*'s theatre critic Michael Billington
becoming a 'monstrous mixture of trade fair, rat-race, audition centre
and showcase for sensation-seekers out to catch the gullible media' that
is 'slowly but surely strangling the international festival' (2002) – it has
also been marked by efforts to challenge or mitigate the excesses of

market-driven logics, and encourage forms of experimentation and risk-taking that are strongly disincentivised by spiralling expenses and the risk of debt. Begun in 1996 at The Footlights and Firkin by Peter Buckley Hill, the Free Fringe has sought to offer an alternative model which charges neither performer for the chance to perform nor audiences for entry. In place of the Fringe's dominant 'pay-to-play' model is an arrangement in which venues – primarily bars, pubs and clubs – give their spaces for free and benefit from increased foot traffic and sales, while performers do not charge for tickets but take home the proceeds of a voluntary collection held at the end of each performance. The overall cost of running the Free Fringe – primarily print costs for the festival's guide, the *Wee Blue Book* – is met through benefit gigs, voluntary contributions from its participants and paid advertisements in the festival's official programme. Though dominated by newcomers, the Free Fringe's sustained success as reflected in a range of awards or nominations for participating acts as well as the festival itself means that it has increasingly attracted established performers away from the paid Fringe mainstream in rejection of the presumed necessity of professionalised debt. As stand-up Stuart Goldsmith asserts, 'Now we've had a Newcomer and the main Best Comedy Show both on the free fringe, there is no excuse for thinking that you have to go up [to Edinburgh] and lose your shirt' (Ajderian 2015).

As a whole, the Free Fringe turns on a model of collective volunteering and commitment: participants are expected to flyer for the festival as they market their own show, carry the organisation's logo on their show's promotional materials and its name in any official Fringe programme entry, and to support other shows by staffing the door before and after their own performance. Performance spaces are minimally equipped with a backdrop, PA system and basic lights – 'When we say basic imagine a switch on the wall and a member of your company switching it on and off' (PBH's Free Fringe 2017) – and the configuration of the stage space and seating must be negotiated with the other shows sharing the venue. Despite its egalitarian principles, the 'ethos and conditions' which govern artists' participation in the Free Fringe take the form of a non-contractual agreement that is notable for forbidding involvement with any of the other nominally free groups at the festival on the grounds that 'we are the original Free Fringe and we are really free. The public know about us and we don't want people confusing us with any of the others' (PBH's Free Fringe 2017). These conditions empower the Free Fringe's organisers to terminate any agreement with a performer at any time, as in the case of stand-up Stephen Carlin who lost his Free Fringe venue midway through the festival in 2015 when Hill discovered Carlin was also appearing in a play on the Laughing Horse Free Festival, a rival organisation created by former collaborators and promoters Alex Petty and Kevin McCarro who split from the Free Fringe in 2006 following creative differences over the direction of the event.

Though the subject of a number of rivalries over the past several years – most notably a dispute over the right to manage the Cowgatehead venue that saw several Free Festival performers lose their allocated spaces – both Free Fringe and Free Festival share a number of viewpoints: that the Fringe mainstream is too expensive for both performers and audiences, that the commercial logic of the Fringe mainstream stifles innovation and favours established acts in larger, well-known spaces, and that the festival as a whole should be a space for risk in creativity. Nonetheless, and in common with many Fringe venues, free festival spaces are programmed in line with the organisers' tastes and sensibilities, with the Free Fringe explaining that it will 'consider any show that we don't deem offensive or not good enough' (PBH's Free Fringe 2016) and the Free Festival addressing a perceived criticism of quality by asserting that 'it is false information, often put around by paid venues and competitors, that free shows are not programmed or curated, they are like any other venues' shows' (Free Edinburgh Fringe Festival 2017). The deeper potential compatibility of free models with the Fringe mainstream is also signalled by the emergence of hybrid 'pay what you want' experiments – led by Bob Slayer's Heroes of Comedy venues – in which audience members choose to either pre-pay full price for tickets (and guarantee their seat) or queue for a chance to attend the show and pay whatever they want upon exit. This model has since been selectively adopted by a number of other venues, most notably C Venues which charges both a hire fee for a performance space (paid in advance) and takes a percentage of audience donations, and by the Gilded Balloon for shows in the Counting House venue – a space developed over nine years as part of the Free Fringe, and which the Gilded Balloon's management were consequently accused of 'poaching' from the free festival economy (see Dessau 2016).

Forest Fringe

If the Free Fringe ecology offers opportunities for artists to present work on terms other than those determined by a commercial mainstream by defraying the cost of taking part, its programming and organisational practices nonetheless mirror many features of the main festival – that is, by largely preferring shows that will be performed over multiple dates if not for the full duration of the festival, by retaining the 'standard' Fringe timeslot of fifty minutes to an hour, and through programmes that are dominated by stand-up comedy and small-scale theatre alongside a smaller range of cabaret, spoken word and live music events. Running in parallel to the free Fringe ecology, Forest Fringe has been distinguished by its support of experimental work that is 'formally adventurous and unusual, whether it thinks of itself as live art, theatre, dance, installation or anything else' (Forest Fringe 2015). Begun in 2007 by theatre-makers and creative producers Deborah Pearson and Andy Field at the Forest Café, Edinburgh – a charitable, volunteer-run café and multi-arts community space – without funding or a theatre licence, the Forest Fringe was born of frustration with 'the fact that the festival had become a callous corporation-driven arts marketplace that promoted a very particular version of success that many artists didn't recognize', and in which support for artists 'extended about as far as showing them where the venue toilets were' (Field 2012). Since joined by performance-maker and writer Ira Brand, Pearson and Field's work at Forest Fringe emerged as a direct critique of the Fringe mainstream as 'a democracy that comes with a £10,000 price tag. It is only open to those who have got money, three weeks to spare and who make work that fits neatly into a 50-minute time slot' (Field quoted in L. Gardner 2008).

Described as a 'no-budget project' by its founders, Forest Fringe's work during the Edinburgh festivals has developed as the result of a particular 'collision of circumstances' (Brand 2016: 41) in and around Edinburgh rather than as the result of a conscious plan or readily reproducible strategy, led by a lo-fi sensibility of 'making-do' which initially resulted in shows 'with an intimate, amateur aesthetic that was at once humorously self-deprecating and charged with a defiant, radical energy' (Field 2016: 12). Though shaped in its early years by the particular opportunities afforded by its venue – a large, high-ceiling hall that had served as the main meeting space of its former residents, the Edinburgh Seventh Day Adventist Church – and by the collectivist sensibilities of the Forest Café, Forest Fringe has increasingly articulated the possibilities of a festival with a 'sort of wild amnesiac vitality to it, able to reimagine and rewrite itself at will' (Field 2012). This willingness to adapt – born of necessity in working with few or no resources in the earliest years of the organisation's existence – was accelerated by the loss of the festival's original venue after 2011 when its owners (another charity, Edinburgh University Settlement) were declared bankrupt. After a year spent between the Hunt & Darton

Café and the Forest Café's new premises in Edinburgh's Tollcross area which saw the publication of *Paper Stages* (2012), a collection of scores, texts and performance-based interventions contributed by former collaborating artists available in return for an hour's donated volunteering, the festival began a longer, ongoing relationship with Leith's Drill Hall, a participatory arts venue run by the arts and education charitable trust Out of the Blue at figurative and literal distance from the main hubs of Edinburgh's tourism-centric festival economy.

Curated by Pearson, Field and Brand, Forest Fringe's Edinburgh programme has encompassed work from both emergent and well-established British, UK-based and international performance artists alongside the artistic directors themselves. While this offer includes a number of companies or collectives (including Action Hero, Figs in Wigs and Forced Entertainment), the majority of artists have presented work as soloists – including Christopher Brett Bailey, Jo Bannon, Season Butler, Rosana Cade, Abigail Conway, Tim Crouch, Richard DeDomenici, Chris Goode, Nic Green, Bryony Kimmings, Tania El Khoury, Brian Lobel, Daniel Oliver, Deborah Pearson, Scottee, Selina Thompson and Greg Wohead. Staging this work free to its audiences, Forest Fringe is distinguished by a level of support which mirrors BUZZCUT in going significantly beyond that offered by any of the other free festivals in promising a space for a performer to present their work, accommodation during the festival, technical support, and in working to ensure that press and promoters see the work. The desire to nurture and sustain arts practices beyond those preferred by the dominant commercial logic of the Edinburgh festivals has involved a conscious recognition on the part of the organisers of the particular ecology of support that might be required by that endeavour – such as that the commitment that 'we will try to ensure that you are free to present your work in whatever way you want, for however long you want' (Forest Fringe 2015) allows artists to present intimate, one-to-one, durational and site-specific work that might otherwise be financially unviable, and likely unwelcome in many mainstream Fringe venues.

Since 2011, the Forest Fringe has also engaged in a programme of year-round UK and international projects that involves curated venues and programme strands within other international arts festivals (such as the UK's Latitude and Fusebox Festival of Austin, Texas), short-term residences developing site-responsive work with visiting and/or local artists (in Yokohama, Bangkok and Hong Kong) and the development of free-standing 'micro-festivals' (as in the 2012 collaboration with Culturgest in Lisbon, Portugal) programmed with artists who have previously appeared in the Edinburgh season. While no one is paid for their work during the Edinburgh festival, artists who appear in micro-festival events are paid a fee by the commissioning venue, with Pearson, Field and Brand paid for their work as curators. In Pearson's words, Forest Fringe's financial model 'is as vulnerable and precarious as the financial life of a freelance artist' (2015a: 80), being dependent on commissions and project funding in which venues approach the organisation to create a micro-festival and other projects because those organisations view Forest Fringe's curatorial model as being unique and capable of being treated, financially at least, as a work of art. Nonetheless, the joint roles occupied by Forest Fringe's organisers as curators and as performers who have presented their own work during the festival complicates the horizontal structure of the event. As Pearson notes, the organisers' ability to determine who appears during the Edinburgh Festival distinguishes them from other artists who might be involved in the larger project of Forest Fringe. Though the group's festival presence has given rise to a number of long-term association, friendships and collaborations, Forest Fringe makes no offer of long-term support, and a stated desire for the communal, creative ownership of the event is complicated by knowledge that 'at its core this community really consists of three co-directors and whoever we are working with at the time' (Pearson 2015a: 80).

After ten years at the festival in 2016, Forest Fringe announced its decision to 'say a temporary no to the Edinburgh Festival — a no shaped pause. Not forever but for now' (Forest Fringe 2016a). In a blog post that acknowledged that what was once only possible at the Forest Fringe could now be achieved in a range of contexts across the city, the organisers expressed frustration that 'the possible ways people have for getting involved with the festival remain annoyingly limited and exploitative, with seemingly little will from the festival as a whole to support greater diversity and accessibility' (Forest Fringe 2016c). In a later post to social media, the organisers explained that the decision was not a protest against the festival or a 'cry for help' as the challenges that faced artists in presenting their work in Edinburgh were not new or significantly worse than in previous years; it was, rather, formed of a more acute awareness of barriers to participation in the festival that had always existed. Taking time away from the demands of the Edinburgh Festival after an unusually tumultuous year would, the organisers offered, allow them the time and space 're-think our presence there so that Forest Fringe remains a radical, hopeful and experimental part of the fringe; somewhere unexpected and unpredictable that invites us to imagine new relationships with art and with artists' (Forest Fringe 2016b). In June of 2017, the organisation took the further decision to withdraw from staging events in Edinburgh during August for the foreseeable future, opting to instead 'explore what else we might do with the collective energy that we have previously dedicated to our presence at the festival' in the creation of as yet undetermined new large-scale projects, in founding a regular monthly art club at Somerset House Studios, London, and in proposing a handbook 'of all the things we think we've learnt in 10 years of making Forest Fringe. It will be a toolkit of good ideas, accidental successes, practical advice, horrible arguments and hard-won lessons' (Brand 2017).

Conclusion

Deferring the question of when and whether one acts freely and autonomously, Isabel Lorey focuses on the degree to which 'self-chosen' precarisation 'contributes to producing the conditions for being able to become an active part of neo-liberal and economic relations' (2009: 187–8). For Lorey, any analysis of 'self-chosen' activity must acknowledge the 'historical lines of force of modern bourgeois subjectivation, which are imperceptibly hegemonic, normalizing, and possibly block "counter-behavior"' (2009: 188). The field of contemporary performance – and solo performance in particular – provides a uniquely powerful analytic for examining this dynamic, and not least because the notion of self-defining subject has been exemplified in the idea of 'the modern male artist subject, who draws his creativity from himself, because it supposedly exists within him, there, where Western modernity also positions sex and has made it the nature, the essence of the individual' (Lorey 2009: 199). While the deployment of talent and creativity as disciplinary regimes may serve to turn the individual into a 'willing work-horse, self-flagellating when inspiration doesn't flow out onto the page', Angela McRobbie nonetheless acknowledges the utopian dynamics described by novel ways of working which articulate 'some desire for a better way of life, a better kind of work. After all, as work is now life, it is hardly surprising that attempts are made to make it pleasant and enjoyable' (McRobbie 2011: 88). To similar ends, de Peuter argues that 'if the cultural worker in nonstandard employment exemplifies tendencies in contemporary capitalism that promote precarity, by the same token, such workers may be a strategic locus of resistance against these tendencies' (2014: 265) with emergent strategies adopted by the creative precariat serving to challenge the acceptability of unpaid work and the uncritical valorisation of non-monetary rewards associated with self-expressive labour.

Such dynamics are evident in the discourse and working conditions of artists engaged in the creation of contemporary performance, and most clearly so in the context of festivals such as BUZZCUT and Forest Fringe where dominant frameworks of individualised entrepreneurialism have been brought into conversation with the possibilities – and challenges – of collaborative and collective working. As such, and rather than merely exemplifying the hegemonic operation of neoliberal capitalism, the figure of the artist as creative entrepreneur in these and other instances may allow us to begin to conceive the incomplete, unstable and unsustainable regime of neoliberalism's processes. At the same time, that figure draws attention to the broader role of self-exploitation within neoliberalism's preferred conception of individual subjectivity: a mode of being characterised by self-reliance, a sustained life-long project of self-invention and, above all, a complicit attachment to the conditions of one's subjection. It is the contradiction within this account – and the way in which solo performance may unravel the oppositions between inside and outside, self and other, on which it depends – that I will explore in and through performance in the following chapters.

2

The martyr: dramaturgies of endurance, exhaustion and confession

Mindful of neoliberalism's preference for subjects who are willing and able to exploit their own well-being and yet drawn to the possibility of testimony which insists that suffering may have transformative political effects, this chapter explores solo performances in which the contested ontology of the martyr articulates the shifting status of endurance as a mode of individual and collective witness. Though endurance in art and performance art can be located within a larger tradition that contains the work of Tehching Hsieh, Mike Parr and Marina Abramović – as well as long-form performances such as George Chakravarthi's *I Feel Love!* (2009), Forced Entertainment's *Quizoola!* (2014) and Action Hero's *Slap Talk* (2015) – this chapter focuses on works which articulate the link between endurance, testimony and confession (rather than, say, endurance and duration, or endurance and pain).[1] As I will explore here and in the following chapters, that link is important because it describes the means through which testimony-as-self-fashioning may be made to serve ends beyond those made compulsory within neoliberalism. Moreover, if the contemporary figure of the suicide bomber positions the martyr as a dangerously unpredictable interloper into civilised spaces – the product of religious or ethnic fanaticism which is strictly 'Other' – this

---

1 For broader discussion of endurance in performance, see Thomas McEvilley's influential 'Art in the Dark', reproduced in his collected essays (2005) and Gonzalez Rice (2016).

chapter focuses on martyrs whose putative and even reliable sacrifices are closer to home, and whose exceptional status serves to constitute the social order from which they emerge and to which they belong. Through that focus, this chapter begins to elaborate two of this book's larger arguments: that exceptional subjects are both useful to the maintenance of hegemonic configurations of power and the public sphere and, at the same time, manifest neoliberalism's incompleteness and inconsistency in a manner that manifests the possibility of resistance, critique and change.

I start, though, in recognition of the martyr's constitution as a figure whose exceptional status resides with their simultaneous and paradoxical embodiment of radical autonomy and complete involuntariness. Arguing that the willingness to suffer and die for a cause has – over the centuries – tended to 'lose its religious orientation and increase its political potency' (2008: 435), historian Lacey Baldwin Smith's study of Western martyrdom emphasises the absolute will of the singular martyr. Though concluding that 'it takes two to create a martyrdom; the actor who sacrifices life and the community that offers the title' (2008: 458), Smith's scholarship returns repeatedly to the idea of the martyr as a figure whose 'aggressively individualistic' tendencies call into question their capacity to represent a larger cause or the interests of others, even though they emerge as 'a group phenomenon, taking strength from their sense of collective identity and representing ... serous rifts within society' (1999: 18). Despite this quality, Smith disputes that the martyr is anything other than anti-social. In recognising a higher allegiance to a cause, martyrs 'by their death present clear evidence that their greatest strength may be their gravest weakness: they cannot live in society with their fellow human beings' (Smith 1999: 15); whether his message belongs to God or history, the martyr is an egotist whose sense of self 'is gratified by fulfilling the mission, even by dying for it' (Smith 1999: 362).

In the teachings of the early Christian Church, Augustine of Hippo addressed the troublesome singularity of the martyr by emphasising their function as a witness rather than a sacrifice, such as that martyrdom was understood as 'an imitation of Christ and a testimony of love for Christ' in which martyrs called 'for everyone to pray to Christ, and rejected any personal veneration' (Dupont 2014: 138). While Augustine taught that it was death and the fear of death which rendered the martyr's testimony credible, he was also careful to emphasise that the martyr did not seek death out: if pain and suffering are desired, he reasoned, then their forbearance meant little as a measure of faith. Opposed to the cult of the martyr, Augustine's teachings on martyrdom are structured by a paradox of self-abnegation – 'by dying, martyrs live; by losing their souls, they gain them, by denying themselves, they find themselves' (Fitzgerald and Cavadini 1999: 538) – in which renunciation is always an act of witness to something other than their own identity. In this mimetic epistemology, the suffering body of the martyr was made one in corporate unity with Christ yet maintained in a careful hierarchy: Christ's death alone comprised a redemptive sacrifice. Through this frame, Augustine ascribed to the martyr a pedagogic function whose exemplary actions might inspire others to join the ranks of faithful while serving as a model of tolerance in accepting whatever adversity God might send. At the heart of Augustine's doctrine, though, is a refusal of suffering as an end or proof in itself: it is not the torture or the punishment which makes the martyr, but the martyr's cause.

Whether framed by sacred or secular values, the martyr – a word derived from the Greek term 'martur' meaning 'witness' – is a privileged observer who does not speak freely or spontaneously. A witness is most often 'someone who saw something others could not see, who heard something others did not hear' whose testimony is politicised because it is called upon the context of a conflict deriving from 'some severe deviance from a (divine, social, legal or political) norm' (Thomas 2009: 93). If the veracity of one's evidence is comprised by its autobiographical certification – in its simplest formation, through the claim that 'I was there' (Ricœur 2004: 63) – then to stand witness is lay the surety of one's self and experiences open to dispute. That risk may be all the more significant for its uncertain relationship to agency. While Elizabeth Castelli proposes that the designation martyr is not an ontological category but a post-event interpretive one in which 'martyrs are produced by the stories told about them' (2006: 1), it is the body and life of the martyr-as-witness which stands as a sort of 'collateral to justify the loan of our credence' (Peters 2008: 29). The paradox of the martyr, in short, is that they belong to themselves as immediately as they belong to the movement to which their suffering stands testament, and they attest to the truth of that cause precisely because that suffering is both self-willed and not of their own choosing.

Reading through and against these cultural traditions, this chapter offers the figure of the martyr as a heuristic for examining the conditions in which politicised subjectivities are allowed – or called upon – to stand as surrogates for others or to speak for themselves. While resilience may be prized within neoliberalism as a feature of self-regulating, responsible citizenship, this chapter explores the possibilities of endurance as a mode of resistance and self-definition which operates through 'the vulnerability and incapacities of the body rather than its prowess' (Warr 2005) – a perspective to which I will return in chapters 6 and 7 in discussion of the misfit and the optimist. Though the following case studies make varying uses of literalness, theatricality and autobiographical material, they share dramaturgies of endurance which implicate their audiences as witnesses to the function and necessity of public suffering. In the first part of the chapter, I explore works by Ron Athey and Kira O'Reilly – situated in a live art tradition in which testimony is an 'irreducible physicality' where 'real blood is really flowing' (Schechner 2014: 151, 154) – to consider arguments made for performative wounding in producing politically progressive or transformative communities of affect. Wary of the selective terms on which exceptional subjects may be positioned as representatives of a universal humanism, I then turn to the post-blood works of Franko B in which strategies of non-literal injury elaborate endurance as a mode of resistance suspended between self-definition and self-excoriation.

The nature of that double-bind – wherein the martyr's imagined powers of self-determination turn on their ability to threaten that same self – is further explored through a reading of Eddie Ladd's *Ras Goffa Bobby Sands / The Bobby Sands Memorial Race* (2009) in which a dramaturgy of 'voluntary involuntariness' frustrates any straightfor-ward claim on the martyr as figure of radical agency. In the final part of the chapter, I consider works by theatre-makers Adrian Howells and Scottee whose staging of self-denunciation further complicate a claim on the martyr as an embodiment of wilful surrender by indicating the relationship between performative endurance and the penitential logic of confession. Where Howells' *The 14 Stations of the Life and History of Adrian Howells* suggests but ultimately frustrates the possibility of expi-atory unburdening through scenes of self-reproach, Scottee's *The Worst of Scottee* asserts a form of confession in which the question of guilt is refused. By moving from endurance through exhaustion to confession, I trace how solo performance's engagement with the cultural logic of the martyr provides a new perspective from which to assess and challenge neoliberal practices of subjectification.

Queering martyrdom: Ron Athey

Since the late 1990s, the figure of the martyr in contemporary perform-ance – and the martyr's potential relationship to self-obliteration – has been closely associated with Ron Athey, whose work is characterised by its engagement with sacred iconographies of endurance and suffering, and the staging of his repeatedly penetrated, HIV-positive body in acts of ceremonial piercing, bloodletting, and scarification. These performances draw on Athey's damaging experiences as a child raised within a Pentecostal household by a schizophrenic mother, and a later decade of drug addiction followed by HIV diagnosis (see Athey 2013). As Dominic Johnson (2008, 2013) has explored at length, Athey's practice reflects a diverse range of contemporary and early twentieth-century literary and artistic influences alongside those of queer and BDSM culture, notably the works of proto-surrealist Georges Bataille and novelist Jean Genet, as well as broad stretches of European art and history. Through work initiated in Los Angeles' punk, club, queer and underground gallery spaces during the 1990s, Athey has repeatedly returned to narratives of sacrifice and bodily endurance and, in particular, the image of St Sebastian through solo and group works that include *Martyrs & Saints* (1992), *4 Scenes In A Harsh Life* (1994), *Sebastian Suspended* (2000) and *Sebastian@50* (2012).

For Mary Richards, Athey's work engages with Christian iconography as to imbue it with contemporary meaning, producing 'the "positive" body as a sort of post-modern secularised saint' whose identification with saintly and Christ-like submissiveness in the face of pain and suffering 'underscores the injustice and lack of mercy shown to both Christ and to those persecuted as H.I.V. positive or as homosexual' (Richards 2003) while simultaneously asserting wilful resistance in the face of potential illness. Reading *Judas Cradle* (2004–5) – performed with opera singer and artist Juliana Snapper – alongside medieval depictions of penitential self-flagellation, Marla Carlson similarly suggests that Athey's masochism serves to rework 'the relation between voluntary suffering, homophobia, and the plague of AIDS in order to present a new martyr who rejects Christianity but finds a sacred subject in himself' (2010: 124–5). In this work, this vision of the martyr is not determined by the morality of an external cause – as in the teaching of St Augustine – but constituted as a figure who challenges a transcendent moral theology which presumes to 'make sense' of suffering. While Athey may repeatedly – and as Fintan Walsh argues, problematically – position himself 'as a sacrificial Christ or Dionysus who endures mutilation in the hope of a second birth' (Walsh 2010a: 112), he does so in a manner which disputes rather than affirms the telos of salvation. In the opening sequence of *Martyrs and Saints*, the first part of Athey's 'torture' trilogy, 'you cannot quite hear what Athey is saying (his lips are sewn together) but among other things he seems to be screaming, "Give up on an AIDS cure"' (McGrath 1995: 24).

At stake in this body of work is the contemporary function of the martyr as a witness 'who attests to the truth by suffering' (Thomas 2009: 95) even as the pursuit of discomfort runs counter to the sensibilities of most Western cultures and when 'seemingly innate rights to physical integrity, to agency over one's body, to respect of and the autonomy of both the living and the dead, and the "property" of one's own body have come under serious stress at the turn of the twenty-first century' (Bouchard 2012: 94). This quandary – and its implications for an attempt to testify to a history of AIDS and queer embodiment – animates Athey's decades-long *Incorruptible Flesh* sequence, first begun in 1997 as a collaboration with Lawrence Steger who later died of AIDS-related pneumonia in 1999, and continued through *Dissociative Sparkle* (2006), *Perpetual Wound* (2007) with Dominic Johnson before concluding in *Messianic Remains* (2013). Structured by ritual scenarios of nursing, healing and grief which address Athey's survivor status alongside acts of exhibitionist, ecstatic masochism, these works elaborate a reflexive history of resistance suspended between self-willed and involuntary acts of endurance. *Dissociative Sparkle* – staged nearly a decade after the series' first episode – extends the final image of Athey's initial collaboration with Steger as a six-hour durational performance: the artist offers himself as sexualised corpse available to the audience's touch, positioned 'on a bed of metal bars, impaled on a baseball bat, with his face fixed into a grimace by hooks tied to the bed's frame' (Doyle 2013a).

In *Messianic Remains* – commissioned by Performance Studies International and debuted during the organisation's 2013 conference at Stanford University – Athey returns to this image in modified form, his body once more resting on a metal rack and penetrated with hooks and baseball bat, and offered to the audience to anoint with grease. Now, though, the staging invokes and appropriates the imagery of pre-Christian culture: Athey wears a false beard 'reminiscent of those donned by ancient Egyptian pharaohs, which were meant to convey their status as living gods' (Hoetger 2014: 60) and his face is covered by a translucent death mask. Athey appears as a monarch lying in state, though the extended endurance of *Dissociative Sparkle* is compressed and gives way to ritual incantation. Accompanied by priest-attendants and invoking Thelemic magic practices drawn from the work of experimental filmmaker Kenneth Anger (influenced in turn by English occultist Aleister Crowley) Athey clears a circle while performing a cut-up text drawn from Jean Genet's debut novel *Our Lady of the Flowers* (1943). In *Dissociative Sparkle*, the audience is positioned as a surrogate for Steger who had anointed Athey in the original scene; in *Messianic Remains*, the audience (re)performs that gesture and engages in a form of restored or 'twice-behaved' behaviour that marks a rite stalled between funeral and resurrection.

Drawing on Agamben's analysis of the state of exception, Matthew Recla (2014) suggests that *homo sacer* may be analogous to the figure of the martyr who is included within a given community because she is excluded from it in death. For Recla, though, there is one crucial difference in that *homo sacer* can be killed but not sacrificed, whereas the martyr can be sacrificed but not killed. Athey's self-martyring suggests the blurring of both outcomes, insofar as the 'incorruptible' flesh of his still-living body describes a form of punitive suspension from the social (marked by Athey's sero-positive status and the consciousness of having outlived so many of his contemporaries) and a resistant persistence, having 'failed' to perform as a morally corrective sacrifice by dying as proof of God's mercy. Athey is (not) dead and (not) returned. A comparable dramaturgy may be found in Turkish born and Netherlands resident artist Anthony Hüseyin Pharaoh's more recent *Playing Possum: My Brothers Might Kill Me* (2015), a work born of being the subject of a familial honour killing threat when an image of Pharaoh perceived as gay appeared online. Imitating the behaviour of the opossum who 'plays dead' as a defensive behaviour and acting in the knowledge that victims of honour killings are often buried without ceremony by strangers, Pharaoh's performance renders his own body at the centre of his own Islamic funeral. In both cases, ritualised death rites become the means by which a queer subject might assert their own persistence.

Arguing that Athey's practice renders its audience both responsive and responsible, art historian and performance scholar Amelia Jones suggests that

> experiencing Athey's elegantly suffering body is potentially upsetting and moving because one is made to take the role of empathetic – or disapproving, disgusted, punitive, angry – witness, rather than distanced spectator. (2013: 176)

For Jones, Athey's self-wounding offers potentially progressive political effects to the extent that it might be understood 'as occurring on/in a body that could just as well be mine' (2009: 55) through an empathetic 'wince' of recognition that has significance for the ways in which we perceive it to have happened to an actual body in the past or to our own body in the future. This empathy is not merely narcissistic – relating only to our personal fear of being hurt – but linked to a sense of our contingent relationship to others, and turns on a radically intersubjective exposure to another even in acknowledgement that one cannot feel as another feels. In this reading, the wound is an opening up to difference, 'a mode of signifying that makes the body of the other available as meaningful through identification. It makes pain readable as inscribed in and through the body' (Jones 2013: 177). To similar ends, Adrian Heathfield argues that Athey's work 'brings to attention a particular quality of being, a precondition of being, that is our singular interdependence, our differentiated co-being' (Heathfield 2013: 209) insofar as it invokes the myth of the sovereign subject in order to dissemble it. For Heathfield and Jones alike, Athey's performances are potentially transformative because they challenge the stability of a given, coherent subject, and render Athey's body as something available to a collective experience of empathetic identification in which the sign of the wounded martyr becomes 'a sign of something larger than the spectacle of the suffering body' (Jones 2009: 56).

Empathy for injury: Kira O'Reilly

The terms of this critique may resonate with the skin and body works of British live artist Kira O'Reilly whose interdisciplinary practice involves visual art, biotechnical processes and conceptual languages, most notably in creation of the interspecies works *inthewrongplaceness* (2005–9) and *Falling Asleep With a Pig* (2009). Through appearances at the National Review of Live Art and performance festivals around Europe, O'Reilly's work may be most widely known for its highly controlled scenes of cutting and scarification – notably *Succour* (2001) in which the artist performs an extended series of geometrically arranged cuts on her body with a surgical scalpel. Positioned at the intersection of fine and live art, O'Reilly's practice challenges what we understand to be the boundaries of the sovereign body and, more broadly, what is means to occupy a human body when it is brought into conversation with the non-human and its surrounding environments. Diverse in form, this work may be unified by O'Reilly's willingness to treat her own body tissue as matter – whether at the micro-scale by growing a living lace out of her own skin cells alongside pig's tissue within *inthewrongplaceness* or at the macro-scale in *Stair Falling*'s (2009) painfully slow-motion collapse, head over heels, down a flight of stairs.

As in Athey's practice, this body of work provokes the complicity of its audience. Performance scholar Rachel Zerihan's account of *Untitled*

Action – a performance which turns on O'Reilly's invitation to audience members to make 'one short cut' in her skin – alongside her experience of the one-to-one work *My Mother* (2003) explores how her role as witness to O'Reilly's self-injury might infer 'wider questions of social violence, trauma and healing, and, essentially, my responsibility in this setting' (2010: 39–40). These scenes of commitment turn on the performative negotiation of consent between performer and audience-participant, a dynamic which produces the subjects capable of giving consent by foregrounding the precarious terms on which they might acknowledge each other's agency. In this frame, consent is not the expression of an already sovereign, constituted subject but the effect of recognising the limits of one's autonomy. Of *My Mother*, Zerihan recalls:

> After I had told her a story about my mother, O'Reilly said, 'I'm going to cut myself now, are you ok with that?' A brief silence followed, and she said to me, reassuringly, 'It'll hurt a little bit but I wouldn't do it if it hurt a lot'. Hearing her acknowledgment of the pain she would experience but 'grading it' as 'little', I gave my consent. (2010: 35)

The terms of this dialogue are complex and suggest how even the explicit pursuit of active consent may invoke uncertainty, with 'are you ok with that?' comprising an enquiry as to Zerihan's emotional state ('do you feel ok about me cutting myself?') as much as a request for permission to proceed ('do I have your agreement to cut myself?').

If bodily action comes to mirror verbal disclosure in a 'physical opening that also spilled' (Zerihan 2010: 35), it does so through a reciprocal gesture of care which is also a measure of complicity in the action that lies ahead: live artist and audience-participant exchange reassurances which simultaneously advertise their uncertain grounds. In *Untitled Action*, Zerihan's description of O'Reilly's process indicates a similar apprehension of transgression, with the artist doing her best 'to put me at ease with vocal reassurances' (2010: 38) while drawing attention to the function of a television screen showing a live feed of the performer and, later, the image of Zerihan cradling the artist in a stylised pietà pose. O'Reilly's discussion of her own practice has sometimes emphasised a relationship with the audience – as viewer, spectator or participant – whose presence serves to 'complete the work with their being' (Chamberlain 2009: 60). Here, that role involves the audience member's understanding of themselves as a witness to O'Reilly's self-wounding and their capacity – or not – to fulfil the role of grieving care-giver.

Exploring similar concerns, Patrick Duggan aligns the possibility of 'kinaesthetic empathy' for a traumatic or traumatised body with the scopic economy of O'Reilly's *Untitled (Syncope)* (2007). Naked but for red stilettos and a feather headdress, her body littered with the scars of past performances, O'Reilly first appears moving backwards but holding a small circular mirror that catches the gaze of her audience to confront them with her own. Taking the hand of one audience member, O'Reilly leads the group into a second space where she reaches down to take a scalpel to her calf muscle: 'blood oozes out slowly and as it collects along the cut it tumbles down towards her ankle, puddling between the skin of her foot and the edge of her red shoe' (Duggan 2009: 310). Accompanied by a metronomic ticking, O'Reilly's breath and muscle movements appear tightly controlled and, at once, the product of mechanistic compulsion. In either case, the body's material presence asserts itself: as Mary Paterson observed of the work in its staging at SPILL, 'the encounter is unsettling. Up to that point we were free to gaze at O'Reilly's beautiful figure, but now it has been given agency – literally, a mind of its own' (2007). Unmistakable for the involuntary bleeding of menstruation – a bodily process staged as durational performance in Poppy Jackson's *Television Lounge* (2014) – O'Reilly's blood testifies to the force of her embodied will.[2]

Echoing the terms of Amelia Jones' response to Athey's body, Duggan's argument for the political efficacy of O'Reilly's practice turns on a sense of 'the reciprocity at work in the creation of the piece: the contract between performer and audience is two-way, without either party it would simply not exist – we are created as a group, an "us"' (2009: 312–13). Yet the terms of something 'larger' (in Jones' reference to Athey) or a communal 'us' (in Duggan's reference to O'Reilly) are precarious and perhaps not inherently radical or progressive. One may not wince when O'Reilly cuts herself but instead – or simultaneously – take sadistic or masochistic pleasure from the spectacle. At the least, Jones acknowledges that the possibility of empathetic recognition may be constrained by the terms of which bodies and subjects we find 'grievable' (2009: 55) in Butler's sense of the 'presupposition for the life that matters' (Butler 2009: 14). While the inclusion of Athey's queer body in the ranks of the grievable might describe the broadening of lives which are liveable in the decades following the first appearance of HIV and AIDS, Fintan Walsh observes that Athey's homosexual body and sero-positive status may nonetheless disqualify him from standing as a sacrificial offering for

---

2 For an alternative deployment of endurance as an exploration of tropes of feminine embodiment, see performance artist Hellen Burrough's *Achillia* (2013), https://vimeo.com/92750302, accessed 1 August 2017.

a broader ('healthy') community (Walsh 2010a: 142). Though the biographical element of Athey's work provides a powerful context for the
'resignification of feminine and associated homosexual attachments',
it also limits his potentiality as 'a representative oppressed everyman'
(Walsh 2010a: 130). It is the specificity of Athey's queer body which
qualifies and refutes his capacity to stand as a martyr for the communities of which he is (not) a part.

Though O'Reilly's work makes limited use of autobiographical
material or associations, we might similarly recognise the degree to
which the capacity of her practice to infer a wider community of responsibility (and response-ability, in Zerihan's phrasing) turns on the singular
status of her body as an exceptional, enduring document of past injury.
This condition – in which the skin might serve as 'the nexus where the
self intersects with society, where ownership and judgment coincide
and sometimes clash between competing domains' (Adler and Adler
2011: 204) – turns on the availability of that body to existing frames
of cultural reference. In this respect, to argue that either O'Reilly or
Athey's queer body might 'exemplify the martyr's suffering' (Schechner
2014: 153) may describe the recuperation of the queer or exceptional
body to established norms of recognition, and ones in which the queer
subject is not only always already wounded but retained and *invoked* as
a wounded subject as proof of liberal humanism's capacity to practice
compassion. The difficulty, then, may be the degree to which the ambition of their expansive humanism turns on the hope that performative
wounding might expand a possible domain of recognition rather than
secure its established terms.[3]

Injury without wounds: Franko B

Challenges to the terms on which an exceptional body might be allowed
to stand as a representative sacrifice are also evident in the work of
London-based Italian artist Franko B. Spanning sculpture, painting,
installation and live art, Franko B's practice is structured by a repeated
back and forth 'between wounding and healing' (Aldarondo 2012) in
which the audience-spectator is implicated as a participant witness.

3 I return to discussion of the potential – and problematics – of vulnerability in chapter 7's
discussion of the optimist.

I Miss You (1999–2005), for example, adopts the form of a catwalk fashion show: naked, shaven and painted white with careful incisions made to the veins of his arms, Franko B walks slowly up and down a strip of canvas, his dripping blood tracing an increasingly dense trail. If the work is consciously exhibitionistic, it is only because it frames the role of the audience as involving something other than disinterested spectatorship. This dynamic may be clearer still in *Aktion 398* (1998–2002) – named for the Vienna Aktionists – which comprised a carefully staged confrontation between individual audience members and Franko B's white-painted, self-wounded body, and its later inversion in *Aktion 893 (Why Are You Here?)* (2005) in which nude audience members experienced one-to-one encounters with the artist who remained fully clothed.

Critical studies of Franko B's self-staging have sometimes emphasised its apparent invocation of sacred iconography in the production of profane images. For Richards, *Oh Lover Boy* (2001–5) – in which the artist appears naked and bleeding on a lit, tilted platform reminiscent of an artist's easel and a dissection table – resonates with the terms of Christ's human/divine suffering by offering a exposed body which 'is at once male (his penis is visible) [and] feminine (he bleeds/he has been penetrated) and aestheticized (he is enclosed in white paint)' (2008: 113). In this account, Franko B's queer body serves to fulfil a certain need: while suffering might be understood as 'anti-thetical to contemporary Western existence, we still look towards the suffering body of the martyr as a body undergoing excruciating physical intensity, a body that has reached towards an altogether transfixing state of sublime unbearable ecstasy' (Richards 2008: 114). On these terms, the martyr figure becomes intelligible as such insofar as it fulfils a pre-existing, seeming-universal function. The difficulty in such a reading, though, may reside in Franko B's reluctance to position himself as a sacrificial everyman as much as in the non-mimetic specificity of his own heavily tattooed and scarred body. In his own words, Franko B is 'not here to give. I am not savior. I am not a cheap Jesus. I am not here to save the world' (quoted in Campbell-Johnston 2001).

Given this resistance, it is significant that the development of Franko B's practice over the past decade describes the pursuit of strategies for affective and visceral wounding which do not rely on literal injury to the body. This trajectory has been informed by the artist's consciousness of his (mistakenly) narrow reputation as a blood-based artist and by a sense of the historical and biographical location of injury at the turn of the twenty-first century. Interviewed in 2015, he observed

I'm 48, not 30 any more. It was important what I did then, but there's other ways of bleeding. In another way, I think we all bleed. Also, for me, I think there's enough blood going 'round at the moment. I bled upside down, I bled lying down, I bled on my knees, I bled on my back ... I just think it's enough. In a deeper sense, I have stopped bleeding. Twenty years ago, we had an AIDS epidemic, a different understanding of infection and blood. We've had the war in Yugoslavia, Iraq ... and the politics of the body changes according to where one finds himself. (Franko B in Who 2015)

This desire to discover 'other ways of bleeding' is apparent in a number of Franko B's performance works produced since 2005 – including *Don't Leave Me This Way* (2006–9), *Because of Love* (2012–14) and *Milk + Blood* (2015–) – in which strategies of performative bloodletting have given way to more consciously theatrical treatments of the body in space. A similar trajectory is apparent in the work of British artist jamie lewis hadley, whose early work making use of controlled incisions or punctures – notably *The Things That Hurt* (2009) and *We Will Outlive the Blood you Bleed* (2014) – has developed in pursuit of 'a visceral punch that does not rely on blood or bloodletting' (hadley 2014).

Working in collaboration with Australian artist and lighting designer Kamal Ackarie, *Don't Leave Me This Way* (2006–9) sees Franko B staged as a sculptural, monumental object. In the first developmental iteration of the work shown in 2006 – staged outdoors at Fresco Bosco, a contemporary art event in southern Italy – Franko B appeared on a platform around which the audience was allowed to move freely, alternately bathed in low red floods and by slowly flashing lights installed at distance.[4] The later studio-based version involves a more calculated attempt to control the audience's perspective, not least through the adoption of a singular viewing perspective designed to frustrate rather than privilege the audience's gaze, with Ackarie observing that 'Franko didn't want the show to be seen' (Ibanez 2006). Seated naked on a chair, Franko B is dimly lit until an array of powerful stadium lights positioned behind him suddenly silhouette his form. These floodlights are dazzling bright: it is uncomfortable if not painful to look directly towards the stage. In the still, pitch-black room at the end of the work, all that is left is the after-image, 'burned into the retina of the spectator. When the light changes, you hold onto the image in front of you' (Holmes 2008). The inverted image of this process may be found in Canadian performance artist Cassils' *Becoming An Image* (2012), originally conceived as a site-specific work for the ONE

4 For footage of this performance, see Ibanez (2006).

National Gay & Lesbian Archives in Los Angeles addressing a history of violence directed towards trans bodies often occluded from historical record. Kicking and pounding a 2,000lb block of clay in a pitch-black room to produce a sculptural record of assault, Cassils' exhaustive labour is illuminated only by the flash of a photographer: as in *Don't Leave Me This Way*, the viewer is gifted an after-image which calls into question their role as a witness, and the function of memory as a form of evidence. Such a dramaturgy – which invites the audience's gaze only to frustrate it – may serve to call further attention to the specificity of the artist's body: a form that cannot fulfil the martyr function because it lacks the quality of resemblance that might allow it stand as a surrogate for a community of others (see Walsh 2010a: 141–2).

If his performance works during the 1990s may be characterised by a dramaturgy of silence in which 'Franko B ... closes his mouth as he opens his body' (Campbell and Spackman 1998: 64), then the most significant aspect of *Milk + Blood* may be the presence of the artist's voice or, rather, how the body and voice interact in a dramaturgy of penitential endurance. First staged in the Toynbee Studio's Court Room, formerly a juvenile court, the performance takes the form of thirteen two-minute rounds in which Franko B spars with a training bag that slowly leaks milk onto the floor. Like the punching bag, his gloves, training gear and head guard are golden and carry the sign of the Greek cross – an image which repeats across Franko B's body in tattoos and as a central motif in his visual arts practice: the symbol of the Red Cross that is redolent of the artist's early years in institutional care. The gold is 'about optimism and desire', an 'artificial and superficial' demonstration of wealth and success and, at the same time, the manifestation of 'positive energy and warmth ... a kind of optimism to get out of the ghetto and to make something of your life, and to share that' (Franko B quoted in Greenall 2016). This composition draws on boxing as a domain of distinctively masculine endeavour which rewards those who endure, and the boxing ring as a space in which 'pugilists must bring their emotions under firm stewardship, relinquish their intimate fears and learn continuously to monitor themselves' (Wacquant 1995: 499). Here, the ritual of shadow-boxing may also describe how mechanisms of self-determination might simultaneously serve the ends of discipline and control – a domain in which one can seek 'the causes of one's own defeats nowhere except in one's own indolence and sloth' (Bauman 2013: 38).

Drawing on the written text *Insignificant* (2015), Franko B's partially improvised speech (pre-recorded but fed through headphones) is heavily structured by repetition of the word 'insignificant' in a manner which seems to qualify and challenge the language which surrounds it.[5] This pattern of speech traces a Derridean play of meaning back and further along chains of signification – 'insignificant, self, insignificant, promoted, insignificant, love, insignificant, more, insignificant, love, insignificant' – in which the possibility for self-expression seems suspended between the demands of others, and the demands or desires that Franko B claims for himself. The associations which run through and against the refrain – prostitution / deluded / untouchable / life / useless / hypocrite – seem accusatory, taking the form of self-reproach and, at the same time, directed outwards in accusation of those who would pass judgement. As the sequence develops, a logic of metonymic, horizontal association seems to assert itself – egotistic / society / trust / given / dying / entertainment / profit – with the effect that the relationship between the terms of individual agency and oppression never settles on a simple account of cause and effect. In delivery, the text is punctuated by the grammar of action: Franko B's punches and his breathing, and the bell which marks the beginning and end of each three-minute round. As he tires, each word is separated by the effort of striking the bag; if the increasing effort required to land each blow marks out exhaustion, it also describes persistence which deepens with fatigue.

As Franko B lands punch after punch, the bag leaks rather than bleeds: a bodily mass doubling for the artist's own form which does not flinch but absorbs each blow. This is penitential speech, tracing a subject indistinguishable from the voluntary acts of punishment by which he composes himself (see Foucault 1988: 42). Yet the refrain which closes the work – a final moment of exhaustion in which a clear if ragged voice seems to struggle free from the text – suggests a claim on language as the means of sustaining a liveable life: 'I have language on my side, I have language on my side.' While the artist's prolonged battle with himself may describe the exhausting work of maintaining oneself through and against self-reprobation, his spoken text provides a score for resistance by measuring out the performative quality of marginalisation – that is, by suggesting how the reiterative process of subjection is a process which might not only be endured without an annihilatory renunciation of the self but provide for new ways of being with others. Perhaps paradoxically, the self persists because it surrenders itself to another: 'Language is the

---

5 The two documented versions of *Milk + Blood* recorded at the Toynbee Studios give a sense of this variation. See *Milk + Blood*, www.youtube.com/watch?v=PoJNcQYxc_U (performed as a livestream on 27 July 2015) and www.youtube.com/watch?v=T3RW2DIGNwU (performed for a live audience on 29 July 2015), both accessed 1 July 2017.

only thing that we can claim for ourselves', Franko B explains, 'It is the only thing that, in a way, we can own, yet nobody can own. Language is a fluid thing. You cannot own it. The moment you express it, it's no longer yours. There is a witness' (quoted in Greenall 2016).

Performing exhaustion: Eddie Ladd's *Ras Goffa Bobby Sands / The Bobby Sands Memorial Race*

The performative rendition of exhaustion similarly animates *Ras Goffa Bobby Sands / The Bobby Sands Memorial Race* (2009), a piece of dance theatre created by Welsh performer Eddie Ladd. A former member of the major Welsh experimental company Brith Gof – whose performances include the large-scale, site-specific works *Gododdin* (1988–89) and *Haearn* (1989) – Ladd's practice as a soloist and collaborator animates a commitment to the past and future of Welsh culture and a consciousness of Welsh-language speech and community as a form of politicised identity. Working in Welsh and English, a recurrent concern of Ladd's work is the notion of colonisation. In *Gaza/Blaenannerch* (2012), a collaboration with director Judith Roberts, Ladd traces parallels between the contested landscapes of Palestine and Wales: the unmanned drones used to patrol airspace around Gaza are tested in the rural landscape near Ladd's home in Ceredigion; the more recent *Dawns Ysbrydion/ Ghost Dance* (2015–16) – co-directed by Ladd with Montréal choreographer Sarah Williams – juxtaposes the nineteenth-century colonisation of North America with the displacement of Welsh-speaking families in Capel Celyn, a village in the north of Wales, to make way for the construction of a reservoir to provide water for the city of Liverpool.

Ladd's practice figures what Lisa Lewis (2004) identifies as the 'resistant body' of Welsh-language minority identity and community constituted by those who persist in speaking Welsh (despite the risk of being misunderstood or rejected) because to cease doing so would be to risk the very existence of the community of which they are part. For Lewis, the persistence of that body is a form of protest: a performance of difference that 'demands the attention of those watching … In phenomenological terms, the protest is a community performing itself – and *becoming* itself' (Lewis 2004: 169). An essential feature of Welshness as defiance is the practice of non-cooperation: a refusal to 'support the authority's way of operating and thereby forcing them to discuss the matter with protestors ... one of the traditional traits of the resistant body is its unwillingness to behave in a specific way' (Lewis 2004: 171). In *Bobby Sands*, the resistant body of the Welsh-language speaker coincides with the non-cooperative figure of the Republican hunger striker, though stops short of inviting straightforward identification between Welsh and Irish nationalist causes. Though Ladd's motion suggests forms of agile resistance and defiance and, as the work progresses, 'a drained body trying to find the power to continue resisting' (Smith 2010), she does not perform Bobby Sands as a character: she performs as herself, and her slight but highly toned dancer's body with close-cropped hair queers rather than resembles the most iconic electioneering image of Sands as a long-haired young man. As such, the association between Ladd and Sands invites critical comparison rather than simple correspondence, and recognition of difference as much as potential congruence (whether between each individual, or the Irish and Welsh identities they might be given to represent).

Running on and around a custom-built, twelve-foot running machine intersected by red sensor beams, Ladd's pre-recorded voice is

Figure 1 Eddie Ladd, *The Bobby Sands Memorial Race* (2009).

heard alongside excerpts from interviews with Sands' biographer Denis O'Hearn and former Maze prisoner Laurence McKeown. Across the performance, Ladd speaks first in Welsh and then again in English, and it is not clear for a non-Welsh-speaking audience whether she is offering a translation or performing two different texts. The material narrates moments from Sands' life and the 1981 hunger strikes, and locates his story in the wider narrative of the Troubles. We are told of the conditions faced by detainees at the Maze Prison and reminded that many inmates were held without trial under the British government's policy of internment. We do not hear any account of the victims of the IRA's actions, with the performance focusing on Sands' personal acts of endurance. In the work's opening moments, we hear an excerpt from Sands' short essay, 'The Loneliness of a Long Distance Cripple', in which Sands juxtaposes youthful vigour and determination in mastery of the race at the age of fourteen with his hunger-strike weakened body as he walks three steps back and forth across his cell, his legs 'heavy and weak and sore and pained' (Sands 1997).

Ladd paces back and forth to trace out the dimensions of that cell, carried by the motion of the treadmill before turning to work against it. At times, Ladd's motion is accompanied by an electro-acoustic score created by the Welsh composer Guto Puw; when the physical score suggests the harsh conditions of Sands' imprisonment, Ladd's movement through the sensor beams triggers an environmental soundscape of harsh, artificial sounds suggesting alarm bells and heavy metal locks. Ladd's movements and the sounds which they trigger are simultaneously voluntary and involuntary, which is to recognise that the form of endurance that she performs involves a certain surrender of agency even within the calculated, time-bound frame of the performance. They describe a voluntary involuntariness – Ladd has sought the terms of the performance and chooses to subject herself to the travel of the treadmill – which is at the same time an involuntary voluntariness: Ladd is forced to keep pace if she wants the performance to continue and avoid being swept onto the floor. As the performance progresses, the sought effect of fatigue comes to challenge Ladd's ability to maintain that effect as a choice; there is a point at which Ladd can no longer choose to be tired or not and in which the theatrical performance of endurance is supplanted by an experience of 'real' exhaustion which begins to interfere with her ability to perform it.

In her study of the rhetoric of suicide, Suzanne Stern-Gillet argues for distinguishing between a suicide and martyr on the grounds of moral responsibility – wherein declaring someone to be a martyr absolves them of personal responsibility and displaces culpability to someone else, a government or an institution (1987: 166). Following Sands' death in 1981, the *New York Times* reported a statement released by the Irish bishops confirming that 'the church teaches suicide is a great evil' but adding that 'there is some dispute about whether or not political hunger striking is suicide or more precisely, about the circumstances in which it is suicide' (Briggs 1981). Then Prime Minister Margaret Thatcher's response to questions in the House of Commons was far less ambivalent: 'Mr. Sands was a convicted criminal. He chose to take his own life. It was a choice that his organization did not allow to many of its victims' (quoted in Apple 1981). Ladd's rendition of Sands, though, may trouble an unequivocal distribution of agency or responsibility: while the work's titular reference to memorialisation might infer an uncritical account of Sands' actions, the internal logic of the performance unsettles an easy valorisation of martyrdom as the product of autonomous self-will. At the heart of that dynamic may be how readily a resistant subject may resemble a penitent one, wherein testimony is resolved as a form of public confession oriented on the creation of 'an individuated self and a defined personage in the social order' (Gutman 1988: 103) whose articulation of culpability and guilt allows their rehabilitation. At the least, a conservative reading of both *Milk + Blood* and *The Bobby Sands Memorial Race* might emphasise the (auto)biographical dimension of each work to constrain the possibility for a structural critique of social and political norms, and re-assert the moral telos of individuated responsibility.

Confession and self-martyrdom: Adrian Howells

Distinguished by its generosity, its rejection of cynicism and the pursuit of generative forms of exchange, the work of theatre-maker Adrian Howells suggests how confessional performance might nonetheless serve ends beyond culturally embedded demands for exhibition or penance so ingrained in Western culture as that we may 'no longer perceive it as the effect of power which constrains us' (Foucault 1978: 60). Most widely known for intimate and one-to-one performances including *Footwashing for the Sole* (2008), *The Garden of Adrian* (2009) and *The Pleasure of Being: Washing/Feeding/Holding* (2010/1), Howells' practice carries implications for an understanding of the contemporary martyr figure – and the queer martyr in particular – for its attempt to renegotiate the relationship between self-exposure, intimacy and self-injury. It is also a body of work which – sometimes uncomfortably – manifests Howells' ability and tendency to 'absorb the bad stuff and sacrifice [himself] for the benefit of others' (Crouch 2016: 287).[6]

Emerging from experiences of performance in which Howells shared details of his own life with strangers in the hope that they would reciprocate – most notably in a series of works as his alter-ego 'Adrienne' – the heavily autobiographical work *The 14 Stations of the Life and History of Adrian Howells* (2007–8) describes how that sacrifice might take the form of self-recrimination. Structured by a return to the scene of wounding experiences which Howells either cannot or will not shake, *14 Stations* is a performance which articulates Howells' self-acknowledged tendency 'not on a conscious level – to play the martyr. I guess I've been comfortable with that, as it's all I've ever known' (interviewed in Johnson 2015: 282). Developed in the early stages of an AHRC-funded Creative Fellowship at the University of Glasgow examining questions of risk and intimacy in performance, the work takes the form of a one-to-one, promenade performance loosely structured by the biblical Stations of the Cross. Each 'station' narrates an episode of suffering or self-excoriation drawn from Howells' life intended to create 'an escalation of uncomfortable experiences' that might 'mirror in some way the idea that Christ carrying the cross to Golgotha [the place of crucifixion, an Aramaic word meaning "the skull"] became a much more intense and painful experience before he reached the ultimate pain and suffering, namely the crucifixion' (Howells in Johnson 2015: 276).

While the structure of the work evokes an identification between Howells and Christ, that parallel is implied rather than explicitly mobilised as a frame for making sense of Howells' life. In this respect, Howells' invocation of Christian martyrdom and absolution is distinct from the strategies adopted within Irish queer theatre-maker Neil Watkins' work – most notably the autobiographical performance *The Year of Magical Wanking* (2010) which was publicised through images depicting Watkins in a bright red 'crown of thorns' and in which multiple comparisons to Christ throughout the play explicitly frame Watkins 'as a martyr or sacrificial figure to be purged and born again' (Walsh 2016: 67). Addressing a personal history of drug use, anonymous sex and continuous self-pleasure – and enacting a form of resistant affinity with other victims of institutional abuse in Ireland (see O'Brien 2013) – Watkins animates shame as a mode of personal insight in service of an

---

6 For extended discussion of the work of Adrian Howells, see Heddon and Johnson (2016).

extra-theatrical, therapeutic intervention in which a willingness to 'stand up, bare [one's] soul and tell the truth' (Moylan 2012) is rewarded with cathartic renewal.[7] This mode of renewal also stands in contrast to Jo Clifford's *The Gospel According to Jesus, Queen of Heaven* (2008) in which the figuring of Jesus as a transwoman through a re-writing of Gospel parables affords a reparative resistance of fear, shame and guilt by re-imagining the world 'as a far better, kinder and more tolerant place' (Gardner 2014a). While Howells' later works share Clifford's orientation on the radical potential of empathy, *14 Stations* suggests the difficulty of extending compassion to one's own self, even in the act of asserting – through the form of autobiographical performance itself – that one might have something of value and interest to share.

As in O'Reilly's *Untitled Action*, Howells' treatment of testimony in *14 Stations* is framed by deliberate dramaturgies of participatory consent, albeit on terms which seem less and less secure as the work proceeds. In a pre-performance briefing captured in filmed documentation of the work in which performance scholar and Howell's friend Deirdre Heddon acts as audience-participant, Howells explains that

> there are going to be times when I will very specifically request your help with certain things, ask you to do things ... but there will also be times where you will be aware that I might have some sort of expectation of a response ... I might not say anything explicitly but, of course, whatever your response is is totally appropriate. (Howells 2007)

Though an audience-participant might refuse that request, they will nonetheless be confronted with their own status as an observer denied the possibility of an alibi – what Derrida describes as the claim on an alleged elsewhere in space (Derrida 2002: xvi).

In biblical accounts, the Stations of the Cross begin with Christ's trial and sentencing at the hands of others. Howells' first station – 'He is Condemned by Others and Himself' – is consciously self-reflexive, and sees him read a series of hurtful and hateful things said to or about him since his childhood: a fellow student from his university years who accused him of being 'so pious and self-righteous that he thinks he's Jesus Christ', the boy who systematically bullied him at school ('You're such a fucking poof, you're like that Quentin Crisp ...'), and an actor that Howells met when he first moved to Glasgow to work at the Citizens Theatre ('when you first meet people, you're just too full on, too OTT

---

7 For an earlier treatment of this dynamic, see Watkins' *A Cure for Homosexuality* (2005), reproduced in Walsh (2010b).

… Anyway, what makes you think people are that interested in hearing all about your life?'). Howells reads this material clearly and plainly and the juxtaposition of plainly homophobic language with more subjectively (and perhaps unintentionally) unkind comments elicits pity while beginning to trace the origins of Howells' self-condemnation in his former identification as an evangelical Christian whose spiritual beliefs led him to regard his own desires as sinful. Reading the monologues of Spalding Gray, David Terry argues that confessional utterances involve the performance of a constative, sinning self in the past and a performative self who, receiving 'some form of salvation for its willingness to confess those same sins', is oriented on the future (2006: 210). This relationship between constative and performative selves is sacrificial in the sense that the former self is given up so that a future self might exist. In the first scene of *14 Stations*, that 'truth' does not disclose an affirmative desire oriented on a future – a new, better, redeemed self – but instead suggests a repeated cathecting to injury as the basis of identity (a dynamic to which I will return in the following chapter).

This impulse recurs across the work, most clearly in a sequence in which Howells uses a conversation with the audience-participant about memories of their mothers to narrate an incident in his childhood when he manipulated his own mother to the point of tears, and again at station six where Howells introduces a series of photographs of unrequited loves. Standing in a corner next to a screen playing a short film of an attractive young, smiling man, Howells puts on headphones and – as though in a memory triggered by whatever music he can hear – begins to cry. Though the station is titled 'Jordan Makes Him Weep', the moment is carefully stage-managed and Howells clearly provokes his own distress: Howells makes Jordan make him weep. Here, an understanding of testimony as 'an autobiographically certified narrative of a past event' (Renaud Dulong quoted in Ricœur 2004: 163) gives way to a sense of how the ritual quality of penitence may undermine its seeming veracity. Jon Cairns suggests that the histrionic force of Howells' emotional display in this moment renders it unreadable: 'His face contorts as he cries, but I'm baffled as to why. What has happened between him and Jordan to occasion such grief? Is Howells mourning, and if so, for what? A death? The end of a relationship? None of this is made known' (Cairns 2012: 367). Jennifer Doyle recalls her own reaction to this moment: 'Instead of being moved to tears, I felt myself shut down. A cold curiosity took over; he was making himself cry, for me, and I didn't care' (2013b: 110).

If the vignettes which structure *14 Stations* describe opportunities for empathetic identification with and for Howells' life experiences, that

Figure 2 Adrian Howells, *The 14 Stations of the Life and History of Adrian Howells* (2007).

Figure 3 Adrian Howells and Deirdre Heddon, *The 14 Stations of the Life and History of Adrian Howells* (2007).

dynamic is held in tension with disclosures which reveal a 'self-abased version of the artist by gradually exposing his "dislikeable" traits, such as selfishness and narcissism, manipulativeness and arrogance' (Cairns 2012: 365), and not merely through memory but by the workings of the performance itself. At station nine, for example, a framed letter details the end of a relationship with someone who had seemingly cared deeply for Howells, and whom Howells had treated very badly. Howells' self-exposure seems to unavoidably involve – if not demand – the exposure of others, even as his own agency is deferred. Though the eleventh station marking the crucifixion is titled 'He is made to suffer', that imperative arises from Howells' own actions and his manipulation of his audience-participant whom he asks to pour a glass of 'that liquid': in actuality cider vinegar – urine-coloured and bitter – of which he is unable to drink more than a mouthful. In later works, Howells emphasised forms of consent that might counter the tendency of his audience-participants to unthinkingly do as he asked for fear of 'spoiling' the artwork (see Prichard 2009). Here, though, a measure of compliant participation is necessitated by the dramaturgy of the piece. After drinking the vinegar, Howells climbs into a shallow child's paddling pool and entreats the audience-participant to pour a jug of ice over his naked back. In the video documentation, we see Heddon pause – saying 'oh gosh, do I have to do this?' – but then obediently carrying out his instructions.

The possibility of empathy for Howells is joined – and even displaced – by a rather more introspective and personal sense of guilt on the part of the audience participant even as Howells' demands structure the work. In the final sequence – following a scene in which Howells crouches in a corner strewn with rubbish and the detritus of deep depression to perform a mawkish version of Céline Dion's sentimental power-ballad *All By Myself* – Howells invites his audience-participant to join him in a clean white bed and spoon with him. After a few moments respite, Howells leaves his audience-participant with a Dictaphone recording of his voice reading Mary Oliver's *Wild Geese* (1993), a poem of solace that gently refuses the necessity of penitential suffering. Yet Howells stands at some distance from this gesture of consolation: whatever measure of comfort is intended for his audience-participant is not something which he allows himself in full share. The work as a whole is dominated by Howells' acts of confession: there is no opportunity for his audience-participant to share their own 'despair', only – as Howells would later reflect – experience 'one thing heaped onto another [meaning that] the participant ceases to have a perspective on the individual actions, or their own complicity in the performance' (interviewed in Johnson 2015: 276).

Refusing repentance: *The Worst of Scottee*

Where Howells' *14 Stations* suggests the difficulties of confession uncoupled from the imperative of renunciation, queer performance artist Scottee's *The Worst of Scottee* (2013) may directly frustrate a narrative of absolution by staging the 'worst' of the artist's adolescent self and refusing to ask for forgiveness: 'I don't feel any guilt. I make it very clear that I'm not sorry, because life happens. We're all fucked up. We've all got shit' (quoted in Rose 2014). Though structured by autobiographical detail and a form of performative self-martyrdom, the performance is also occupied with a cultural moment in which the presentation of a public self seems compulsory. Developed during his time as associate artist at London's Roundhouse venue, *The Worst of Scottee* began as a response to habits of the YouTube generation – 'blogging, putting our lives out there' (quoted in Walters 2014) – alongside the more specific cultural economy of professional development as a solo artist. In interview, Scottee recounts the experience of watching 'a bunch of my peers trying to sell themselves' (Brewis 2014) at the Edinburgh Fringe Festival and the expectation that he should produce a solo show as a kind of showcase so that people in the industry would know what he is 'all about' (see Jankovic 2014a). In response, *The Worst* was intended an act of 'anti-salesmanship' intended to reject a culture of relentlessly positive self-promotion that might distance Scottee from performers 'desperate to sell themselves as an attribute to the arts' (Barrett 2014).

Part confessional and part 'vlog', the show was initiated through an invitation to past friends and acquaintances to be interviewed on camera and share stories of Scottee's worst behaviour and its consequences: 'people who no longer speak to me … ex-lovers, ex-friends, ex-acquaintances and people I have had altercations with' (Scottee 2013). The subjects of the interviews did not meet Scottee in person but instead were told by the production team that an artist was making a show about the things they had done in the past, and invited to talk to a psychotherapist – the critic and author Charlotte Cooper – and guess who he or she might be. Of ten potential participants, four agreed to meet Cooper and three consented to take part in the performance once Scottee's identity was revealed; in the desire to respond honestly and ethically to this material, Scottee played no role in the interview process, and saw the edited interviews for the first time in the rehearsal room (Jankovic 2014a). Appearing in photo booth-cum-confessional styled to resemble a slightly oversized model of

Figure 4 Scottee, *The Worst of Scottee* (2013).

Berlin's Photoautomats – the site of the 'vintage' selfie – Scottee performs to a camera; the audience sees him live, side-on, and simultaneously on a screen on the side of the booth.[8]

In the opening sequence, Scottee performs the torch song *Cry Me A River* (1953) and cries thick, black rivers of liquid from behind over-sized, round, glossy dark glasses; at the end of the song, he removes the glasses and pulls the concealed tubes that fed his 'tears' from under his

8 For further solo works exploring the format of the confessional, see Martina Von Holn's *The Seal of the Confessional* (2006–9), and Richard DeDomenici's more recent *Shed Your Fears* (2017) project. See http://dedomenici.com/shedyourfears, accessed 27 June 2017.

shirt. Heart-break and self-pity is theatricalised and dissembled: unlike
Howells' real-but-theatrical tears, Scottee's tears are staged first so that
the biographical detail which follows – accompanied by the emergence of
'Scot' from beneath costume and make-up – might acquire the veneer of
documentary truth. As it develops, the performance is intercut with filmed
interviews with friends and acquaintances and structured by stories from
his life between the ages of ten and eighteen: stealing money from his
parents to buy chips for the boys on the estate where he grew up, getting
expelled from school, seeking attention and sympathy by claiming that his
first girlfriend had committed suicide and telling his first employer that he
had AIDS when he was fired for turning up late for work once too often.
Though confession may serve as a form of 'parrhesia' – a mode of rhetoric in which candid truth-telling coincides with a knowledge of the self
(Miller 2006: 28) – such speech might not resolve in a singular account
of a stable subject: each story is punctuated by the flash of the camera;
he draws the curtains on the booth and a new version of Scottee appears.

The episodes from Scottee's life appear out of chronological
order, with jumps in time advertising omissions which raise their own
unanswered questions and complicate the assumed relation of a penitent
subject to their 'past' self. As Michael Brindley (2014) observed in his
review of the show's appearance at the Melbourne Fringe, in one story
Scottee is seventeen and seemingly abandoned by his parents when they
move from London and make it clear that he has no part in their new
life; in another, he is thirteen and falsely accused of the sexual assault of
another boy, and his family is fiercely supportive. But what has changed?
These stories intertwine moments of personal irresponsibility and deception with tales of unjust persecution and abandonment, and begin to
question the limits of individual responsibility and agency. Juxtaposing
details in stories that are in turn shocking and banal, the work seems
both masochistic – centred on the performer's interrogation and humili-
ation of himself and the persona 'Scottee' – and laced with an 'element
of accusation of the audience for their complicity in cruelty and intoler-
ance … an implicit criticism of the audience for their ghoulish "sympathy"' (Brindley 2014). Here, the autobiographical framing of Scottee's
public persona – the sharply funny, sometimes bitchy, 'outrageously glam
femme-chub' (Costa 2013) performer – serves to question both his and
his audience's role as witnesses to his past misdeeds. Who have they – and
he – turned up to see perform?

Echoing Howells' staging of past hurt, there is a sense of how Scottee
and his audience alike are invested in his image as an enfant terrible of
queer performance, a reputation which may or may not be grounded in

fact. As critic Daniel Yates notes, 'the taped interviews of the people he told lies to, or upset, which overlay Scottee's image on the screen come to this with a clear fondness and bemusement rather than aggrievement' (Yates 2013). As in *14 Stations*, there is a sense that past hurt may be more significant to the performer than its victims: 'No-one feels as much ill-will towards Scottee as Scottee himself', Maddy Costa offers, 'he could be taking confession except the only place absolution is going to come from is himself' (Costa 2013). Where the one-to-one form of Howells' performance renders confession an intimate (if not wholly private) affair, Scottee's claim on the 'worst' of himself is directed towards a public hearing – but, crucially, without any demand for a finalising retribution, reconciliation or redemption from that public. As if to make this point plain, Scottee closes the show by facing the audience to sing Édith Piaf's signature song *Non, Je Ne Regrette Rien*. In his more recent show *Bravado* (2017), Scottee offers a more linear autobiographical narrative of growing up in the 1990s in a work which grapples with working-class masculinities, violence and the desire to be desired by one's abusers. Here, too, though, the work's dramaturgy refuses the status of confession as a spectacle oriented on a penitential subject: Scottee is entirely absent from the stage, and the script is performed by a volunteer audience member reading from a screen.

Conclusion

Foucault offers in the first volume of *The History of Sexuality* that 'since the Middle Ages, at least, western societies have established the confession as one of the main rituals we rely on for the production of truth' (1978: 58). The figure of the martyr in performance, though, suggests the highly conditional terms on which individual testimony comes to stand as a form of witness – that is, as a mode of truth-telling which extends beyond the singularly exceptional body or circumstances of the performer to become available as the site of communal identification and feeling. Perversely, the qualities which distinguish the martyr as a representative figure are also those which may serve to disqualify them from standing as a political figure whose actions constitute a demand for change, or may serve to challenge normative regimes of recognition. While the works explored here suggest the demands that make the Western subject 'a confessing animal' (Foucault 1978: 51), their staging of endurance also describes the possibility of a resistant and potentially transformative relationship between acts of witness and the communities of complicity which they might invoke. Such acts do not involve a straightforward claim on autobiography and lived experience as unmitigated proof of one's integrity as a subject, but instead deploy such material to expose, examine and transform the field of power within which subjectivity gives rise to personhood and where, through the logic of exception, subjects are neither granted nor denied legitimacy but instead occupy a suspended, threshold position in relation to the social sphere.

In this respect, the martyr's figuring of voluntary involuntariness signals how the proximity (if not indistinction) of subjection and subjugation may be made to serve a critique of dominant conceptions of the subject. Nonetheless, and though Bauman has argued that modernity's pursuit of immediate satisfaction and personal reward mitigates against the conditions which produce martyrs (2005: 45–6), it is clear that martyrs remain useful in neoliberal times. While the martyr's public suffering may enable a form of 'solidarity with a smaller and weaker group, a group discriminated against, humiliated, ridiculed, hated and persecuted by the majority' (Bauman 2005: 42), it may yet serve an exemplary function for that majority's worldview by narrativising the primacy of individuated agency and responsibility. This dynamic – and its difficult relationship to a history of the queer subject as an outcast – is explored in the following chapter.

3

The pariah: queer outcasts and the politics of wounded attachment

The figure of the pariah represents one of the key paradoxes of exceptionality: though conventionally despised and avoided by the majority, found to be untouchable or unspeakable, the pariah nonetheless persists within the social scene. The pariah is an outcast who 'sticks around', intelligible as a breach of social norms because he or she remains within their frame of reference. While the pariah may constitute the limit conditions of the social – describing both the kinds of subject who can be successfully assimilated and those who must be excluded – such a subject may also articulate the difficult demand for alternative orders of value and sociability. If the figure in performance can be understood as 'a structural entity that concentrates or disperses figurative and abstract elements' that allows us to 'see and follow meaning' (Pavis 2013: 311) then this chapter animates the pariah to examine the structures of meaning that characterise contemporary liberal narratives of inclusivity and assimilation, and their relationship to history. While – as explored in the Introduction – we might conceive of community as 'definable only on the basis of the lack that characterizes it' (Esposito 2010: 16), I am interested here in how the figure of the pariah begins to give such lack a body – and, in turn, how that body in performance might produce a particular, critical understanding of the historical function of that lack. Following closely on from the account of the martyr offered in the previous chapter, that history is one in which the pariah remains useful within a contemporary cultural discourse of exception – not simply illustrating the work of reformist progress that lies ahead, but functioning to generate, justify and constrain the terms of that project. At the same time, I am also interested in examining how an affective history – what Elizabeth Freeman (2010) describes as an 'erotohistoriography', discussed below – may function not just 'to make visible some thing lost, but to urge us to think about the present in political (and material) ways' (Campbell 2016: 235).

In figuring the pariah, this chapter is framed by a complex social and political genealogy marked by colonial appropriation of the Indian caste system during the 1800s, the constitution of different religious and ethnic minorities by various states and governments across several hundred years of European history and, more immediately, by the status of the person with HIV/AIDS as the pariah-at-home following the mid-1980s. It also acknowledges the place of the pariah as an embodiment of rebellious critique in twentieth-century theatre and literature, perhaps most clearly in the works and lives of Jean Genet and André Gide. In Genet's universe, 'the isolated pariah is seen as a proud, independent, self-reliant rebel' (Plunka 1992: 47), an outcast amongst outcasts closely associated with the traitor whose betrayal of his own kind marks an absolute break with sociability. In *Our Lady of the Flowers* (1942), the pimp Darling eagerly sells out his friends and fellow criminals to the authorities because he enjoys how it 'dehumanizes' him. In turn, Gide's character Menalque in *The Immoralist* (1902) challenges the limits of possible solidarity that one might share with others when 'the quality of being different … constitutes the worth of a human being' (Pollard 1991: 309).

Though these figures remain significant to what Jonathan Dollimore (1991) has explored as a history of sexual dissidence, this chapter reads against an understanding of the pariah as a figure of isolation to emphasise Hannah Arendt's account of the 'conscious pariah' – a figure who appears across her writings on Jewish political identity in critique of the ambiguity of freedom ensured by Jewish emancipation and, more sharply, the treachery 'of the promise of equality which assimilation has held out' (Arendt 1944: 100).[1] This figure first appears in Arendt's essay 'The Jew as Pariah: A Hidden Tradition' (1944) in which she draws on the work of literary critic Bernard Lazare to distinguish between an assimilationist 'parvenu' who is the result of social emancipation and a critically conscious pariah who articulates the demand for political emancipation. Whereas

---

1 For Arendt's further writings on the pariah see 'Between Pariah and Parvenu' in *The Origins of Totalitarianism* (1951) and *The Jew As Pariah: Jewish Identity and Politics in the Modern Age* (1978).

the parvenu seeks acceptance within an existing social order – and is willing to abandon signs of Jewishness and affiliation with other Jews in order to achieve it – the conscious pariah remains an outcast because he refuses to regard his normal human rights of autonomy and association 'as privileges bestowed by the "powers that be"' (Arendt 1944: 119). Rather than seeking social integration through the suppression of difference to create a 'false sameness' (see Hammer 1997: 326), the conscious pariah has an awareness of themselves as an outsider who actively rejects the limited and conditional acceptance that would require them to live as something other than their true self. In this dynamic, the figure of the conscious pariah does not anticipate recognition from his peers but instead 'serves to act instead as a member of a group of outsiders against the prevailing community' (Ring 1991: 441). The intervention articulated by the conscious pariah 'is not a simple demand for "inclusion," but a complex demand made *against exclusivity* per se as an unethical principle for building a polity' (Jones 2015: 467).

The readings of performances offered here seek to elaborate and problematise that thinking in the context of late twentieth- and early twenty-first-century narratives of social progress. Beyond the terms of Arendt's analysis – and conscious of the complex relationships between queer theory and Jewish identity (see Boyarin, Itzkovitz and Pellegrini 2003) and between Arendt's work and the politics of sexual liberation (see Kaplan 1995) – I am interested in how attachments to the figure of the pariah might serve to historicise the conditions of exceptionality, not only as a product of a selective narration of the past but as a cultural logic which continues to shape our possible futures. This approach draws on Heather Love's (2007) contention that we might resist a dominant narrative of recuperation and recovery of 'lost' or isolated queers in the past in order to examine the political significance of affects which may be resistant to affirmation. Noting the dominance of cultural projects which have recognised 'sad old queens' and 'long suffering dykes' most often in order to 'save' them, Love suggests that 'the emphasis on damage in queer studies exists in a state of tension with a related and contrary tendency: the need to resist damage and to affirm queer existence' (Love 2007: 3). This tension finds expression in projects as varied as Doug Wright's *I Am My Own Wife* (2003), Rebecca Lenkiewicz's *Her Naked Skin* (2008), Alexi Kaye Campbell's *The Pride* (2013) and in revivals of Robert Anderson's *Tea and Sympathy* (1953) and Lillian Hellman's *The Children's Hour* (1934) as well as in the public reconstruction of Alan Turing as a hero whose war-time achievements warranted a posthumous royal pardon for the crime of 'gross indecency' (an exception not extended to the many thousand still-living men convicted of the same offence). Such exceptional treatment reflects what Halberstam identifies as the discursive patterning of a 'representative individual' model of minority history which elides structural issues relating to gender, class and race by focusing on the lives of a few extraordinary individuals (2005: 23–44).

My figuring of the pariah as a subject who is 'aware of himself in history, or at least aware of the way in which history has shaped his life' (Ring 1991: 441) is not intended to resolve the tension between (selective) affirmation and the resistance of damage but instead serve the task of 'writing a history in the present; self-consciously writing in a field of power relations and political struggle' (Roth 1981: 43) wherein exceptional individuals are put to task in service of political agendas of different kinds. Though, like Love, I am interested in the terms of a future apart from the promise of redemption and offer a critique of forms of acceptance characterised by a liberal LGBT mainstream, I am also concerned with how the singular figure of the pariah might illustrate how one of the overriding political affects of neoliberalism is complicity: a sense of one's paradoxical involvement in and attachment to discourses that one might reject, or even from which one is excluded. Though Neil Bartlett's sequence of devised works *A Vision of Love Revealed in Sleep* (1987–90), explored below, may draw on the life of Simeon Solomon in order to elaborate a poetics of reparation for historical injury, I suggest that it does so by acknowledging Solomon's refusal of social recuperation within his own lifetime in order to offer that resistance as a mode of survival and critical intervention in the present. This pattern of resistance is explored through two more recent works inspired by the life of nineteenth-century aristocrat Henry Cyril Paget – known as the 'dancing marquess' – by theatre-makers Marc Rees and Seiriol Davies in which Paget's self-indulgent excess is presented as a cipher for non-conforming queerness and, moreover, a means of resisting a narrow historical telos of rescue from ignoble defeat.

In the second part of the chapter, I move from works structured by their relationship to a historical past to consider performances more directly concerned with the late twentieth century's liberal politics of equality and assimilation. While we might read the drag rendering of Margaret Thatcher as cabaret superstar in Jon Brittain and Matt Tedford's *Margaret Thatcher Queen of Soho* (2013) as a kind of satirical inversion of the ex-prime minister's antipathy towards gay subjects during the 1980s, I contend that the work articulates attachments to Thatcher that are not merely ironic, and which may serve to critique the forms of memory on which mainstream narratives of LGBT progress depend as modes of 'wounded attachment' that describe the investment of politicised identities in their own history of injury. In turn, I argue that performance artist David Hoyle's acerbic critique of homogenised desire and homonormative consumerism within mainstream gay culture is inflected by an awareness of the performer's own complicity within those same discourses of desire, and the fragility of his own capacity to enact radical alternatives. Running through the chapter as a whole is a regard for the ways in which history and progress narrativise each other through the figure of the pariah – a claim which first requires a step back from the start of the twenty-first century to examine the unfinished business of the twentieth.

Rehabilitating Simeon Solomon

Neil Bartlett's sequence of works *A Vision of Love Revealed in Sleep* – titled after a prose poem by the nineteenth-century artist Simeon Solomon – suggests how the material practices and historical contexts of performance might inform a contemporary critique of the social function of the pariah. As Dominic Johnson observes, a central technique in Bartlett's prolific work as playwright, director, performer and writer 'involves charged collisions between distinct historical moments, for example the affective shuttling between late-nineteenth- and late-twentieth-century gay London in his ground-breaking scholarly novel *Who Was That Man? A Present for Mr. Wilde* (1988)' (Johnson and Keidan 2012: 152). In *A Vision of Love* – originally staged in 1987 and since revived in 2017 at Tate Britain – that collision is informed by the moment of its enactment (the AIDS crisis at the end of the 1980s following a decade of Thatcherism) and Bartlett's parallel history of activism and lobbying for lesbian and gay rights, and AIDS awareness. These histories frame the work's encounter with Solomon, an artistic prodigy born in 1840 to a middle-class Jewish family whose life and career at the heart of London society was interrupted in 1873 when Solomon was arrested in a public toilet along with a sixty-year-old stableman and charged with committing buggery. As the *Oxford Dictionary of National Biography* recounts: 'Although the incident was not reported in the newspapers his public career was effectively at an end ... Most of his former friends disowned him and he began an obscure and precarious existence which led him to the workhouse' (Cruise 2004).

Twentieth-century accounts of Solomon have frequently adopted the narrative of downfall and shameful exclusion as the lens through

which his life and work might be understood and brought to bear
upon the present. Alfred Werner's (1960) plea for the recognition
of Solomon's artistic talent, for example, performs a kind of tactical
admonishment that attributes Solomon's flaws to his Jewishness and
the excesses of youth. For Werner, Solomon's failing is the product of a
kind of intense naivety, having 'the earnestness and pent-up emotions
of *Yeshivah bocher* [taking] everything seriously, drinking no less than
homosexuality' (1960: 399). Solomon's openness to 'abnormal' sexuality and alcohol is thus tied to his Jewishness; he drinks and 'learns'
homosexuality as fervently as he might study the Talmud. Werner's
appeal for empathy (Solomon's story is titled a 'sad ballad') is correspondingly constrained by a sense of disapproval for the artist's erotic
attachment to his subjects:

> Magnificent as were the color sense and the draftsmanship of the artist, there
> was something sickly, something faintly degenerate about all he produced at
> the height of his career, that is to say, when he was around thirty. (Werner
> 1960: 400)

Gayle Seymour's far more sympathetic narration of Solomon's life –
published some thirty years later – notes Bartlett's *A Vision of Love* alongside the presence of Solomon's work within collections such as Brian
Reade's *Sexual Heretics* (1970) and Richard Dellamora's *Masculine Desire*
(1990) to propose that 'paradoxically, Simeon Solomon's arrest for sodomy
at age 33 had the immediate effect of erasing him from High Art circles,
but of allowing his resurrection as a subject of interest to post-Stonewall
gay cultural historians' (1997: 98). In turn, cultural critic Roberto Ferrari
aligns Solomon's transition 'from sodomite to queer icon' with the evolution of gay studies as a whole, arguing that discussions of the artist 'in
many ways reflect the transformation of the social and critical acceptance
of homosexuality over the past century or so' (Ferrari 2001: 11).

A Vision of Love Revealed in Sleep

If Werner's rehabilitation of Solomon sustains homophobic beliefs,
Seymour and Ferrari's accounts view Solomon through the lens of the
reform and progress to find in Solomon an emergent gay subject whose
intelligibility rests on the affirmative cultural changes that have followed
his death. In contrast, Bartlett's *A Vision of Love Revealed in Sleep* sequence

frustrates the certainty of these narratives by blending a re-telling of Solomon's poem with experiences of being a gay man during the AIDS crisis. Rather than aligning Solomon with a telos of progress, Bartlett's work seems to insist on the discomforting contemporaneity of the past and a failure to learn from history by presenting the portrait of an unrepentant, flawed and transgressive social outcast (see Dau 2017: 40). First published in 1871, Solomon's prose poem takes the form of a dreamlike vision in which the artist is guided through a series of allegorical encounters with Love and Death by a representation of his own soul.[2] As he journeys, Solomon discovers the angelic figure of Love, wings falling 'weak and frayed' about his perfect body and wearing a broken garland whose leaves and blossoms fall to the ground. That vision is a warning 'in good time' of a future which Solomon might evade, and the poem closes in a beatific image of Love restored and ascendant, 'primaeval and eternal, compact of the white flame of youth, burning ineffable perfection' (Solomon 1908: 54). While the allegorical scenarios which structure Solomon's original poem might be read as raising bodily desire to an ultimately chaste spiritual plane (see Morgan 1996), Bartlett's text insists on the manifest materiality of a desiring queer subject, and its exposure to injury.

The first part of the sequence – *A Vision of Love Revealed in Sleep: Part One* (1987), devised by Bartlett with artist and designer Robin Whitmore – was performed at London's Battersea Arts Centre as a solo work in which Bartlett appeared naked, shaven and powdered as to resemble 'a marble statue, an artist's model, a painting', wearing a flaming red beard with shoulder-length hair (Bartlett 2005: 17). Bartlett – named as 'Neil' in the published script – figures the signs of Solomon's Jewishness and, as 'a boy draped in silk', embodying the desired subject of Solomon's paintings. This identification marks out the doubled conditions of Solomon's pariahdom: abjected as both queer and Jewish. Later performed as *Part Three* (1989) with drag artists Bette Bourne, Regina Fong and Ivan the Terrible (aka Ivan Cartwright) as 'a choric voice of the unacceptable face of gay history' (Bartlett 1990: 83), *A Vision of Love* involves a form of what Freeman theorises as erotohistoriography: an anachronistic embodiment that offers an encounter with history in which contact with the past is coded as 'a meeting of sensate body, historical understanding and representation' (2010: 105). That meeting does not conflate past and

---

2 The poem was later republished in *The Bibelot*, a yearly literary anthology published by Thomas Bird Mosher between 1895 and 1914, alongside works by Algernon Swinburne, William Morris, Robert Louis Stevenson and Oscar Wilde. The full text can be found online at https://archive.org/details/bibelot00ferggoog, accessed 9 January 2015.

present but instead signals the kinds of creative, affective labour that might be required for acts of historical understanding to take place.

Though the performance opens in the claim that 'everything I say tonight is true, and everything I say tonight is written here in this book, and this book was written in 1871' (Bartlett 2005: 19), the performance text is a conscious hybrid of nineteenth- and twentieth-century sources: the work of Charles Dickens, 1980s homophobic tabloid demagoguery and immediately recognisable governmental AIDS health warnings: 'Don't Die of Ignorance.' Here, the notional 'untouchability' of the AIDS pariah inaugurates a social scene of heightened vulnerability in which touch is not denied but amplified as violence. Solomon's 'wounded love' takes the form of someone Neil recognises, 'someone I'd spent the night with', lying bloodied in the road as a victim of homophobic assault. Rather than warning of a future injury to be escaped, Bartlett's vision describes a reality which may not be averted because it is already taking place: it is a work which refuses to treat AIDS 'as an epidemic of the future rather than a catastrophe of the present' (Bersani 1987: 199). The relationship to history is neither reparative nor recuperative in the sense of performing a 'rescue' of queer subjects but one which describes what it is like 'to bear a "disqualified" identity, which at times can simply mean living with injury – not fixing it' (Love 2007: 4).

In recognition that 'I think we're running out of time; I don't think you can ask us to wait to be happy' (Bartlett 2005: 29), *A Vision of Love* shifts from a re-telling of Solomon's poem to the most notorious events of Solomon's life: his arrest in 1873 in a public toilet for a sexual encounter with an unemployed stableman. Faced with social scandal, Bartlett's Solomon refuses the telos of shame that might allow his return to polite society. Where Werner wistfully imagines an alternative path in which the artist might have 'given up heavy drinking' so that 'society might have forgiven him and after some years rewarded him with a membership in the Royal Academy' (Werner 1960: 401), Bartlett's Solomon is gloriously unrepentant:

> And he never, never, never, never, never apologised for what he had done. And his friends came to him and they asked him to come back and he said no; and his family came to him and asked him to come back and he said, no, my behaviour has been perfectly disgraceful, I cannot possibly ask you to forgive me. (Bartlett 2005: 38)

Uncoupled from the promise of redemption, Solomon's confession takes the form of a refusal – one in which Solomon persists by failing to die young as an icon of talent and excess ('sitting on the toilet, from an overdose of barbiturates') and instead living for another thirty-two years in increasing poverty.

Recalling Arendt, Solomon is a conscious pariah not merely because he is an outcast but because he refuses the premise of acceptance on which his rehabilitation would depend: he cannot apologise because to do so would require him to live as something other than his true self and come to hold up the social order from which he would otherwise be excluded. Though Solomon's status as a pariah is not of his choosing, his refusal of rehabilitation describes a form of agency by which the role of the outcast in confirming narratives of liberal inclusiveness might be frustrated. It is for this reason that the work's manifestation of 'the pull of the past on the present' (Freeman 2010: 62) describes something other than the inevitability of injury as the basis of queer identity – gesturing, instead, towards an 'anti-teleological dialectic producing knowledge in opposition to destiny' (Dollimore 1991: 229). If Solomon is a 'strange, sad' and 'disquieting' role model (Eyres 1990) – as in the words of a reviewer for *The Times* – then it is only because his dissident refusals continue to bring to light the normative values on which liberal tolerance and approval depend.

At the same time, the non-linear history that emerges from *A Vision of Love* marks a resistance of history as a destiny that cannot be re-written – an assertion that is also apparent in several of Bartlett's more recent solo works: *Helpless* (2007), created for the Royal Vauxhall Tavern to mark World Aids Day, and *What Can You Do?* (2012), performed to close a 'queer retrospective' of Bartlett's solo works at the Theatre Royal in Brighton dedicated to the workers of The Sussex Beacon, a care centre for people living with HIV and AIDS. *Helpless* opens with a confession – 'I can't stop. I just *can't*' – in which the pejorative belief that gay people are prisoners of their (sexual) impulses and that change is not possible – 'We can't cope … We can't care. We can't talk. We can't share' – becomes a rallying determination to keep fundraising, to keep arguing and to keep taking pleasure from fucking 'some impossibly handsome Danish twenty-eight year old in Denmark Hill' (Bartlett 2012: 17). In *What Can You Do?*, Bartlett invokes former Prime Minister David Cameron's Conservative Party conference claim that 'we're all in this together' to unpack its cruel irony:

> we all knew the moment he said it, the moment he said it, that he *meant the exact opposite*; which was perfect, which sums the whole bloody situation up really, because everyone knew, and knows, *everyone* knew, the moment they heard it, that they only way we're all in this together is that we're all equally and absolutely and exactly *in this* … On Our Own. (Bartlett 2012: 66)

In both works, the knowledge and value of what gay subjects have been able to achieve singularly and as a community exceeds the conditions which made those achievements necessary to assert another world – of desire, and of being together with others – which is already possible.

In the closing moments of *A Vision of Love*, Neil reads a letter from Solomon addressed to the present moment – 'I hear that London is just the same these days, or worse. Please, try not to be too frightened' (Bartlett 2005: 46) – before showing the audience that the page is blank. Whatever else, the form of transtemporal identification involved in Bartlett's figuring of Solomon is one which acknowledges that an encounter with a queer past may demand impossible acts of transport. This sensibility structures Bartlett's play *Stella* (2016), concerning the life of Victorian bank clerk, performer and top-billed 'female impersonator' Ernest Boulton, where a resistance to linear biography manifests in the work's dramaturgy as a 'one-man show for two bodies' in which 'a single life is being scrutinized from two different perspectives' (Bartlett 2016: 10). Echoing the logic of *A Vision of Love*'s closing epistolary gesture, *Stella* plays with the conceit that a person in the future might seek solace from their same self in the past and that a younger person might turn to their older selves for advice. In the final scenes of the play, the work's two versions of Boulton appear to address each other – though this possibility rests in the willingness of the audience to desire it, as the comfort that might be extended to a historical life exists only as a possibility that we might wish for ourselves in the present. If – following Freeman – drag signals backwardness, retrogression and delay (2010: 62) and thereby the existence of lives lived on terms other than those of the present, it may also mark the unavailability of those lives to knowledge without giving up a claim on the present as a critically detached and somehow objective perspective rather than one charged with present affect. Revived for a single performance in 2017 to coincide with Solomon's inclusion in Tate Britain's *Queer British Art 1861–1967* exhibition – and performed some thirty years after the development of antiretroviral therapies to manage HIV/AIDS – *A Vision of Love* calls attention to the complexity of how we might come to recognise progress *as* progress from any given moment in time.

Historical pariahs: *Gloria Days* and *How to Win Against History*

The desire for an encounter with a queer past set apart from the historical destinies of wounded victory or ignoble defeat is also apparent in Marc Rees' *Gloria Days* (2007) and Seiriol Davies' *How To Win Against History*

(2016), two works concerning the life of Henry Cyril Paget, the flamboyant 5th Marquess of Anglesey. Born in 1875 to an aristocratic family and isolated in childhood following the death of his mother at an early age, Paget inherited his title on his father's death at the age of twenty-four before proceeding to spend the family's considerable fortune on elaborate clothing and ornaments, and on staging lavishly costumed productions of contemporary and classical plays across the UK and Europe. Though income from his family estates was equivalent to £11 million in today's money, Paget mortgaged his life interest several times over before eventually being declared bankrupt with estimated debts of £50 million to be framed as a cautionary example in *The Complete Peerage* as 'only to have existed for the purpose of giving a melancholy and unneeded illustration of the truth that a man with the finest prospects may … have lived in vain' (Cockayne 1910: col. 141). While claimed by early gay rights campaigner H. Montgomery Hyde as the 'most notorious aristocratic homosexual' of his period and an 'extreme example of the effeminate transvestite type' (1970: 153–4), there is little evidence of Paget's relationships. For theatre historian Viv Gardner, Paget resembles a 'classic narcissist' unable to love or make love to anyone but himself, with his extravagance and theatricality 'all point[ing] to some form of compensation for "not being as other men" in a world that still demanded manliness from its ruling class' (V. Gardner 2008: 29).

While both Rees and Davies' works enact a queer claim on Paget through recognition of gender non-conformism, they are more profoundly structured by a sense of his suspended relationship to history itself: his personal papers burnt in shame by his ancestors but his name and reputation preserved the logic of hereditary succession and the public spectacle of his downfall. In the solo dance theatre work *Gloria Days*, Rees performs Paget on a mirrored black glass floor which allows him to return repeatedly to his own reflected image. Circling the stage dressed in a crisp white suit, he recites a long list of Paget's belongings sold to meet a fraction of his debts – 'a diamond and platinum chain. A diamond windmill pendant. A pair of diamond heart-shaped sleeve-links' – with the sharp tapping of his heel marking the crack of an auctioneer's hammer. In a later projected film sequence, Rees appears in a diamond face mask: a figure in a forest dressed in a fur coat with a handful of elaborately jewelled rings. While Rees clearly figures Paget, he also stands at a distance by invoking Roland Barthes' *Camera Lucida* (1980) to tell us:

> In the many, many photographic portraits of the 5th Marquis, we see him playing to the social game, almost hear him declaim not 'I think therefore

I am' but 'I pose therefore I am'. 'I pose, I know I am posing, and I want you to know that I am posing'.

Rees doubles as Paget while drawing attention to his own game of 'posing', and the desire to recuperate Paget as a gay man unrecognised in his own era sees Rees project his own desires for the present backwards in time. As in Bartlett's figuring of Solomon, the past and present make each other possible. Rees staging recovers Paget's identity from illegibility in the past even as its very existence in that past allows Rees to perform himself as a gay man in the present. This game of reflexive agency frames the closing moment of the performance in which Rees speaks the words attributed to Paget in an interview given to the *Daily Mail* in the final months before his death:

> I must apologise for not appearing before you in peacock-blue plush wearing a diamond and sapphire tiara, a turquoise dog-collar, ropes of pearls and slippers studded with Burma rubies; but I prefer, and always have preferred, Scotch tweed.

In Rees' delivery, this admission is queerly sincere, with the opulence of the language playing against the claim on instinctive conservatism. Paget's final performance, in other words, describes a wilful act of self-fashioning intended to put the idea of a historically authentic straightness forever in quotation marks.

The possibility of a queer resistance constituted in apparent defeat is more sharply felt in Davies' *How to Win Against History*, initially developed at Roundhouse in London ahead of staging at the Edinburgh Festival Fringe in 2016. Structured as a musical comedy and performed by Davies alongside Matthew Blake and Dylan Townley, the show cuts a roughly chronological path through the major stages of Paget's life: his childhood at Eton, his rapidly annulled marriage to his cousin, his inheritance and profligate spending, and premature death from 'some sort of lung thing'. Davies' Paget is a wide-eyed, queer man-child whose narcissism is only occasionally punctuated by flickers of self-awareness. Visited by absurdly theatrical ghosts who tell him that history has great expectations and deliver the singular advice to 'be yourself', Henry commits to 'wear lovely, lovely dresses' and proceeds to stage increasingly lavish and obscure theatrical spectacles in which he plays the starring roles – including a version of the real Paget's own 'Electric Butterfly Dance' (thought to be inspired by the sinuous movements of modern dance pioneer Loie Fuller).

Henry's moment of imagined self-recognition and acceptance through performance at an avant-garde club in Berlin – 'I have always been / Tongue tied / Now my soul / Is outside / I'm a butterfly!' – is undercut by the audience's refrain, taught through call and response: 'Ich bin höflich aber verwirrt' (meaning 'I am polite but confused'). The moment is also followed by news that Henry is bankrupt and must sell all of his possessions. Rather than struggle onwards to fulfil his prophesied destiny, Henry vows to 'give up so flipping hard' and 'retire, in exile, to live like a peasant – a pauper – in Monte Carlo'. The final turn of the show, though, sees Henry realise that he can win against history after all by giving his 'greatest, and arguably finalest' performance of being 'normal', and the interview with the *Daily Mail* journalist plays out as one final burst of camp excess that is, paradoxically, Henry playing 'straight':

> I mean in an ideal world I'd have literally everything of tweed: trouser of tweed, jacket of tweed, pant of tweed, pancreas, man face, lungs … I mean a tweed suit of armour's what I really need. (Davies 2017: 80)

Henry dies, and while his family's attempt to erase him from their history is 'regrettable', the show closes on his insistence that he existed: he was an aristocrat, he was rich, he was lonely, he was fierce and he was 'a crossdresser' and for all those reasons he 'sort of won' (Davies 2017: 84).[3]

Margaret Thatcher Queen of Soho

If Bartlett's Solomon and Rees and Davies' Paget serve as potentially representative pariahs for the queer community because they stand as outcasts excluded from a cultural mainstream, Brittain and Tedford's figuring of ex-Prime Minister Margaret Thatcher inverts that scene by offering identifications *with* Thatcher as the agent of such exclusion through her association with the passage of anti-gay legislation known as Section 28 that was intended to prevent the 'promotion' of homosexuality (Greer 2012: 105–6). Though the work presents a satirical re-writing of British political history, it also suggests the ways in which British gay cultural history – shaped by the moral telos of historical injury – has come to depend upon Thatcher as the figural representative of past intolerances, and the measure by which progress may be judged. Neither plainly antagonistic nor merely celebratory, *Queen of Soho*'s imagining of

---

3 For an alternative treatment of the happy queer outcast, see Dafydd James and Ben Lewis' *My Name is Sue* (2009) centred on James' anti-drag performance of a Welsh prophetess haunted by visions of the apocalypse.

Thatcher as cabaret star and supporter of gay rights can be understood in light of what Dominic Janes has explored as the 'queer afterlife' of Thatcher as a gay icon whose gender performance 'helped gay men and lesbians to construct and develop their own subjectivities' (2012: 213). As Heather Nunn (2002) has argued, the fact that Thatcher both troubled and endorsed unequal gender and economic divides has allowed her supporters to read in her politics support for a range of different personal aspirations, whether in the form of escape from traditional gender roles or the acquisition of private wealth.

While gay male commentators have variously framed Thatcher as a model of 'pure elegance, feminine perfection, perfect dress sense, and sheer determination to change society' (Coleman 2007) and as an embodiment of the 'steely power to self-transform' (Flynn 2006), *Queen of Soho* suggests how 'identification with, and desire *for*, may coexist with parodic subversion *of*' (Dollimore 1991: 321, original emphasis).[4] Focused on – if not dominated by – Tedford's performance as Thatcher, *Queen of Soho* joins a tradition in which Thatcher's status as 'a drag queen of sorts herself' (Baker 1994: 256) sustains a history of contentious attachment – whether in impressionist Steve Nallon's popular performances as Thatcher for TV satire *Spitting Image* and at Pride marches during the 1980s, or in more recent portrayals by performers such drag artist Myra Dubois, whose show *TURNING! Lady Thatcher Returns* capitalised on her death in 2013 with a 'jukebox musical romp' with 'the first person to rise from the grave since Jesus Christ', and burlesque performer Honey Wilde, whose 'The Lady Is For Turning' act sees her lip-sync to a fragment of Thatcher's 1980 Conservative Party conference speech – 'To those waiting with bated breath for that favourite media catchphrase, the "U-turn", I have only one thing to say: "You turn if you want to. The lady's not for turning"' – before performing a kind of fem-dom striptease accompanied by Depeche Mode's track *Master and Servant* (1984).

Presented as a play within a drag act – with Tedford's Thatcher accompanied by two 'wets', Hessel and Tine, played by Nico Lennon and Ed Yelland – *Queen of Soho* imagines an alternative history in which the former prime minister has gone into showbiz: 'I used to be the Barbra Streisand of politics, now I'm the Margaret Thatcher of cabaret' (Brittain and Tedford 2015: 8). Interviewed ahead of the show's first appearance at the Soho

---

4 See, for example, Amy Lamé's staging of her love–hate attachment to the pop star Morrissey in her 'party-slash-show-slash-party' *Unhappy Birthday* (2012) and the mock accusation that Morrissey is to blame for making her a lesbian.

Theatre, London, Brittain framed *Queen of Soho*'s aesthetic as a response to the seeming seriousness of the other works planned for Theatre 503's 2013 event *Thatcherwrite*, an evening of plays inspired by the legacy of Thatcher in which the show first appeared as a short sketch.[5] *Queen of Soho* reflected the desire to make a play 'on the surface, as stupid and silly and ridiculous as possible' even though 'there is a point underneath, because it is about Section 28 and gay rights and what she could have done if she'd chosen to' (Brittain quoted in Fleming 2013). Though *Queen of Soho*'s script mocks its own narrative coherence, historical accuracy and theatrical acumen, the work's dramaturgy manifests skill and conviction: Tedford's appearance in twin-set, pearls and handbag is carefully rendered, his voice reproducing both Thatcher's husky lower register (itself the product of voice coaching following media commentary that she sounded 'shrill') and the characteristic intonation of her speech. While the show makes use of parodic grotesques in depicting Conservative MP Jill Knight, activist Peter Tatchell and ex-Prime Minister Winston Churchill (the latter as an animated portrait who fondly recalls cottaging in the Houses of Parliament), Thatcher is accorded a certain respect. It is also, perhaps paradoxically, Tedford's ability to produce a committed drag performance as Thatcher that gives affective significance to the later misapprehension of Thatcher – explored below – as a failed drag queen.

Riding low in the polls in her third term of government, facing a hostile press and sensing dissent amongst members of her own Cabinet, Thatcher is in need of a measure that, as one of her ministers suggests, 'will satisfy the whim of the party, titillate the press, and appeal to the prejudices of the general public' (Brittain and Tedford 2015: 16). Such a plan of action is handily provided by Jill Knight, one of the original sponsors of Section 28, who appears as a pantomime villain against whom Thatcher is allowed to narrate herself as a kind of honest pragmatist whose actions were the result of political pressure rather than deliberate homophobia. Knight's concerns take the form of lurid and barely restrained fantasies of desire – 'I sit at home in the dark every night and imagine all the disgusting, immoral and sweaty things they [homosexuals] do to each other' (Brittain and Tedford 2015: 18) – to which Thatcher deadpans a non-response. While Knight's outrage at Susanne Bösche's children's book *Jenny Lives With Eric and Martin* (1983) involves a rather threadbare appeal to decency – 'Look at this filth, both men sat up in bed having breakfast and neither one is wearing an undershirt' – Thatcher's

---

5 These plays included Kay Adshead's satirically eulogistic *I Am Sad You Are Dead Mrs T* and Jimmy Osbourne's Falklands war playlet *1888*.

Figure 5 Matt Tedford (centre) with Ed Yelland and Nico Lennon, *Margaret Thatcher Queen of Soho* (2014).

Figure 6 Matt Tedford, *Margaret Thatcher Queen of Soho* (2014).

retort is campily misplaced: 'And look at that crockery!' (Brittain and Tedford 2015: 19). Though Tedford performs with Lennon, the sequence emphasises Thatcher's singular, narrative perspective: Lennon provides Thatcher's (self-serving) version of Knight as much as it indulges the audience's desire to see Knight mocked.

Dismayed by the tenor of debate and threatened by Knight with a vote of no-confidence in Parliament if she does not support Section 28, Thatcher takes a walk to clear her head but finds herself lost in the middle of Soho. Unable to find a taxi, she is verbally abused by a banker and a policeman who refuse to believe that she is the prime minister. Catching sight of herself in a shop window, Thatcher narrates the terms of her own (mis)recognition:

> The rain had caused my make-up to run and become garish, my hair had come loose in the wind and had begun to look like the most awful wig, and my tiredness and unease had conspired to give my usually feminine features the very vaguest hint of masculinity. (Brittain and Tedford 2015: 38)

If the audience does not respond in audible empathy, Thatcher cajoles them until they have sympathised to her satisfaction. While Thatcher's rejection turns on her (mis)apprehension as a gay man in drag, the terms on which she is then welcomed by the gay community does not involve a straightforwardly affirmative recognition of her 'true' identity.

Invited out of the rain and into the club, Thatcher hesitates for fear of rejection but is warmly welcomed by name: 'Do you want a drink Maggie? ... Oh we love you, Thatcher!' (Brittain and Tedford 2015: 39). In this scene of (mis)recognition and uncertain affirmation, multiple and conflicting possibilities for acknowledgement emerge in the layering of a dramatic representation of the historical person of Thatcher, the mis-recognition of that person as a gay man in drag, and the presence of a real world performer – a gay man in drag – who is playing that part. Identification is invited simultaneously *with* Tedford's Thatcher as the non-gender-conforming subject of misogynistic homophobia, and *against* the real world historical figure of Thatcher as someone unable or unwilling to empathise with those faced by the same experiences. That doubling of drag as recognition and, simultaneously, misrecognition frames the imagined acceptance of Thatcher by the counterpublic of a gay community as something other or more than revisionist wish-fulfilment. Instead, its consciously playful camp theatricality marks the politically charged affective labour that might be involved in remembering Thatcher as something other than a pariah for the gay community.

If, as Love proposes, our sense of progress is tightly bound to regress as a function of 'the reliance of the concept of modernity on excluded, denigrated, or superseded others' (Love 2007: 5), *Queen of Soho* might articulate how Thatcher has come to stand as a figure of 'regression' on which a contemporary conceptualisation of the progressive gay subject depends. The closing moments of *Queen of Soho* are indeed direct – if not blunt – in narrating the functional quality of cultural memory. Having raced to Parliament to successfully block Section 28, Thatcher resigns and leaves for the cabaret circuit, pausing to imagine what could have been if people had not had 'a hero to praise, or even a villain to hate' and merely 'a person, much like any other, to try and understand. But luckily that was not the case. You've had me, and I've been fabulous' (Brittain and Tedford 2015: 44). Beyond a history lesson which reminds a younger audience of the recent past, the backwards drag attachments of *Queen of Soho* might also allow better recognition of the ways in which a history of anti-homophobia politics structures a mainstream politics of equality, and in which the historical injury described by Section 28 – in which older gay men and women were imagined to 'promote' homosexuality to impressionable youth – continues to shape affirmative attempts to bring young people up queer (even as the lessons for growing up straight have become more clearly enshrined in the UK's national curriculum through the affirmation of marriage and 'family life'). The injury of Section 28 is not only the founding cause of the UK's Stonewall group but that which continues to shape what recovery – and progress – feels like, namely access to existing (heteronormative) frameworks of legitimacy and recognition.

Wounded attachment

More significant still may be an elaboration of what Wendy Brown (1995) theorises via Nietzsche's concept of *ressentiment* as a process of 'wounded attachment' – that is, the creation of a form of politicised identity which is structured by an investment in its own subjugation.[6] That attachment takes the form of the discovery of an external figure to blame, the satisfaction of moralising revenge on that figure, and, most significantly, the acquisition of recognition through a history of subjection (Brown

---

6 For a parallel discussion of wounded attachment as a dynamic in the work of Ron Athey and Franko B, see Walsh (2010a).

1995: 70) with the consequence that such identity is unthinkable apart from that history of injury. Brown writes:

> In its emergence as a protest against marginalization or subordination, politicized identity ... becomes attached to its own exclusion both because it is premised on this exclusion for its very existence as identity and because the formation of identity at the site of exclusion, as exclusion, augments or 'alters the direction of the suffering' entailed in subordination or marginalization by finding a site of blame for it. (1995: 73–4)

Suffering is made meaningful and put to use by describing the exclusion of subjects from a normative field of reference for liberal citizenship as described by the entitlements of male, white middle-class subjects – a dynamic which Brown argues reverses without subverting the political function of blame in aligning moral standing with social status.

In this regard, the attachment described by *ressentiment* differs from the kinds of identification with injury and exclusion characterised by a social poetics of camp which 'works to drain suffering of the pain that it also does not deny' (Halperin 2012: 186). In 'gender disillusionist' Dickie Beau's show *Blackouts: Twilight of the Idols* (2011), for example, the drag tradition of lip-synced playback performance serves to animate Marilyn Monroe and Judy Garland as icons who 'speak to queerness because they were outsiders' (Beau quoted in Megarry 2015). This identification is not straightforward but involves a triangulation through drag itself: Steve Farrier observes that Beau's performance of Garland and Monroe's iconicity involves its 'undoing' through mimicry and gestural vocabulary that is at once well-observed and 'exaggerated and grotesque, which emphasizes its artifice as performance' (2013: 57). Consequently, the queer quality of Garland's pain centres on the 'pain of being authored by others' in which 'Garland as icon gets undone in the sense that the audience is encouraged to witness her as a person pained by her situation' (Farrier 2013: 57–8). In this dynamic, identification with/ as an outcast involves a sense of the split between the public and private dimensions of a self in which Garland and Monroe's private speech in the form of private, archival recordings manifests a form of self-authorship elided by the demands of public image. Accordingly, gay male identification with Garland's 'strength and suffering' (Dyer 1986: 149) plays out as an account of a psychic – which is to say internal – structure in which the queer self is split between its capacity to self-define and the forms of social (mis)recognition forced upon it on entry to the public sphere.

In *Queen of Soho*, the site of blame is given an externalised form – Thatcher – that narrates and sustains a history that is not only predicated on past injury but in which the attachment to that hurt seems part of the pleasure of the work. As such, Thatcher's impossible 'fabulousness' and the alternative history that it represents might well remind us once more of the political limits of imagining outcast subjects only in terms of their eventual acceptance within a normative social sphere, while prompting knowledge of how – as Love puts it – 'feeling bad about being queer can serve as a reminder that the magical solution of affirmation is inadequate and push us toward different kinds of responses' (2009: 258). At the same time, the spectacle of the work's largely youthful audience – and, frequently, younger gay men who came of age after Section 28 – gathering for 'selfies' with Thatcher at the end of every performance may prompt us to recognise the possibilities of forgetting: not an erasure of history, but a re-ordering of the role that history plays in constituting identities constituted through *ressentiment*. To this end, Brown proposes a subtle shift in our political language: from the claim on 'I am', loaded with 'its defensive closure on identity, its insistence on the fixity of position' to the language of 'I want this for us', an articulation of desire in the formulation of identity prior to its wounding (Brown 1995: 75). Claiming the figure of Thatcher as something more than a site of injury and blame might form part of such a project.

Complicity and resistance: David Hoyle

If the first parts of this chapter have read the pariah to think about subjectivity in its relation to history and the past, my emphasis shifts at this point towards an understanding of the pariah as offering a critique of the forms of complicit attachment that constitute the experience of a neoliberal present. I do so by reading the work of performance artist David Hoyle as offering a direct response to the psychosexual pathology of the 'happy queer', the 'conventional albeit white, gay, middle-class male concerned with the reproduction and protection of property and money, and whose politics are entirely compatible with the workings of neoliberalism' (Blackman 2011: 192). Hoyle's performances are not opposed to happiness but invested in a suite of affects that Halberstam argues are often occluded from the gay male archive, and which may run counter to easy claims on togetherness: 'rage, rudeness, anger, spite, impatience, intensity, mania, sincerity, earnestness, overinvestment, incivility and brutal honesty' (Caserio *et al.* 2006: 824).[7] These affects challenge the field of values through which any claim on community and the common might be successfully articulated and, to invoke Brown, become intelligible as a claim on what 'we' might want for 'us'. I read Hoyle as a conscious pariah, then, for the ways in which his work cuts against the premise of assimilationist inclusion which leaves the terms of an existing social order intact.

Hoyle first rose to prominence in the 1990s through the character of The Divine David, an anti-drag queen at the centre of the 'anti-gay gay crowd' characterised by 'a sensibility deeply at odds with all the consumerist paraphernalia that purports to define gay style' (Gray 1996) whose acerbic critique of gay mainstream consumerist narcissism was matched by acts of self-recrimination and, sometimes, self-harm. Success on the queer and alternative circuit led to two television series for the UK's Channel 4 – *The Divine David Presents* (1998) and *The Divine David Heals* (2000) – following which Hoyle 'killed off' the character in a final show staged at the Streatham Ice Arena, titled *The Divine David on Ice* (2000). Following a period of illness, Hoyle reappeared in the Channel 4 sitcom *Nathan Barley* (2005) and in live performance through Manchester's Queer Up North festival and the touring stage show *David Hoyle's SOS* (2006). In the following, I focus on Hoyle's *Magazine*, a series of shows staged in 2006–8 at the Royal Vauxhall Tavern, London, to explore a critique of hetero- and homonormative culture that is inflected by a sense of its own precarious complicity. While Arendt's work suggests we might understand the pariah as one who stands as 'a member of a group of outsiders *against* the prevailing community' (Ring 1991: 441), Hoyle's practice calls for a closer consideration of the terms of any such 'outsider' identification, and the precarious terms on which any re-politicisation of that community might take place.

Structured by recurring elements of action painting and guest interview (and, more often, heated debate), each of *Magazine*'s interlinked shows addressed a different 'issue' – in the 2007 sequence, Celebrity, Cookery, Crime & Punishment, Immigration, Dogging, Media Studies, HIV unt AIDS, The Women's Issue, Antique's Roadshow and Alcoholism. These titles served as markers for explicit enquiries or interventions – as in Hoyle's inclusion of his own HIV test results received only hours prior to the performance – and as the jumping off point for more open-ended, abrasive and sometimes obscene encounters with the audience and Hoyle's guests. Tonally, *Magazine* shifts back and forth between camp

---

7 For an expansive interview with Hoyle, see Johnson (2015).

triviality and keenly consequential social commentary. The introduction to Hoyle's celebration of women, for example, finds its self-declared 'political edge' ('why now are young women ignorant of the fact that the suffragettes ever existed?') before immediately digressing into an appraisal of British gay porn film company TRIGA, and the HIV edition sees Hoyle naked but for a short towel in a smoke-filled stage set to invoke a gay sauna: 'Well, who hasn't been here, ladies and gentlemen? Knowing deep in your heart you're an effeminate homosexual but you're trying to butch it up to try and get some trade' (Hoyle 2008a).

While Hoyle's transgression of polite social discourse is sharply funny in itself, Hoyle's willingness to confront and draw humour from difficult, controversial or plainly distressing material – from mental illness, suicidal thoughts, drug use or graphic descriptions of taboo sex acts – also manifests as a kind of ethical obligation to give voice to frequently unspoken elements of gay cultural identity. In rejecting romanticised accounts of persistence and demanding that we take our 'built-in obsolescence' (Hoyle in Johnson 2015: 259) seriously, Hoyle's work may run in close parallel to the forms of subversion found in the pages of radical AIDS 'zines such as *Diseased Pariah News* and *Infected Faggot Perspectives* which refused representations of people with AIDS as sentimentalised victims, and embraced the role of sexual and medical pariah as a practice of uncensored, performative self-representation.[8] Nonetheless, Hoyle's 'tragic-comic reworking of his autobiographical narratives of "unhappy affect" (of loneliness, abuse, mental collapse and alcohol and substance abuse)' (Blackman 2011: 193) to address issues faced by gay communities does not lend itself easily to an affirmative politics of communal belonging. Rather than merely asserting the shared authenticity of lived experience, the autobiographical elements of Hoyle's work serve to foreground the provisional terms on which identification as part of a community constituted through injury might take place. As the history of LGBT activism makes plain, the notional shared interests of non-heterosexual subjects provide for only tenuous bonds of solidarity.

Reading the improvisational, chaotic register of Hoyle's performance, Daniel Oliver suggests the quality of Hoyle's 'car-crash' style is characterised by sudden shifts from 'reassuring order to disturbing messiness', dwelling 'on the slippery border between the intentional and the accidental' (Oliver 2012: 1) in producing incidents and aftermaths which both seduce and repel our gaze. Structured by shame, the feelings generated by Hoyle's performances may be 'equally and simultaneously

8 See Long (2000).

identity-defining and identity-erasing', constructing the 'singularity and isolation of one's identity through an affective connection to the shaming of the other' (Crimp 2009: 70). The effect – and, perhaps, affect – is a relationship suspended between complicity and culpability, between ethical responsibility for what is unfolding onstage (won't *somebody* stop him? Won't somebody stop him *before he hurts himself?*) and a sense of involvement with others in the commission of something which may be morally questionable. In consequence, the implication of Hoyle's audience in the conditions of the queer outcast is as often characterised by guilt as by reassurance, figuring the pariah as one who 'knows his outsider status is not of his own making, yet recognizes that he has some choices and indeed some responsibility for what he does with it' (Ring 1991: 441).

The terms of such responsibility, though, are not easily identified. If Hoyle is more than willing to aggressively confront those with whom he disagrees, his performances also seem to question any personal claim to moral or political superiority, and the queerly sincere register of his speech seems intended to draw attention to what a normative paradigm of conviction-based political speech excludes (see Butt 2007). Interviewed by Gavin Butt following a heated stage confrontation with transsexual media personality Lauren Harries – in which Hoyle attacked Harries as a 'right wing cunt' and Harries had accused Hoyle of failing to acknowledge his own transsexuality – Hoyle suggested that 'I'm interested in questioning and betraying my own ignorance and prejudice rather than sounding PC-ed up to the eyeballs' (quoted in Butt 2008: 31). Hoyle's tirades are not structured by self-justification but often inflected by an awareness of their seeming contradictions, aggressively confronting 'his male spectators for aping oppressive forms of machismo with their gym-honed bodies, only to admit, in the next breath, his own desire to fuck them' (Butt 2013: 50). If the claim on an inherently transgressive queerness might offer what Jasbir Puar describes as 'an alibi for complicity with all sorts of other identity norms, such as nation, race, class and gender' (2007: 24), Hoyle's speech works to advertise its own inconsistencies and attachments. It is this troubling of an exculpatory queerness – in which the act of transgression performs a kind of absolution from guilt – that might describe the function of the contemporary pariah as a political agent who refuses critical distance as the basis for action.

I will quote Hoyle at length to give a sense of how he ricochets between castigating gay male homogeneity and demanding authentic 'difference' in a manner that exposes the precarity of those judgements, even as they are put into play.

Gay men aping heterosexuals make me [spits]. 'Please regard me as a man,
please see me as being sexy.' Well, I suppose if the chips were down I wouldn't
kick you out of bed. But you're not real. You're not authentic. We've all been to
bed with a greased monkey, haven't we? Up and down the scaffolding. Who
here hasn't had a lucky moment? When you've had intimacy with a real man
and he's got his body – his hard body – from manual work. Not from going
to the gym four times a week, because if he was truly honest with himself he
lives in a lonely hell … It's one of the perversities of life that the oppressed
then dedicate their every waking hour to emulating their very oppressors!
Oh yes, you see these gay men going to the gym. You know why that is?
Guilt, guilt, guilt! Deep down inside, they know they're different because
if everyone went gay, there'd be no more fucking children. Which I'm all
for. 'Please take me seriously. I want to come across as a type of man who
might say yes to war with Iraq, to considering the annihilation of Iran and
Syria. Please confuse me with the straight men who make these decisions.
Please. I don't want you to look at me as dangerous and different and potentially hyper-creative. I want to castrate myself! I want to emasculate myself!
I want to look like those cunts who rule the world!' (Hoyle 2008b)

In this passage, Hoyle's speech resembles Leo Bersani's concern for how
a logic of sameness which underpins claims on liberal equality threatens
the very possibility of queer identity, where in the attempt 'to convince
straight society that we are only some malevolent invention and that we
can be, like you, good soldiers, good parents, and good citizens, we seem
bent on suicide' (Bersani 1995: 42). That rejection of sameness, though,
remains laced with seeming acknowledgement of the allure of 'authentic'
male heterosexual embodiment which is the product of masculine labour.
In a more recent interview with Dominic Johnson, Hoyle has described
the liberation of no longer desiring men and the accompanying realisation that 'humanoids who *identify as men* are my enemy … humans
who identify as "men" are pathetic, cancerous, old-fashioned, dangerous
and an absolute obstacle to the progress of society' (quoted in Johnson
2015: 243). Here too, though, the dead seriousness of Hoyle's claim –
mirrored in a frequent call for his audiences to 'kill all in authority' – is
laced with a deadpan consciousness of its excess; prompted by Johnson to
recognise his sense of humour, Hoyle observes that he is from Blackpool,
after all, and that Blackpool has three piers.

In the discussion above, I have inferred how the figure of the pariah
might elaborate the more challenging aspects of queer collectivity,
whether through recognition of forms of historical injury and practices
of persistence (as in *A Vision of Love*) or in acknowledgement of illicit
pleasures in identification with/as the pariah (as in *Queen of Soho*). That
project is not easily continued through Hoyle's work. As Bojana Jankovic

offers in her review of Hoyle's *I, Victim* (2014) – centred on the victim-isation and self-victimisation which surrounds mental health diagnoses – the 'constant attacks at traditional masculinity often metastasise into a surge against men in general' (Jankovic 2014b) such as that an iden-tification with the hurt and wounded precludes masculine-identifying men who may be subjected to – and wounded by – patriarchal norms. Though Hoyle's performances repeatedly invoke – if not demand – an egalitarian, communal experience, his performative rhetoric works to call the terms of that communality into question through what Oliver has explored as a 'bait-and-switch attitude towards audience interaction and communal, relational activities' (Oliver 2014: 112). Where it exists, the collective experience of Hoyle's audience might be an uncomfortable one and, indeed, constituted through discomfort. Reading *Dave's Drop-in Centre* (2009) – structured by the premise of a psychiatric day-care centre – Fintan Walsh observes that 'Hoyle's method is raucous and some-times quite shocking as he shouts at the audience' (2012: 67), with Hoyle pausing at one point to hold his own performance to ransom: 'I won't do this painting, ladies and gentleman, unless you convince me that if you've got an unaware, ego-driven, egocentric, self-delusionary cunt in your life, that you won't get rid of them. They need to die tonight' (Hoyle 2009).

This recurrent unease, I suggest, stems from how Hoyle's attempts to orchestrate the communal turns on the presence of his own distinctively assertive performance persona: 'There ain't nobody here more important than any other fucker. Other than me of course, it's my fucking show' (Hoyle 2008a). The singular speaking position which allows Hoyle to demand radical change also undercuts its capacity to enact it. On the one hand, Hoyle's rhetoric frames the queer subject as counter-normative (as quoted above, 'dangerous and different and potentially hyper-creative'), manifesting a politically charged rejection of homogenised forms of desire and desirability. On the other hand is his sense of how claims on dis-tinctive individuality might work to deny one's obligations towards others:

> Yes, it's nice to stand out, to be a little bit different. But if your individuality comes at the cost of your humanity, please kill yourself. And I mean that in a lovely way, ladies and gentleman. Some of us believe in reincarnation, and maybe it's time that you moved on. (Hoyle 2010)

The distinction, perhaps, is between an individuality born of a queer humanism that acknowledges and values difference, and one in which the claim on individuality betrays an indifference to suffering through 'childish self-interest, and a conscious reluctance to grow up and connect with other humanoids' (Hoyle in Johnson 2015: 243).

Figure 7 David Hoyle, *I, Victim* (Chelsea Theatre, London, 2014).

Conclusion

While Hoyle's affirmation of the human often resolves as a desire to recognise a common need for care and affection, his refusal of a readily
identifiable (and, perhaps, totalising) political position from which to act
may also prompt recollection of the terms of Esposito's conceptualisation of communitas, discussed in chapter 1: an understanding of community not as a corporation in which individuals are founded in a larger
individual or a state of mutual, intersubjective 'recognition', but as an
exposure of the subject to that which it is not: 'a dizziness, a syncope, a
spasm in the continuity of the subject' (Esposito 2010: 7). The kinds of
communality demanded – but found only in uncertain terms – in Hoyle's
work may be exactly those which resist exchange between autonomous
subjects, marking instead an obligation towards others which cannot
be completely fulfilled: an encounter that marks an ongoing exposure,

burden and debt. To return to Love, the impossible demands of Hoyle's performances may also elaborate how while historical losses may 'instil in us a desire for change, they also can unfit us for the activity of making change' (Love 2007: 149). That unfitting does not preclude the possibility of change, but demands recognition of how possibilities for political intervention may be occluded by an insistence on a subject position marked as already 'inside' the social or, at least, oriented on their return.

To return to the larger frame of this book: what may be at stake in the figure of the pariah is a refusal of the kinds of exceptional subjectivity entertained within neoliberalism precisely because they are essential to its continued project, describing agency within existing frameworks of power and social recognition that serve to reinvigorate and legitimate its selective recognitions. In this, we might begin to understand the queer pariah as one who makes abjection a duty in the sense that it is an obligation that arises from the conditions of one's subjectivity in protest of those conditions. The wilful figuring of the pariah enacts the realisation that 'the limits to liberation are to be understood not merely as self-imposed but, more fundamentally, as the precondition of the subject's very formation' (Butler 1997a: 33). The demand for emancipation articulated by the figure of the pariah, then, is not merely the call for a more expansive public sphere in which formerly excluded outcasts – in the past or present – might take part, but a concern for how the desire to recuperate 'lost' subjects might be all too readily co-opted. If the figure of the pariah reminds us that

> one may enter the mainstream on the condition that one breaks ties with all those who cannot make it – the nonwhite and the nonmonogamous, the poor and the genderdeviant, the fat, the disabled, the unemployed, the infected, and a host of unmentionable others, (Love 2007: 10)

it also describes how such subjects are not intended to be fully assimilated – and, indeed, are *required* to remain at the outer edge of sociability in defining the narrow terms of individual difference which are found to be acceptable even as difference is demanded as an expression of 'free' and autonomous individuality. This double-bind – and the ways in which threshold subjectivities called upon to participate in their own exclusion may yet provide a means of critical resistance – is explored in further detail in the following chapter's exploration of the killjoy.

4

The killjoy: public unhappiness and theatrical scapegoats

The feminist killjoy, writes Sara Ahmed, 'is a spoilsport because she refuses to convene, to assemble, or to meet up over happiness' (2010: 65). Though the killjoy is an anti-social figure she does not stand quite far enough apart from her social scene to go unnoticed. Like the pariah, the killjoy's anti-sociability has a recuperative quality that insists upon her relationship to the public sphere. In plainer language, we might understand that the killjoy is only a killjoy insofar as her unhappiness takes place in public where others can be touched by it. When the killjoy is accused of bringing 'everyone' down, it can only be because she is already present and because sociable happiness is assumed – in advance – to be something in which everyone can share. If the killjoy brings others down, she also holds others back: she is a hindrance on progress who insists upon her complaint and will not 'let it go' or 'get over it' in order to move 'forward', and in that refusal becomes a scapegoat who stands in for 'it', whatever the object of complaint might be. The killjoy does not have a problem: she *is* the problem, either by drawing attention to what someone else has said, or merely because she is less than enthusiastic about the forms of happiness she is expected to pursue (Ahmed 2010: 65–6). For Ahmed, then, happiness is a political condition rather than a merely personal state, evident in the ways that 'happiness is unequally distributed amongst social groups and individuals, disproportionately experienced by those subjects who occupy privileged cultural positions'

(Stephens 2015: 278). If 'getting along' requires one to 'go along' by participating in certain forms of solidarity – by learning to 'laugh at the right points' (Ahmed 2010: 65) – then the killjoy laughs in the wrong places or refuses the premise of the joke because she knows that she is part of a tradition that makes her the joke's object.

In response, this chapter animates the figure of the killjoy to explore through performance the terms on which dysphoria, recalcitrance and other refusals of public happiness become intelligible as forms of social critique. In doing so, I offer the killjoy as a way of thinking about the centrality of ideas of agency, choice and empowerment to both neoliberalism and postfeminism as discourses in which we are required to behave as though we are free to choose no matter what obstacles or personal disadvantages are placed in our way. Informed by Ahmed's understanding of the feminist killjoy as a figure who 'exposes the inequalities, unfairness, or happiness of others as a precondition for the happiness of the privileged' (Bissenbakker Frederiksen 2014: 109), I deploy the killjoy to examine a contemporary paradigm in which the demand for 'getting along' (and the rhetorical claim that we are 'all in it together') clashes with neoliberalism's preference for individuated subjects capable of seeking private, biographical solutions for social problems. Out in public, the killjoy's unhappiness (which, as Ahmed notes, may only take the form of the absence of signs of joy) threatens the stability of that compact by challenging the narrow terms on which such togetherness is construed: a neoliberal discourse in which 'being an individual … means having no-one to blame for one's own misery' (Bauman 2013: 38).

While the contested notion of postfeminism exhibits a number of relations to feminism 'ranging from complacency to hostility, admiration to repudiation' (Genz and Brabon 2009: 12), I am also interested in how the killjoy might elaborate how beliefs that feminism is no longer needed retain earlier forms of feminism as 'a source of prohibition against which to (gratifyingly) "transgress"' (Aston and Harris 2012: 143) in ways that are particularly compatible with neoliberal imperatives of individuation. Angela McRobbie suggests that 'for feminism to be "taken into account", it has to be understood as having already passed away' (2004: 255) while also being retained as a ghost against which the 'new' female subject is able to position herself as autonomous and unfettered by supposedly proscriptive demands for the critique of conventional femininities which characterised earlier generation feminisms. One of my intentions in naming this spectre as the killjoy is to acknowledge and examine how critical voices – and in particular women's voices – have been rendered historically as voices of mere complaint, often before they are even heard.

Doing so involves understanding how the anticipatory quality of the killjoy – figured by Ahmed as the eye-rolling response of others even as the feminist opens her mouth to speak (2010: 65) – is structured as a long-standing rhetorical device: 'a convention, a plot trick, a setup, a narrative structure, a character type' against which one cannot easily argue without reproducing the logic of the trope rather than challenging it (Tomlinson 2010: 1). If the feminist killjoy shares the same horizon as the female troublemaker for finding the promise of happiness not quite so promising (Ahmed 2010: 59–69), it may be because her disruption of happiness-as-sociability is part of a tradition in which women have been 'pathologised as unstable, deceitful, naturally inferior and irrational' (Bankey 2001: 38) and in which women's speech is always vulnerable to being named and transformed 'into a kind of nonsense, chatter, hysterical or seductive patter' (Berlant 1988: 244).

Beginning in readings of performances by Bridget Christie, Ursula Martinez and Adrienne Truscott, I explore the persistence of the trope of the humourless killjoy at a cultural moment in which even highly gendered identity practices are 'divested of singular oppressive meanings, and can be adopted ironically or reframed as actively chosen and enjoyed rather than imposed by the patriarchy' (Harris and Dobson 2015: 148). Across these artists' works – each punctuated by laughter as a space of counter-hegemonic sociability – I consider how identification and counter-identification with the figure of the humourless killjoy might draw attention to the bad feelings 'that get hidden, displaced or negated under public signs of joy' (Ahmed 2010: 65) and the logics of gratitude and responsible sociability on which they depend. Informed by feminist and postfeminist sensibilities, these works also indicate how the figure of the killjoy is retained – in common with the pariah – as a regressive figure against which claims on progress may be constructed. Turning to the multi-disciplinary work of dancer and live artist La Ribot, I consider how killjoy performatives may disrupt this logic by positioning the body against the conceit of an ordered, sovereign social subject. By reading works in her *Distinguished Pieces* series, I examine how La Ribot's practice offers commentary on the female body as a particular kind of cultural object while simultaneously questioning the public affects of togetherness which might be attributed to it.

This framing of the killjoy as a public figure who calls both sociability and subjectivity into question is further explored through Cristian Ceresoli's *La Merda / The Shit*, performed by Silvia Gallerano. Informed by the sexual politics of contemporary Italian media culture, *La Merda* shifts between the twin rhetorics of self-improvement and self-excoriation to elaborate contradictory demands to cultivate a work ethic and responsible constraint while simultaneously manifesting a voracious appetite for consumption. Through a reading of this double-bind as a form of 'bad faith' self-deception, I turn to Gary Owen's *Iphigenia in Splott* – set in austerity-hit Wales – to re-frame the killjoy as an unhappy scapegoat whose disorderly public affects advertise the personal sacrifices she is required to make on behalf of her community. Through these works I construct an account in which the killjoy's capacity to challenge gendered norms for speech and conduct might also address neoliberalism's sustained and contradictory demand for individuals to make 'free' decisions as socially responsible agents, even in acknowledgement of the lack of capacities or resources to fulfil that duty without damaging ourselves.

'Getting away' with feminism: Bridget Christie

Actor, comedian and stand-up Bridget Christie is best known for her solo shows at the Edinburgh Festival Fringe and broadcast comedies for BBC Radio 4. Her live shows include *The Court of King Charles II* (2007) and *The Court of King Charles II – The Second* (2008), both performed in the persona of the regency monarch, *My Daily Mail Hell* (2009), *A Ant* (2010), *Housewife Surrealist* (2011), and the Fosters Comedy Award-winning *A Bic for Her* (2013), named after the pen marketed by Bic as 'designed to fit comfortably in a woman's hand'.[1] Two series of *Bridget Christie Minds The Gap* for BBC Radio 4 – the first of which won Best Radio Comedy at the Rose d'Or International Broadcasting Awards – and the book *A Book For Her* (2015a) have incorporated or extended with various elements of this live work; a further live show – *Stand Up for Her* – was released by online streaming service Netflix in 2016. Though the politics of gender runs as a thread through much of her work, *A Bic for Her* was Christie's first expressly feminist hour of stand-up, inspired in part by an awareness that

---

1 The Fosters Comedy Awards (now the Edinburgh Comedy Awards) were the direct successor of the Perrier Comedy Awards (named for their original sponsor). Led by theatre producer Nica Burns since 1984, the awards' past winners include Eddie Izzard, Steve Coogan, Lee Evans, Jenny Eclair, Peter Kay and Rich Hall. Christie is only the second woman to win the main prize since Eclair's success in 1995.

her babysitter was earning more than Christie for an evening's work (see Moses 2013). While *A Bic for Her* narrates the development of Christie's consciousness as a feminist, it also describes a negotiation between a desire to practice feminism and a primary identification as a 'professional idiot' whose job is to 'stand in front of people and try to make them laugh. That's my main objective. It may not always look like it, but it is. Sometimes I try to raise awareness for things too, if I think I can get away with it' (Christie 2014). Nonetheless, Christie's practice of 'getting away' with feminism has regularly taken the form of an explicit, repeated identification as a feminist and, with greater consequence, as a *humourless* feminist. In this, Christie's interrogation of the relationship between feminism and humour serves as a structural device that allows her to explore the constraints on women's speech, and on feminist speech in particular.

If the figure of the humourless feminist serves as a trope designed 'to delegitimize feminist argument even before the argument begins' (Tomlinson 2010: 1), it does so in part through a punitive reading of affect which frames anger as irrational, excessive and illiberal, and – as in Helen Paris' biting comic solo *Family Hold Back* (2004) – presents the requirement to moderate one's anger as a simple matter of good table manners. In response, Christie's stand-up proceeds by asserting angry humourlessness in a manner that anticipates anti-feminist sentiment in order to appropriate and invert its force. The second radio series of *Bridget Christie Minds the Gap* (2015), for example, begins with the assertion that

> I'm a feminist. All that means is that I'm extremely hairy and hate all men. Collectively and without exception ... Us feminists hate being complimented, praised or having our lives improved in any way by a man. (Christie 2015b)

All men are rapists, including Christie's three-year-old son (and that, she confirms, is how she sees him). Christie's appropriation of the feminist killjoy does not involve irony in the sense of invoking cool, critical distance but instead manifests in overly enthusiastic commitment – what Slavoj Žižek theorises as a 'too-literal identification' (1999: 99) with the edifice of ideology that threatens its surety. This over-identification sees Christie embrace rather than directly contradict the absurdity of antifeminist rhetoric to scoff at the idea that feminists hate all men by asking 'How could I have possibly met all men?'[2]

By provoking laughter at the image of the humourless feminist while simultaneously acknowledging its cultural force, Christie's work serves

---

2 For a contrasting example of subversive identification with the stereotype of the man-hating feminist, see British stand-up Jo Brand, interviewed in Wagg (2011).

to re-politicise the terms on which we do or do not 'meet up' in communal laughter. In this, Christie's animation of negative tropes of feminism describes a history that continues in the present: a rhetoric of disdain that persists in 'ironic' form, allowing anti-feminist claims to be sustained through disclaimed responsibility for their utterance in what Judith Williamson (2003) has described as 'sexism with an alibi'.[3] Christie continues: feminists only listen to one song on a loop: k.d. lang's *Constant Craving* (1992). It is a small joke that does quite a lot of work at once; constantly craving, feminists are unsatisfied and can never be satisfied. Feminism is constituted as having a complaint that can never be resolved because feminism is itself complaint. In any case, Christie reminds us:

> In the entire history of feminism, no one has ever told a joke … If a feminist is made to pull a cracker at Christmas, she quickly eats the joke so that she doesn't have to tell it … Feminists don't laugh at jokes either. (Christie 2015b)

A game is played in which the audience is made complicit, and in which complicity comes to articulate a critique: Christie's persistent identification as an unfunny feminist makes us laugh, meaning that neither she nor we can be feminists, us for laughing or her for being the cause of laughter.

While feminists might laugh, Christie's performance of refusal directs us to consider the selectively enforced imperative of good humour in legitimating certain forms of political speech, and delegitimising others – where having a 'good sense of humour' is understood both as the mark of robust individuality and the capacity for fair-minded participation within a sociable public sphere. Like happiness, laughter may have a normative bent in performing a regulatory 'act of expulsion' akin to disgust which moves us 'literally and figuratively … away from the thing, the object or figure that we laugh at' which creates a distance between 'them' and 'us' (Tyler 2008: 23). Yet if laughter serves to verify and even impose normative cultural values, tastes and conventions, it may also allow for alternative communities of identification: forms of subaltern counterpublic in resistance of dominant cultural values permitting 'oppositional interpretations of … identities, interests, and needs' (Fraser 1990: 67). On those latter terms, Christie's performance of humourlessness may work to offer an alternative space for an audience to meet up in and over the laughter of frustration and complaint.[4] In this, we might begin to understand how

3 For further discussions of ironic sexism see Mills (2008).
4 For performances exploring counterpublics of individuating envy rather than complaint, see Rachel Mars' *Sing It! Spirit of Envy* (2014), the precursor to *Our Carnal Hearts* (2016) as noted in the Introduction.

spoiling one kind of fun – the joke at the expense of the feminist – may work to generate other orders of sociability without recourse to what Tomlinson describes as the imaginary ideal of an 'impartial' discursive arena (2010: 2).

As such, Christie's work suggests a wariness of any straightforward claim on laughter as a counter to the image of the feminist as a woman with 'the complete inability to smile—let alone laugh' (Douglas 1994: 165). Though a headline for an interview feature in the *Telegraph* timed for International Women's Day in 2013 persisted in the claim that 'Bridget Christie is trying her hardest to make feminism funny', Christie's act has repeatedly challenged the idea that feminism has an obligation to be entertaining in order to achieve its goals. An extended sequence in *A Bic for Her* sees Christie re-enact the beginning of Martin Luther King's 'I have a dream …' address and imagine her disappointment at the lack of jokes: 'Unfunny civil rights, it's not for me. I think I'll carry on being a racist.' When, asks Christie, did having a sense of humour and 'being up for sex all the time' become an integral part of the fight for equality? While a male comic's commitment to an issue might be understood as principled, sincere and passionate, a female comic's speech is more readily understood as 'whingeing' or 'moaning', or overly personal and trivial: either not political, not political enough, or enacting a commitment to the 'wrong' kinds of politics. As Christie riffs in the opening moments of *A Ant*'s thinly-veiled commentary on women in comedy while wearing a deliberately absurd home-made ant costume, 'even before an ant has reached the microphone, you've started to make assumptions. "Oh, no. Not another ant going on about jam and the division of labour"'.

Christie adopts and subverts the accusation of improper political speech in advance, segueing into discussion of the issues that are important to her by imagining a heckle from a male member of the audience which accuses her of triviality:

> What's that? Why are you talking about pens when you've got honour killings and sex trafficking and domestic violence and female genital mutilation?

One of the consequences of Christie's juxtapositions of the weighty and the absurd is to begin to place the banal qualities of everyday sexism in conversation with larger institutional and structural systems of gendered oppression. To address female genital mutilation alongside absurdly gendered marketing of pens, yoghurt and clothes is not to trivialise the former, but to begin to examine how agency and autonomy is selectively framed as 'freedom of choice' through consumer logics that mark certain issues as having individual rather than public significance, and wherein labioplasty is available as a self-affirming cosmetic procedure.[5] In this respect, Christie's performance may also foreground the particular, privileged speaking position of white Western feminist complaint, inflected by Christie's own consciousness of the predominantly white and middle-class composition of her audiences. In her 2016 show *Because You Demanded It* – written at speed following the narrow British referendum result in favour of leaving the European Union – Christie plays her own acute anger at the outcome and the upswell of racist incidents which followed against acknowledgement that a proportion of her audience may well have voted for it.

Performing (in)tolerance: Ursula Martinez

The question of happiness may contain less significance if we understand that underlying 'problem' with the killjoy is that she is too much of an individual – or, more accurately, too assertive in her individuality in ways which violate ordinarily unspoken rules of heterosexual sociability. Live artist, burlesque and queer performer Ursula Martinez's (re)staging of her choreographed strip-tease magic act *Hanky Panky* (2005) within her later work *My Stories, Your Emails* (2010) can help us understand this dynamic as one in which claims on personal agency are shaped by gendered standards for sociable conduct. In form, *Hanky Panky* is structured by the narrative of a magician's hanky which 'keeps disappearing and reappearing in various items of her clothing which are removed as part of the search' (Aston and Harris 2012: 148), concluding in the apparent production of the hanky from Martinez's vagina. The authorised documentation of *Hanky Panky* featured on Martinez's website emphasises her control over the display of her body, the skilful performance of the disappearing hanky magic trick and her active exchange of gaze with the crowd through winks, glances and expressions directed at individual audience members.[6] These gestures – and their foregrounding in the act's documentation – resonate with Claire Nally's account of neoburlesque's capacity to disrupt a linear audience-performer visual economy through

5 See Braun (2009).
6 See Ursula Martinez, 'Hanky Panky Magic Striptease' (2012), www.youtube.com/watch?v=RbVz5V6DCds, accessed 22 June 2016.

an assertion of the performer's agency (2009: 637–9).[7] The resulting effect/
affect is playful and humorous; as Martinez offered in a 2010 interview,
the act is 'funny and entertaining and cheeky, and yet provocative, but
primarily cheeky and funny and entertaining. I [have] never associated it
with eroticism and I don't feel erotic when I'm performing it, I feel funny'
(Martinez on RN Breakfast 2010).

When footage of the act originally broadcast during Montreal's Just
for Laughs comedy festival was published online without her notice in
2006, Martinez received a large number of unsolicited emails – primarily
from male fans 'making assumptions about who she is, what she [was]
looking for and why they [were] just the person to supply it' (Edwardes
2010). In My Stories, Your Emails (2010), Martinez revisits and reframes
Hanky Panky by re-staging both the act, the footage which appeared
online and her consternation at that decontextualised disclosure alongside personal, autobiographical anecdotes. In the first part of the show,
Martinez appears in the same smart suit and red lipstick worn for Hanky
Panky to tell stories about her life, career and family, leaving the stage
during a second sequence in which the uploaded footage is projected
before returning in more casual, loose-fitting clothes and without make-
up to read from a selection of sexually suggestive and sometimes unnerv-
ingly aggressive emails received after the footage of her act went 'viral'
online. Considering My Stories, Your Emails alongside theatre-maker
Nic Green's Trilogy (2009–10), Sarah Gorman examines Martinez's work
in terms of self-determination: 'an individualistic insistence upon self-
realisation and a developed sense of agency' which articulates the possibility of 'control' by insisting on the importance of both intention and
context (2013: 57). Reading against critiques of immanence or disavowal
of the human body and acknowledging Martinez's capacity to assert
the context for her own performance, Gorman theorises the work as 'a
celebration of individualism' which evades the pitfall of essentialising
women's bodies by offering individual experience as a complex and sometimes contradictory plurality (2013: 62–3). Echoing Debra Ferreday's
sense of burlesque's potential as a form of critical drag which might
destabilise 'the ways in which dominant feminine identities become
normalized' (Ferreday 2008: 49), Gorman suggests that 'the exaggerated
winks and quasi-macho pelvic thrusts' performed by Martinez in Hanky

---

7 For an alternative treatment of the male gaze and female agency, see Tania El Khoury's
   site-specific work Maybe If You Choreograph Me, You Will Feel Better? (2011), a one-to-
   one performed for exclusively male audience members who gave remote instructions to
   El Khoury, performing on a public street.

Panky 'work to consolidate the sense that the performer has elected to strip to undermine or ridicule the form, rather than to titillate' (Gorman 2013: 58). This sense of heightened citation informs Gorman's reading of the deliberately mundane removal of clothing which closes *My Stories, Your Emails*: Martinez undresses rather than strips to assert her occupation of an 'ordinary' human female body.

The moment is, as Martinez teased before the show's UK premiere, an 'anti-climax' (Szalwinska 2010) directed towards a live audience who have been cajoled from the outset to recognise that they have come to see 'a bit of minge'. Here, the work's final comic image in which Martinez turns to reveal a piece of toilet paper stuck to her naked bottom plays against the culturally designated unfunniness of a 'heteronormatively sexy' female comic body by exploiting 'the gap between being a body and having a gendered body' (Ballou 2013: 182). In this, we might understand Martinez in relation to the figure of the killjoy for the ways in which her performance disrupts the certainty of a heterosexist visual economy in which women's bodies exist as erotic objects for the male gaze. The form of sociability which Martinez 'spoils' is the presumptive, entitled space of heterosexual male fantasy or, more accurately, the naked female body as the meeting place for such fantasy.

I am particularly interested, though, in the ways in which broader, positive critical reception of *My Stories, Your Emails* still framed Martinez's performance of complaint in terms of its failure to abide by an implied social contract between the performer and her erstwhile contributors. Broadsheet and online reviews of the show in the UK often raised the question of consent in Martinez's use of the unsolicited emails that she had received within the show and suggested that her gentle mockery of male fantasy and machismo mirrored rather than challenged her own treatment. Jane Edwardes' largely positive review for *Time Out*, for example, expressed concern that there was gradually 'an uncomfortable feeling that she too is guilty of making assumptions about others' (Edwardes 2010) and Lyn Gardner's less enthusiastic coverage for the *Guardian* similarly cautioned that Martinez ran close to 'double-dealing dealing in its treatment of the deluded men who contacted her' (L. Gardner 2010). In turn, Ian Shuttleworth's review for the *Financial Times* protested that

> Martinez's programme note complains that these mails 'strip me of my ordinariness as a human being', but she either does not realise or does not care that she is doing precisely the same to them, and moreover doing so in public. Her own intimacies are hers to peddle; other people's, even if sent to her unsolicited, are not. (Shuttleworth 2010)

Common to these reviews is an assumption that Martinez owed a duty of care, respect or confidentiality to the men who sent her unrequested emails and images: that she might engage in good faith with expressions of male heterosexual interest, even though those expressions might be aggressively self-entitled, even though Martinez is a lesbian, and even though – as Gorman observes – 'for female audience members who have been intimidated and harassed by unwanted sexual attention, the ridicule provides a welcome opportunity to recognise a supposedly innocuous practice as a form of abuse' (2013: 59).

Martinez is a killjoy and a spoilsport, though, because she refuses to engage in practices of liberal tolerance by managing, enduring or 'putting up' with sexism, and for appearing to shame the men who wrote to her by refusing to empathise with their desires. If the subversive possibilities of the naked female body in performance may be haunted by the possibility of 'being (mis)read as a reproduction of normative heterosexuality' (Ferreday 2008: 53), it is because that body is assumed to be both available and responsive to such desire. Ahmed observes that compulsory heterosexuality 'shapes bodies by the assumption that a body "must" orient itself towards some objects and not others, objects that are secured as ideal through the fantasy of difference' (2004: 145). Here, that orientation is couched as an unspoken condition of 'getting along', and is one which the lesbian killjoy refuses as a premise of her participation in the public sphere.[8]

Re-appropriating rape humour: Adrienne Truscott

One of the possibilities presented by the killjoy is her capacity to force a reconsideration of liberalism's conceit of universal, egalitarian participation. Nancy Fraser observes that amongst the assumptions which ground a masculinist, bourgeois public sphere are the beliefs that 'it is possible for interlocutors in a public sphere to bracket status differentials and to deliberate "as if" they were social equals' (1990: 62). In this, the claim on

---

8 Martinez's more recent show *Wild Bore* (2017) – created and performed with Adrienne Truscott and comedian Zoe Coombs Marr – offers a direct commentary on theatre criticism through a re-performance of the artists' own unfavourable reviews.

participatory parity imagines subjects who are able to engage in public discourse without prior constraint, and without facing disproportionate consequences for their participation. Such an analysis pushes from view structural inequalities as well as how violence and the risk of violence accrues unevenly to non-male, non-white bodies, as well as those who depart from the appearance of normative gender. Viewed through that lens, Australian performer Adrienne Truscott's award-winning show *Asking for It: A One-Lady Rape About Comedy Starring Her Pussy and Little Else* (2013) describes a challenge to the framing of women's 'responsibility' for their bodies as a simple matter of common sense in which the ability to exercise such responsibility is always within reach, without constraint or consequence.

Better known as one half of New York act The Wau Wau Sisters whose work straddles burlesque and performance art, Truscott's debut hour of comedy interrogated the rise of rape jokes in mainstream UK and US comedy, appearing at the 2013 Edinburgh Festival Fringe as part of a broader wave of feminist comedy alongside shows by Mary Bourke, Nadia Kamil, Sarah Pascoe and Kate Smurthwaite.[9] In claiming the trope of the rape joke for her own ends, Truscott's act shifts emphasis from discussion of the victims of rape – 'the worst version of which is "you asked for it", and the best version, "that shouldn't have happened to her"' (quoted in Brockes 2014) – to address the assailant who, given the frequency of sexual assault, is likely already present in the room. In the show's opening moments, Truscott appears in blond wig, denim jacket and high heels but otherwise naked from the waist down to perform a redundant anti-striptease, lifting a wig from her head to reveal another underneath and unhooking her bra to reveal more clothes before asking 'Anyone here been raped? Or has anyone raped anyone?' In the awkward moment that follows, Truscott pushes the point: 'Statistics say there's at least one of you.'

Originally staged in the intimate space of Bob & Miss Behave's Bookshop – a 'pay what you want' venue programmed under Bob Slayer's Heroes of Fringe banner – Truscott's body was unavoidably present, with little distance between stage and front row where Truscott's groin appeared at eye level, and audience members unable to leave the room without crossing the performance space. Acknowledging the confrontational staging of her body and the challenging nature of her subject material, Truscott invites her audience to take responsibility for a rape

9 For further context, see Logan (2010).

whistle: 'if you don't like what I'm doing, you can blow this and hopefully I'll come to my senses and stop'. As the show progresses, Truscott projects footage of male comedians and rappers onto her naked body, juxtaposing date-rape lyrics and jokes on rape by male comedians with George Carlin's defence of rape as a topic for comedy: 'Don't seem right, but you can joke about it. I believe you can joke about anything. It all depends on how you construct the joke.' In recontextualising that material on her own body, Truscott addresses the laziness of the rape joke as the hallmark of 'edgy' material through a sight gag that renders her pubic hair as male facial hair whilst simultaneously prompting recognition that sexual assault happens to bodies (and most often female bodies at that).

If *Asking for It* re-appropriates the rape joke as 'a feminist tool [for] challenging entrenched cultural attitudes surrounding rape and parts of the stand-up scene that have failed to move beyond a misogynistic past' (Czajkowski 2015), Truscott's account of her practice suggests a more careful identification as a feminist performance artist in foreknowledge of how it might be perceived. Interviewed ahead of an appearance at the Brisbane Festival in 2015, for example, Truscott suggested that identifying as a feminist might inhibit her from playing to a 'mixed' audience in which difference would create productive, enjoyable tension: 'I don't think you'd find any performers who had a really great time performing to an audience that's really monolithic' (interviewed in Aly 2014). A tactical resistance of identification with feminism might be understood as a strategy intended to pre-empt the dismissal of Truscott's work as *merely* feminist, a measure running alongside the use of nudity as an 'inexpensive and effective costume' (Spring 2015) which, as one journalist speculated, ensured that 'a good part of her audience are men who've come to look at her bits, *rather than just earnestly nodding women*' (Merritt 2014, emphasis added).

Given this framing of feminism as socially and politically homogenous – where going along with feminism is perhaps imagined as not standing up for one's individual interests (Hill and Paris 2006: 57) – it is not incidental that praise for *Asking for It* invoked the trope of the killjoy as a condition of the show's success. Kate Copstick's review for *The Scotsman*, for example, congratulated Truscott for having broken free from 'all the humour-free, cliché-ridden, post-feminist carping and whinging' of stand-up by women who had 'the easy tourist path up the mountain of stand-up' (Copstick 2013). Reviewing the show in its post-Fringe appearance at London's Soho Theatre, the *Guardian*'s Brian Logan similarly reported that it was 'exhilarating to see the ugliness of rape discourse taken on, and bested, not with humourlessness or censoriousness, but with firecracker wit, sophistication and luminous humanity' (Logan

2014). Truscott's work, in other words, was viewed by some critics as successful because it evaded the anti-social errors of the killjoy: repetitive complaint ('carping and whinging') and a lack of sociable good humour (the ability to laugh, to cause laughter and be laughed at). Such a logic retains the killjoy as a predictable menace and a cautionary lesson, even when she is nowhere to be seen: a ghostly threat to sociable happiness summoned to demonstrate how we have 'moved on'.

Disorderly bodies: La Ribot

If liberalism and neoliberalism's 'excessive freighting' of the individual with powers of self-making, agency and personal responsibility works to 'eliminate from view various norms and social relations' (Brown 2006: 17) which constrain, position and subordinate subjectivity, killjoy performatives may serve to draw attention to such constraint by deploying the body against the conceit of an ordered subject whose affects – and their social intelligibility – are a matter of easily demarcated individual agency and responsibility. The possibilities of such perform- ance are apparent in the work of Spanish-born dancer, choreographer and transdisciplinary live artist La Ribot, whose performances are pre- occupied with the manipulation of objects and the body as an object. Since 1993, La Ribot has developed a sequence of solo works known collectively as the 'Distinguished Pieces' series. These are comprised of *13 Distinguished Pieces* (1993–94), *Más Distinguidas* (1997), *Still Distinguished* (2000) and the omnibus work *Panoramix* (2003), origin- ally developed for front-on theatre spaces but later designed for gallery spaces or as installations.

The premise of the original distinguished pieces series was that the contents and duration of each piece 'would be negotiated with its "distinguished proprietor" – individuals or businesses who would acquire each distinguished piece from La Ribot' (Lepecki 2006: 76). This sequence has since been continued through works which interrogate the place of La Ribot's persona in her own practice – notably *Anna y las Más distinguidas* (2003), a collaboration with dancer Anna Williams reinterpreting *Más Distinguidas*, and *PARAdistinguidas* (2011), an exten- sion of the distinguished pieces series performed by La Ribot with four dancers and a chorus of twenty extras. As such, 'distinguished' describes the conceptual logic of the performance works while offering playful acknowledgment of the aura of the soloist as singular auteur, the ephemerality of performance art within an institutional arts economy, and the status of the artist as creative entrepreneur. The term 'distinguished' also invokes a measure of reserve and, perhaps, dubious superiority: La Ribot cites the French idiom 'avoir l'air distinguee' to mean 'a sense of distance ... something like British' (Peter 2003).

As La Ribot suggests in Luc Peter's documentary *La Ribot Distinguida* (2003), this work frequently treats the (most often naked) body as 'but yet another thing' alongside shoes, suitcases, occasional items of clothing and folding chairs. Rebecca Schneider suggests that the 'habitual scene of the female body' is a locus of 'culturally inscribed misrecognition—an image of such a body, say, draped on a car, is agreed to be misrecognized as "woman"' (1997: 96). La Ribot's deployment of her body may pre-empt this discourse by purposefully invoking its visual logic in order to ascribe within it new and subversive possibilities, whether by refiguring a beauty queen as cargo, as in *Outsized Baggage* (2000), or in staging her body as mass-produced object with its own instructions for use, as in *Manual de uso* (1997). As Mark Harvey offers in his reading of La Ribot's prolonged slow fall in *Zurratada* (2000) – a work whose extended contortion may find a resemblance in Kira O'Reilly's *Stair Falling* (2010) – 'we are invited to reflect on our role as the audience viewing a naked female body and the complex politics associated with it' (Harvey 2013: 86). At the same time, humour – and a particular kind of dead-pan humour in the guise of the idiot who is 'the fool, the rebel, the buffoon, the clown ... who is marginal and an outsider' (La Ribot quoted in Weaver 2013: 259) – laces the possibility of knowingness with uncertainty: we do not know exactly where La Ribot stands.[10]

This sensibility is apparent in the *Distinguished Pieces* series' precursor work, *Socorro! Gloria!* (1991), a dance solo which sees La Ribot perform simultaneously as a flustered woman attempting to give a public speech and as a professional stripper who removes garments only to discover another (and another, and another) layer of clothing. Each persona affirms while simultaneously undercutting the other, with both playing against the erotic narrative of a striptease and the audience's expectation that the performer will eventually appear naked. In one of the earliest *Distinguished Pieces*, *Narcisa* (1996), La Ribot take three Polaroids of her naked body with the camera held at arm's-length when she then tapes to the corresponding parts of her body. As the Polaroids develop, there is a shifting and uncertain

---

10 For an alternative deadpan deployment of the female body as a performative object, see Grace Surman's *...White* (2003). See https://gracesurman.wordpress.com/white-2003/, accessed 7 July 2017.

sense of the relationship between the representational image and the body in the room. This transitory moment suggests something akin to Susan Sontag's observation that to possess the world in the form of images is to 'reexperience the unreality and remoteness of the real' (1977: 164). Though the work nods towards Rene Magritte's *The Treachery of Images* (1929) – in which 'Ceci n'est pas une pipe' ('This is not a pipe') prompts us to acknowledge the presence of a representation rather than the real thing – it also resonates with the visual humor of British visual artist Sarah Lucas' roughly contemporaneous *Self Portrait with Fried Eggs* (1996).

In *Another Bloody Mary* (2000), distinguished proprietors Franko B and Lois Keidan, La Ribot enters the gallery performance space naked and proceeds to carefully lay out pieces of red clothing, clothing and objects before lowering herself into the splits and arching herself backwards to rest on the floor. Wearing a wig that covers much of her face and another which covers her pubis, La Ribot's body figures the uncanny hypermobility of joints on a child's toy and, at the same time, the contortions common to fashion photography which must be adopted without any expression of exertion, only disinterested poise. La Ribot inhabits but unsettles this expectation of form: the female body is fragmented or compartmentalised but still living, and La Ribot seems to propose a version of her subjectivity which resists rather than reifies 'a logic of identity associated with the sovereign subject' (Gutiérrez-Albilla 2015: 372). For Adrian Heathfield, La Ribot's solo performances figure 'the wound at the centre of the experience of embodied subjectivity itself', continually tracing the inability of a body to constitute itself 'with solid boundaries and integrity' (2006: 195) that might distinguish it from other, non-human objects. Here, the figure of the killjoy becomes a source of social unease for the ways in which she is unable – or unwilling – to constitute herself as a coherent, self-ordered subject. If La Ribot's work presents a relation between 'the self and the social body that it meets in its performances' (Heathfield 2006: 195), that social body is refused the security of distance and instead brought uncomfortably close to that which threatens its integrity. It is a closeness which does not describe the fullness of a shared experience but threatens recognition of a shared lack: an exposure to a 'spasm in the continuity of the subject' (Esposito 2010: 7) which exists at the heart of the social.

The killjoy's disruption of communal sociability – or, at least, its assumed and normative terms – is further suggested by *Laughing Hole* (2006), a six-hour durational work performed by La Ribot with dancers Delphone Rosay and Marie Caroline Hominal. Dressed in identical housecoats characteristic of cleaners or domestic staff and wearing ungainly flip flops, the three women laugh continuously while attempting to take strips of corrugated card which carpet the floor, and affix them to the walls of the space. Each card carries a text of two or three words, 'like an image caption, or a speech bubble, or a piece of signage, the title of the event' (Kelleher 2008: 57), drawn from a lexicon that is political (Guantanamo, war, occupation), personal (over 40's, mum) or refers to *Laughing Hole*'s performance actions (laughing, falling). Each of the performers wears a microphone and a sound engineer – Clive Jenkins – mixes and remixes the sound of their voices in real time to broadcast laughter through speakers distributed around the walls. Though the performers are laughing at the same time – looped to create a chorus of thousands of voices laughing before dropping into nothing – they do not appear to be laughing together or 'with' the audience. In La Ribot's earlier work *40 Espontáneos* (2004) performed by forty non-professional dancers, continuous group laughter has the quality of co-operative, supportive play. Here, though, laughter cuts against the possibility of togetherness: not 'an open invitation to laugh with or a complicit avowal of another's slips and stumbles that incites laughter in the onlooker' but rather that which 'seems to work against laughter as cathartic release' (Joy 2014: 82).

While the signs that carpet the floor in *Laughing Hole* are held up and then carefully taped to the wall without overlapping, they are not directed *towards* anyone as to be read. For Joe Kelleher, the effect which emerges is such that written language is 'abandoned to mere visibility' (2008: 59) and emptied of its intentionality. The signs also mark a gap between the space of the studio and other disputed places – signalled in THIS IS GUANTANAMO and GAZA OCCUPATION (but also ILLEGAL BAY, SECRET BUILDING and DYING IN DETENTION) – to trace the 'gathering up of the lexical waste of our contemporary state of exception' (Kelleher 2008: 58). While Ramsay Burt suggests that both *40 Espontáneos* and *Laughing Hole* refer tangentially to 'outsiders forgotten or ignored within twenty-first century western society', he observes that the performers do not in any way 'become or represent these others' (Burt 2008: 15) and are, rather, engaged in an effacement of self.

Bad faith and self-harm: *La Merda / The Shit*

While I will return in the following chapter's discussion of the stranger to examine the persistence of subjects 'included in the political in the form of exclusion' (Ziarek 2008: 90) at the site of border regimes, my concern here is for how such exhausted labour – suspended between voluntary and involuntary action – might inform a bad faith critique of sociability. In the work of Jean-Paul Sartre, the notion of bad faith describes a pattern of self-deception: it is a lie one tells oneself in denial of one's ability to make free choices. The nature of that deception is paradoxical as the person who deceives and the person being deceived are one and the same; in fact, 'I must know the truth very exactly in order to conceal it more carefully' (Sartre 1956: 49). Sartre describes this as a 'metastable' situation wherein contradictions are held in unsettled relation that threaten to fly apart at any moment, but which might yet nonetheless constitute an 'autonomous and durable' form of life (1956: 50). Thinking about the killjoy as the figural embodiment of such contradiction allows an examination of its normative and punitive dimensions, wherein the apparent stability of a self turns on its willingness to do violence that same self. Moreover, while the conventional understanding of a scapegoat involves a sense of the victim's innocence, the killjoy-as-scapegoat invokes knowledge of complicity and culpability – that is, a guilt in one's own involvement which cannot be resolved by the defence of involuntariness.

That the killjoy might figure neoliberalism's predilection for self-harm is grimly apparent in Italian playwright Cristian Ceresoli's *La Merda / The Shit*, a monologue play first performed in Italian in Milan and Rome in Spring 2012 and premiering in English at the Edinburgh Festival Fringe later that year. Since 2013, the work has toured Italy, Europe and internationally, been translated into French, Danish, Czech and Brazilian Portuguese, and published as a bilingual English–Italian text. Since its inception the work has been performed by Silvia Gallerano, with whom Ceresoli developed the play through scratch and studio performances.[11] Structured by three movements – the Thighs, the Cock, the Fame – and a counter-movement, Italy, *La Merda* addresses the imbrication of gender, sexuality, power and the media in contemporary Italy while also articulating a broader dynamic of neoliberal subjection: that which Susan Bordo describes as a 'bulimic' economy in which the imperative to cultivate the work ethic and repress the desire for immediate gratification meets the demand to display 'a boundless capacity to capitulate to desire and indulge in impulse; we must hunger for constant and immediate satisfaction' (Bordo 1993: 199).

11 For an early scratch performance of *La Merda / The Shit* in Italian, see https://youtu.be/oVg6_rmiGOI, accessed 1 May 2017.

While *La Merda* plays out many aspects of this discourse – shifting from a starvation diet and electro-stimulant 'beauty' therapy in the Thighs to the pursuit of corpulence in the Fame – it also locates Bordo's 'work ethic' within a cultural economy of media celebrity that in Italy has been dominated by former Prime Minister Silvio Berlusconi's Fininvest media empire whose output was characterised from the late 1980s onwards by the practice for 'broadcasts of all types – sports, satires, comedies, quizzes, talk shows – to feature, alongside men in conventional clothes, girls of pleasing appearance in revealing bikini-style outfits who were called upon to dance or pose, but who often said little or nothing' (Gundle 2009: 69). If the promotion on Fininvest-owned channels of young women and girls as constantly sexually available was 'implicitly legitimated by virtue of Berlusconi's position of authority as Prime Minister' (Galetto *et al.* 2009: 194), that association was strengthened by Berlusconi's decision to field young women with a background in television – but no political experience – as candidates in national and European elections, and by the various widely reported sexual scandals concerning private parties held at Berlusconi's residencies.

In its staging, *La Merda* explicitly addresses the relationship between objectification, power and display to demand that its audience consider the terms of its own gaze. In its published form, Ceresoli's script establishes the space of the stage as that of heightened scrutiny:

> Five most powerful spotlights focused centre stage, stark, glacially cool, give back a desaturated vision of the woman, just as in a perfect commercial. The interpreter, nude, is already there under that stark and cold light, sitting on a pedestal, when the humanity (or audience) comes in. (Ceresoli 2012: 6)

In my experience of the work – staged during the Edinburgh Festival Fringe 2015 in the Summerhall venue's stark and stripped back Demonstration Room – the shallow, tiered rings of anatomy theatre seating framed Gallerano as both instructor and dissection study. While reviews of Gallerano's performance have often emphasised her mouth – a 'slick of blood red lipstick' (Love 2012) marking 'a gash like a wound' (Gardner 2014b) – in performance we see the texture and weight of an unsupported body, breasts hanging on her chest and thighs resting on the bare metal plinth with her feet dangling high above the ground.

The lighting is stark and – to use the euphemism which gestures towards a fear of actually seeing bodies as they are – 'unforgiving'. On Gallerano's form we see the birth marks and ordinary imperfections of human skin that fashion photography works so hard to conceal, and which Gallerano makes no attempt to hide. In this, theatrical mediation

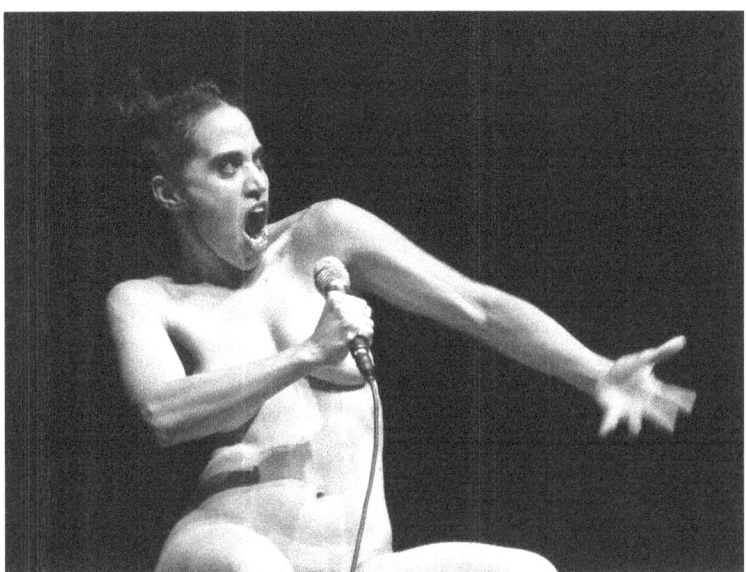

Figure 8 Silvia Gallerano, *La Merda* (2012).

Figure 9 Silvia Gallerano, *La Merda* (2012).

appropriates and inverts the frame of the camera's lens and we begin to see the ways in which such mediation invites us to *look*, searching for imperfection or imperfection's trace. Though Gallerano holds her arms against herself, the gesture does not register as self-consciousness in exposure; later in performance as the voices of her father, casting agents and her beautician possess her, Gallerano's arms and legs fly out at sharp, even cartoonish angles, face contorting and limbs splaying to show her groin, her fingertips, the soles of her feet and her gums. In contrast to the disembodied Voice of Samuel Beckett's *Not I* (1972), *La Merda*'s interpreter always knows where she is, even when she moves through memory: she is in her body. A similar register may be traced in Annie Ryan's monologue *A Girl Is A Half Formed Thing* (2015), adapted from the novel by Eimear McBride, and Tim Etchells' *Sight Is The Sense That Dying People Tend To Lose First* (2008) – albeit on contrastive terms – as works in which fragmentary but embodied delivery comes to exhaust language's claim to transparent communication.

In *La Merda*'s first movement, the interpreter hungers for fame and success, and models agency within the frame of a Situationist-like spectacle: it's 'not a becoming rich 'n famous kind of thing, but it's more about making your life happen yourself, instead of watching it from the sofa' (Ceresoli 2012: 7). The solution is not to resist or reject the spectacle but to enter more fully into the economy of images that might secure the full promise of bios as social life. Making 'life happen' is an act of self-fashioning – through torturous beauty treatments at the hands of a self-made business woman 'making *her* own decisions about *her* own career and *her* life and *her* future' – that pays tribute to her deceased father and the red-shirted volunteer soldiers who followed the Italian general Giuseppe Garibaldi to 'beat the shit out of the Austro-Hungarian empire and made our nation' (Ceresoli 2012: 9–10). Yet that happy agency is annihilatory: finding the 'courage' to act and make the necessary sacrifices in order to succeed takes the image of her father's apparent suicide under the wheels of a commuter train.

Returning home from his funeral, she starves herself through a one-week diet of only apples and when cramps of hunger threaten to wreck her chance to be a 'brand new woman', a body produced by the logic of self-governance rediscovers itself as an autophage drawn to cannibalise itself in the knowledge that 'the *solution*, the real *final solution* … will be *to eat* these thighs of mine, and it's only like this, by eating them and tearing them off by bites … taking them away from me forever and shitting them out of my ass once eaten, these thighs of mine, will let me be *free*, free to be the woman I am and to sign thousands of autographs and to be adored and to feel a thousand claps pinching my ass' (Ceresoli 2012: 11–12, original emphasis). In the final movement – the Fame – the interpreter prepares for an audition for which she must be 'fat, fleshy, opulent and large' by gorging herself on sweet and fatty foods. As she fills herself – 'sucking. Eating. Ingurgitating' – she holds her breath, puffing herself out and refusing to go the toilet. But her body resists and rebels, and she shits out everything she has swallowed but never digested: a personal history mixed with the detritus of her national culture, the red carpets, the autographs and 'the girls who want to make it' (Ceresoli 2012: 30).

In a sickly-triumphant gesture of control and bravery – she was almost fat, she had almost made it – she chokes it all back down in the same unprocessed state: 'Take back the shit, all the shit, into my mouth. Yes. Like this. Bit by bit, all the shit and my whole country into my mouth. Eat. Eat. Eat. Yes, I'll eat. Eat' (Ceresoli 2012: 30–1). In fulfilment, the image of the autophage – who must self-cannibalise in order to balance the demands of continuous self-scrutiny and relentless appetite – is transformed into a copraphage, the shit-eater who dines on waste. Here, the figure in performance enacts a kind of metonymic slip between taste as the 'acquired disposition' of class and culture (Bourdieu 1984: 466) and taste as that which we are not only willing to swallow but eager to consume; taste only marks the distinction between different kinds of consumption, not the rejection of consumption itself (in revulsion, in the gag reflex, in something one cannot 'stomach'). If discontented societies are simultaneously anthrophagic and anthropoemic, voraciously devouring and steadfastly ejecting people marked by difference (see Young 1999: 394), *La Merda*'s final movement spells out how the mechanism by which that process is sustained is the capacity of individuals to internalise it as a matter of personal responsibility.

The killjoy as scapegoat: *Iphigenia in Splott*

Though the relationship of the killjoy to the social may be one of suspended inclusion – recalling here the conceit of the exceptional subject as both inside and outside the frame of the social – it nonetheless marks the point at which a process intended to isolate a risk to the social serves to reintroduce a contaminating threat. Esposito suggests that the function of a sacrifice is to neutralise a violence which is already present within a community, and does so through a process of 'externalization' in which the sacrificial figure becomes a 'magnet' for that violence in such a way as to separate the situation of the victim from that of the aggressors (2011: 38). To fulfil this role, the sacrificial victim is made 'other' so that her death might decontaminate a community from its own violence, transforming 'the disastrous violence of all against all into the healing violence of all against one' (Girard 2004). Yet, Esposito observes, the capacity of an 'outsider' to stand in for the community is compromised by an act of recognition which marks her as already present within that same community.

Set in the austerity-hit south of Wales, Gary Owen's monologue play *Iphigenia in Splott* (2015) suggests how such logic may be occupied so that it might be identified for critique, and wherein the killjoy becomes intelligible as an unwilling scapegoat for wider forms of social injustice. Performed by Sophie Melville and first staged at Cardiff's Sherman Cymru (itself only a short distance from the working-class district of Splott) the monologue reworks the myth of Iphigenia, figured in Euripides' tragedy as Agamemnon's eldest daughter whose death is required to appease the gods and allow the Greek fleet to sail to Troy. Summoned to her father under the pretence of marriage to Achilles, Iphigenia petitions for her life but ultimately goes willingly to her death when her father pleads with her to sacrifice herself for family and nation. In this, Iphigenia's actions re-establish religious and cultural social order by turning 'the threatened lynching into an orderly and voluntary ritual … through her youthful love for her father and his ideals' (Foley 1985: 101). If classical and neo-classical renditions of the Iphigenia myth frame sacrifice as a duty owed to the greater good of one's community – with Friedrich Schiller's 1788 translation asking 'Can there be anything more significant or sublime than the – ultimately willing – sacrifice of a young blossoming princess for the happiness of so many nations assembled together?' (quoted in Linton 2008: 50) – Owen's Ephigenia, Effie, is profoundly and confrontationally ungracious. She has suffered harm and 'you lot, every single one / You're in my debt' (Owen 2016: 249).

Effie knows that how others see her means that they cannot meet her face to face: she knows that she resembles – or knows that she *is* – a 'chav', a member of the poor, white and working class animated through middle-class disgust as excessive, drunk, fat and vulgar (see Skeggs 2005; Tyler 2008). In any case, Effie is consciously and wilfully anti-social: unemployed with no interest in looking for work and aggressively confrontational. Out drinking, Effie catches sight of a man looking at her and takes him home where she discovers that he is a soldier and the victim of an IED: one leg stops at the knee. They spend the night together and by the morning Effie has found a sense of purpose: making her lover 'better' and in 'being his better half I'll be so much better than I've ever been' (Owen 2016: 271). But this 'perfect and certain thing' is a lie: she's been 'fucked and dumped' and left pregnant by a married man. Tracking him to his home and about to challenge him at his doorstep, Effie sees him drop his crutches – limping, staggering, half-falling – to pick up his young daughter, and in that instant chooses to walk away. Yet this sacrifice is not rewarded as Effie loses her baby to premature birth when the ambulance carrying her comes off the road in a storm, leaving her stranded with paramedics who are unable to help. Armed with a 'no win, no fee' lawyer, Effie pursues a settlement for the death of her child. But the cuts, the midwife explains, mean that there are fewer beds than ever before and a compensation payment will see even fewer. In the final moments of the play, Effie surrenders her claim on revenge: 'I took this pain / And saved every one of you, from suffering the same' (Owen 2016: 306).

Though the play has been broadly received as a protest against the conditions of contemporary austerity (see Gardner 2016 and Trueman 2016a), Effie's choices are not easily read as the expression of a resistant moral agency, and not least because the framing dramatic logic of tragedy may establish Effie-as-Iphigenia's sacrifice as an inevitability given in advance. While the close imbrications of marriage and sacrificial rites in Euripides' text might resolve the tension between private interests of the individual or family and the public interests of the community (see Foley 1985: 77–8), Effie's actions are uncomfortably suspended between a claim on self-determination (she chooses to 'take the cut' in self-willed defence of her community) and the narrow terms on which such individual agency is animated and made available (the logic of the injured party who sues the state for negligence). Effie's choice is circumscribed by a particular logic of individuality in which singular subjects are required to find singular solutions to systemic problems and, accordingly, can only be beneficiaries of personal reparation at the cost of their communities. It is precisely and perversely because Effie remains a member of her community that she cannot accept compensation, for the lack which constitutes community 'cannot be closed by any sort of compensation or reparation if it is to continue in fact to remain shared' (Esposito 2011: 139).

Such thinking troubles critical narratives in which Effie's anti-sociability is redeemed through the idea that it masks an underlying nobility: a belief that her actions ultimately honour a social contract in responding to the burden of *munus* as 'the gift that one gives, not the gift that one receives' (Esposito 2010: 5). In Ben Lawrence's (2016) review of the London transfer for the *Telegraph*, for example, Effie 'goes on a voyage of self discovery' before making a decision which seems 'little short of revolutionary' because it counters the narrative of social disempowerment for young women that makes 'life choices' seem unimaginable. Reaching similar conclusions, Tim Bano's review for *Exeunt Magazine* suggests that Effie is an emblem for the choice 'between taking the individual responsibility that every person can take to care for others, or to remain blind and to remain selfish and to live out the solipsism that's encouraged in us' (Bano 2015). In this narrative, the killjoy's antisocial conduct is absolved through her imagined social conscience, and her public unhappiness is redeemed as a social good because she wills that unhappiness as a moral agent. Moreover, it is Effie's willingness to surrender her happiness in the name of a common good which offers a 'glimmer of hope' (Lawrence 2016) and – paradoxically – marks the supposed return of powers of self-determination.

Aleks Sierz suggests that it is problematic that Effie's 'final gesture of political protest is an individual act, not a collective one. Instead of showing a community coming together to make a point, Owen focuses on one person's clenched fists' (Sierz 2016). This is, I think, the crux of the play's killjoy performativity: the framework in which Effie is required to make a sacrifice is one in which agency is only accessible, indeed only legible *as* agency, when it is enacted by individuated subjects capable of 'taking the cut'. It is the primacy of individualisation as a default political ontology – animated here through the logic of the singular scapegoat – which makes 'collective identity or action difficult to adopt, on either a theoretical or practical level' (Evans 2015: 46). Those who are called upon to 'take the cut' are those who are always those 'who have to take it / When the time for cutting comes' (Owen 2016: 306) and austerity comes to revive rather than immunise violence, ricocheting back upon itself to multiply its victims and 'threatening to unloose onto the community the same forces it was intended to save it from' (Esposito 2011: 42).

If nothing else, we might still take seriously Effie's insistence that her sacrifice comprises an unrepayable debt rather than a selfless gift, and one which threatens to overturn rather than confirm the social order which has made it necessary. In the closing lines of the play, Effie wonders

> just how long
> Are we gonna have to take it for?
> And I wonder –
> What is gonna happen
> When we can't take it any more? (Owen 2016: 306)

Though the scapegoat is conventionally characterised by their relative lack of power within a particular social scene – someone 'conspicuously marginal who cannot retaliate' (Culbertson 1993: 59) – the killjoy-as-scapegoat's agency derives from their refusal of the social contract of which they remain an unhappy part.

Conclusion

In performance, the killjoy animates how the conditions of neoliberalism require us to participate in our subordination as though it were the mechanism of self-realisation and happiness, and even when we suspect or know the opposite to be true. While going along with the duty of happiness might mean 'simply approximating the signs of being happy – passing as happy – in order to keep things in the right place' (Ahmed 2010: 59), the killjoy's recalcitrance suggests how refusing to 'go along' may expose the uneven distribution of social and political agency while also gesturing towards alternative configurations of the social – that is, of the possibility for 'things' to be in different places. More significant, though, is the killjoy's animation of what Linda Hutcheon has theorised as a complicitous critique – one which 'acknowledges that it cannot escape implication in that which it nevertheless still wants to analyze and maybe even undermine' (Hutcheon 1989: 4). Such a critique is valuable because it informs what Nikolas Rose describes as the necessary step of abandoning 'the political calculus of domination and liberation. This is not because we live in some consensual universe. It is because power also acts through practices that "make up subjects" as free persons' (1999: 95). Within the broader discourse of exceptionality, then, the killjoy may serve as an attempt to trace the fault-lines within processes of subjectification that are 'simultaneously individualizing and collectivizing' and in which 'identifying with one's proper name as a subject one is simultaneously identifying oneself with a collectivized identity, and differentiating oneself from the kind of being one is not' (Rose 1999: 46). It is this process – whereby the imperative to give an account of oneself is implicated in the disciplinary distinction between the individual and the collective, and between 'us' and 'them' – that I turn to examine in the following discussion of the stranger.

5

The stranger: performing 'out-of-placeness' in the UK and Europe

In a rapidly expanding field of scholarship concerning performance and migration, this chapter animates the figure of the stranger to consider the function of (mis)recognition and undecidability in a range of solo performances made in relation to contemporary border regimes. Recent works including Alison Jeffers' *Refugees, Theatre and Crisis* (2011), Yana Meerzon's *Performing Exile, Performing Self* (2012), Victoria Sam's *Immigration and Contemporary British Theatre* (2012) and Agnes Woolley's *Contemporary Asylum Narratives* (2014) all point towards the significance of theatre in tracing a contemporary European migration 'crisis' fostered by economic inequalities, political upheaval and climate change. Though Thomas Nail argues that 'the twenty-first century will be the century of the migrant' (2015: 1), this discussion takes the stranger rather than the migrant, the exile, the refugee or asylum-seeker as its starting point for a number of reasons, central to which is a concern for the exercise of power encoded in distinctions between these terms.[1] Human rights scholars Laurie Berg and Jenni Millbank note that the LGBT refugee is most likely to be seen 'when she or he looks like

1 The United Nations 1951 Refugee Convention defines a refugee as a person recognised as having a 'well-founded fear of being persecuted' forced to flee because they lack the protection of their own country. In contrast, an asylum-seeker is a person who has lodged an application for protection but has yet to receive formal recognition of refugee status. For discussion, see Zetter (2007).

"us" or, when that is not possible, looks like what is being looked for'
(2009: 197) – and as the performances discussed below will elaborate, the
capacity to look, see and determine the terms of 'us' are carefully reserved
rather than freely available to all. While the stranger has been claimed as
a universal subject who is the product of globalisation to the extent of the
claim that we are 'all strangers now', I am attentive to Sara Ahmed's observation that such rhetoric functions to 'elide the substantive differences
between ways of being displaced from "home"' and sustain the processes
by which the stranger becomes fetishised as a figure in itself – that is,
invested with life of its own to the extent that it is cut off from its constituting history (2000a: 5). As elsewhere in this study, the specificity of
performance provides a means to re-assert and examine that history and
its relationship to the disciplinary individuality demanded and sustained
by neoliberal logics.

Originally writing at the beginning of the twentieth century, sociologist Georg Simmel distinguished the stranger from both the outsider –
who has no connections to a group or community – and the wanderer
who 'comes today and goes tomorrow' (Simmel 1971: 143). Being a relative newcomer who does not belong to a group from its 'beginning' and
gifted with an enviable mobility in being able – at least in principle – to
return to their place of origin, the stranger's social status is characterised
by a synthesis of 'nearness and distance' which marks them as simultaneously foreign and familiar. Simmel writes:

> The stranger is close to us, insofar as we feel between him and ourselves
> common features of nationality or social position, of occupation or of gen-
> eral human nature. He is far from us insofar as these similarities extend
> beyond him and us, and connect us only because they connect a great many
> people. (Simmel 1971: 147)

Suspended between the particular and the universal, the proper and
the common, the stranger does not merely come from elsewhere but
occupies a particular place in the social structure that marks them as a
person who is '*in* the group but not *of* the group' (McLemore 1970: 86).
Accordingly, the stranger's membership within a given community
involves 'both being outside it and confronting it' (Simmel 1971: 144) – a
position which gives them a particular and even enviable critical distance.
Lacking the commitment to the 'unique ingredients and tendencies of
the group' that might characterise original membership, the stranger is
gifted with objectivity: the freedom to 'experience and treat even his close
relationships as though from a bird's-eye view' (Simmel 1971: 146). The
stranger, in short, is an outsider who is also an insider, and an insider who

is also an outsider – a figure of exception whose inclusion is characterised by their exclusion.

Drawing on Simmel's work some eighty years later, Zygmunt Bauman's rendition of the stranger describes an existential threat to the categorical certainties of modernity as a third term which challenges the integrity of oppositional logic. While friends and enemies are defined against each other as variations of the opposition between inside and outside, they function equally to sustain the domain of the social in that each term allows the other to be recognised as another subject, 'construed as a "subject like the self", admitted into the self's life-world, be counted, become and stay relevant' (1990: 144). For Bauman, the stranger threatens the stability of this opposition – and the principle of oppositionality itself – because as neither friend nor enemy, the stranger may be both. In this light, the stranger 'is one (perhaps the main one, the archetypal one) member of the family of undecidables' who, following Derrida, are 'all neither/nor, that is simultaneously either/other' (Bauman 1990: 145–6). Framed as invaders who threaten the distinction between here and elsewhere, strangers 'befog and eclipse the boundary lines which ought to be clearly seen' (Bauman 1995: 1) and in so doing challenge the bonds of individual and collective identity. In short, the stranger 'is a constant threat to world order' (Bauman 1990: 149) and represents all that has been – or must be – excluded from modernity to preserve its ordered reality.

Reading against both Simmel and Bauman, Sara Ahmed's *Strange Encounters* (2000a) elaborates the shifting status of 'stranger danger' within multicultural discourse wherein a perceived threat might instead be welcomed as a source of (desirable) difference. Disputing Bauman's more recent affirmation of a postmodern stranger whose difference must be protected and preserved, Ahmed questions whether the stranger's very 'figurability' might 'conceal the histories of determination which were already concealed in the discourses of stranger danger' (2000a: 4). Rather than taking the figure of the stranger for granted, Ahmed directs our attention towards the registers of knowledge which render the stranger 'familiar in its very strangeness' (2000b: 49), asking

> How do you recognize a stranger? To ask such a question, is to challenge the assumption that the stranger is the one we simply fail to recognize, that the stranger is simply *any-body* whom we do not know. It is to suggest that the stranger is *some-body* whom we have *already recognized* in the very moment in which they are 'seen' or 'faced' as a stranger. (2000a: 19, original emphasis)

In Ahmed's account, stranger recognition circulates as a performative that produces the subject to which it refers insofar as 'the act of welcoming "the stranger" as the origin of difference produces the very figure of "the stranger" as the one who can be welcomed in' (2000a: 97). Status as a stranger is not simply something that one 'is' or 'has' by dint of difference in origin, as Simmel's narration might suggest, but is instead the outcome of a particular kind of located encounter in which habits and knowledge of belonging in a given place produces certain subjects as *not* belonging. Understood on these terms, the figure of the stranger 'comes to be faced as a form of recognition: we recognise somebody *as a stranger*, rather than simply failing to recognize them' (Ahmed 2000a: 19, original emphasis). The stranger is not merely 'any-body' but a particular kind of marked, socially differentiated body, 'constructed through a process of incorporation and expulsion – a movement between inside and outside' (Ahmed 2000a: 54) that occupies a suspended relation to the social sphere.

In theorising the stranger as a site of conditional, politicised recognition wherein migrants are rendered vulnerable to exclusion while positioned unequally 'within the symbolic economy, the public sphere, and the labor market' (Luibhéid 2008: 174), I begin by examining the dynamics of testimony and (mis)recognition within Kay Adshead's drama *The Bogus Woman* (2001) alongside Zodwa Nyoni's play *Nine Lives* (2014). Noting the works' proximity to social and applied theatre projects intended to 'give voice' to refugee and asylum-seeker communities, I explore the plays' staging of how a system intended to confirm the identity of a prospective refugee comes to insist upon their strange(r) ness through forms of compulsory testimony that dispute the ability of applicants to give an account of themselves. In tracing potential resistance of this regime, I move to consider Oreet Ashery's *Staying: Dream, Bin, Soft Stud and Other Stories* (2010) – inspired by the lengthy administrative procedures by which non-heterosexual asylum-seekers are required to 'prove' their sexual identity – as a project which side-steps the demand for accuracy and singular accountability by elaborating autobiographical practices that allow for slippages, gaps in memory and intersubjective forms of self-identification. This practice, I suggest, can be read in the larger context of Ashery's use of alter-egos to explore forms of 'belonging through not-belonging' wherein a collaborative process of creating group-authored identities reflects experiences of uncertainty and deportability within the asylum process while also making possible heterotopic spaces of belonging and self-recognition.

If the stranger's undecidability describes a space of possibility for self-recognition beyond the forms demanded by border and migration regimes, it nonetheless remains a space of projection in which the relationship between inside and outside is structured by liberal fantasies of

European cosmopolitanism and mobility. Recalling Simmel's emphasis on the synthesis of proximity and distance within the figure of the stranger – and mindful of Ahmed's observation of the ways in which the stranger may become fetishised – I consider Nassim Soleimanpour's *White Rabbit, Red Rabbit* (2010), a work created when the playwright was unable to leave Iran and of which each performance requires a new, unrehearsed actor to act as Soleimanpour's surrogate. While critical reception of the work has emphasised its status as a creative response to Iranian censorship, I trace how such celebration also serves the narration of the West as a space of free expression, mobility and cultural exchange that elides the stringent controls placed at its outer borders. In further locating the 'problem' of the stranger within rather than beyond the literal and imaginary space of Western liberal states, I close by focusing on interdisciplinary performance artist Tanja Ostojić whose work concerning migrant women's experiences stems from her own origin as a citizen of the former Yugoslavia. Rather than acting as a tabula rasa or blank slate, the undecidability of the contemporary stranger is shown to be rooted in the specificity of her material and historical conditions – and not constrained to the border or frontier spaces of the nation state, but emerging as a structural feature of its internal logic.

Forced misrecognition in asylum narratives: *The Bogus Woman*

The contemporary refugee system across Europe and the West is centred on the obligation for applicants to tell their story in a manner which is intelligible to immigration authorities (Berg and Millbank 2009; Millbank 2002). In responding to the UK's treatment of asylum-seekers, Kay Adshead's *The Bogus Woman* describes how the possibility of giving an account of oneself becomes an imperative which paradoxically delimits the ability to be heard and recognised. Initially staged as a short during The Red Room's 1998 'Seeing Red' mini-festival of performances responding to the first year of Blair's New Labour government, the play underwent further development at the Watermans Arts Centre in West London before premiering as a full-length work directed by The Red Room's artistic director, Lisa Goldman, at the Traverse, Edinburgh during the Festival Fringe in 2000 starring Noma Dumezweni as the work's titular woman (and performing the fifty-something other roles within the piece). The play is structured by two parallel stories: the violent assault and rape of a young black woman following the murder of her family and one-day-old baby in retribution for human rights journalism in an unnamed African country, and that same woman's experiences within the UK's border and immigration system before she is deported to her country of origin where she is murdered alongside three friends who had sheltered her. Both narratives are composites drawn by Adshead from a range of documentary materials and refugee stories including evidence provided by The Medical Foundation for the Care of Victims of Torture and The Refugee Council and the transcript of the 1997 trial in which nine black West Africans were charged with 'riot and violent disorder' following disturbances at Campsfield House Immigration Detention Centre (the site of multiple hunger strikes in protest against conditions of indefinite detention).

This use of documentary evidence has formed a central element of the work's reputation as the creative synthesis of several different first-person accounts: a 'fictional account in as much as it is the story of no particular woman's life [and] a documentary account in that it draws on the facts of many lives' (Clapp 2000). Nonetheless, *The Bogus Woman*'s expressly theatrical device of multiple roles performed by a single actor distinguishes it from approaches adopted by groups such as ice&fire Theatre whose ongoing projects *Asylum Monologues* (2006), *Rendition Monologues* (2008) and *Afghan Monologues* (2011) emphasise the primacy of individual testimony and its documentary basis through stagings in which actors read first-person verbatim materials with script in hand. Such work, observes Derek Paget, is a 'very specialized, stripped-down performance-for-a-purpose' in which performers 'speak for' rather than 'stand for' absent others and act as authorising agents for the exhibition of evidence (2010: 180–1). A similar register of performance is also apparent in several recent verbatim and documentary works concerning LGBT asylum-seekers that include Clare Summerskill's *Rights of Passage* (2016) and Sam Rowe's *Hearts Unspoken* (2011). While the (re)performance of refugee testimony by professional actors may contribute to their silencing – perhaps most clearly when black or minority ethnic testimony is delivered by white Europeans – it may nonetheless provide a useful 'disarticulation of body and voice that throws into question the divisions that describe who can be seen and heard' (Farrier 2012: 434). Invoking but without laying claim to documentary truth, *The Bogus Woman*'s text and dramaturgy suggests how such disarticulation may also be produced by the compulsory testimony required of the asylum process – and to punitive effect

Told at different points of the UK's immigration process, *The Bogus Woman* describes how a system of detention – in which the asylum-seeker has no leave to remain and no leave to leave – coincides with the double-bind of a discursive field that demands testimony of a well-founded fear of persecution while simultaneously installing doubt and suspicion as a condition of such speech. Noting that testimonial speech acts are essential in establishing the credibility of the asylum-seeker, Sarah Gibson (2012) reads the work alongside Timberlake Wertenbaker's *Credible Witness* (2001) to identify a pervasive culture of disbelief in which applicants are tasked with proving that they are not lying. Perversely, it is the capacity of a subject to testify which disputes the veracity of their speech: the young woman's testimony is considered unreliable because she lives to deliver it when, as the interrogator asserts and Gibson observes, expert evidence from humanitarian organisations gathered over the years has established

> That a woman / in the situation / you describe / from the area / you claim / to come from / would more likely be raped / *then* killed. (Adshead 2001: 87)

Though the asylum process requires 'authentic' detail to confirm and corroborate testimony, it is that same detail which threatens an applicant's ability to self-authenticate. While the suffering of strangers en masse may be sacralised through a rhetoric of sublime, pure endurance (see McKinney 2007), 'the particularity of a single person's "stories" and "claims" is suspect' (Malkki 2007: 337); for trauma to convey veracity, it must be presented in experts' terms or within a general framework for 'as soon as one returns from the general to the particular ... the evidence weakens' (Fassin and d'Halluin 2007: 325).

In tracing the demands of the asylum process, Adshead's drama suggests how the process of producing an 'authentic' refugee claim requires the formulation of biographical experience in a manner that allows an individual claimant to become 'charismatic as universalized humanity' (Malkki 2007: 339). At the same time, *The Bogus Woman*'s scenes of interrogation point to how the intelligibility of such 'humanity' turns on its proximity to notions of Western, cosmopolitan citizenship characterised by mobility and consumption. In an early sequence, two interrogators feed the young woman the story which she is expected to confirm through confession in return: 'it says here you have a sister studying fashion drawing in London / Perhaps you came over to see her / have a holiday / do a bit of seasonal shopping / see the sights / and then stay on / just a few weeks' (Adshead 2001: 17–18). In this exchange, the figure of the tourist haunts the figure of the refugee, acting as a preferred point of reference for assessing legitimacy and movement across borders. While the refugee has no place to go to – or, rather, no place to return to – the cosmopolitan subject is gifted with 'world-making' potentiality whose mobility, curiosity and willingness to 'risk' encounters with difference (see Swain 2009) are an expression of agency and, moreover, grounded in an ability to enjoy such difference by paying for it. Ironically, we later learn that this is precisely the fiction that the young woman rehearsed and delivered at the passport control of her own country in order to be able to leave: the innocuous story of 'a holiday / two or three weeks' (Adshead 2001: 19–20). It is the highly desirable fantasy of tourist mobility which structures the stranger's supposed threat as one whose uncertain commitment to place and community cannot be regulated by market logics. It is this fantasy which rationalises the necessity of detention as a remedy of the 'fear of flight' imagined for all asylum-seekers, even though they may have nowhere else to go.

Echoing concerns explored above for the ways in which compulsory forms of testimony might foreclose or frustrate the ability of a person to speak for themselves, Elaine Aston offers that the play's presentational register allows the young woman to double as both centre and margin, speaking from the margins of racialised experience but doing so from the (presumptively white) centre in a manner which exposes 'the way in which the immigration system "authors" the young woman's representation as "bogus" and refutes the truth of her story' (2003: 12). Viewing the work in the intimate space of the Royal Exchange Theatre's studio space in 2001, Aston describes how Dumezweni sought out and maintained eye contact with individual audience members who – unable to look away – were 'made to feel the weight of a colonial past/present looking back at them not through the submissive gaze of the victim, but through the resistant gaze of the rebel' (Aston 2003: 12–13). This oppositional gaze – framed by Aston in terms of bell hooks' description of a look which might 'change reality' (hooks 1992: 116) – exposes how the black 'bogus woman' is a fictive construction of the white gaze. Aston's point, I think, is not that the gaze or the body simply speaks where the voice cannot, but rather that performance of/by a gendered, raced body might resist the erasure of the specificities of oppression in favour of a universal, humanist refugee subject – and, consequently, challenge an audience's investment in the stranger as a blank slate for liberal concern, and whose supposed 'blankness' turns on their readability through reference to white, Western European norms.

LGBT asylum and conditional hospitality

One of the broader perspectives that *A Bogus Woman* enables is how
the stranger's seeming familiarity turns on their resemblance to norms
of recognition which precede and constrain possible knowledge of specific experiences of displacement. This dynamic may be more sharply
articulated in the case of LGBT asylum-seekers who are called upon
to narrate their sexual identity in ways readily intelligible to immigration decision-makers 'even though there are no universal or trans-
historical sexualities and genders into which diverse migrants could
be expected to fit' (Luibhéid 2014: 1036). Berg and Millbank observe
that the perceived coherence of LGBT asylum-seekers' narratives is
dominated by a stable model of LGBT identity development prized by
Western gay communities that is characterised by a 'linear process of
self-knowledge moving from denial or confusion to "coming out" as
a self-actualized lesbian or gay man' (2009: 206) – an approach which
imagines coming out as a single event over which one has full control.
While recent UK Home Office policy guidance forbids decision-makers
from drawing conclusions of credibility by stereotyping the behaviour or characteristics of LGBT individuals or communities and are no
longer permitted to consider whether it is possible for an applicant to
live 'discreetly' in their country of origin (see Gray and McDowall 2013),
assessors are still directed to consider how a claimant would 'behave'
on return to their home country if refused asylum and assess whether
they would likely be perceived as gay or lesbian. Reflecting on the UK's
self-depiction as a space of hospitable shelter despite its continued willingness to deport claimants to countries where homosexuality is pun-
ishable by life imprisonment or even death, Thibaut Raboin observes
that perceptions of LGBT claimants' credibility involve homonationalist
discourses which make tolerance 'a product of "our" British culture (as
opposed to the barbaric others)' (Raboin 2016: 669) in which narratives
which do not link queerness with a life in the UK through a narrative of
liberation appear less compelling. Part of the process of LGBT asylum
therefore requires a 'performance of queer abject disclosure' (Johnson
2011: 62) in which the claimant renders themselves 'known' as an
oppressed other for whom the law must take responsibility.

In Zodwa Nyoni's *Nine Lives* (2014) the fraught relationship between
LGBT recognition and conditional hospitality is played out through
the character of Ishmael, a Zimbabwean asylum-seeker who has been

'dispersed' to Leeds while he waits to hear if he has been granted refugee status and whose temporary residence is signalled in the original production by the persistent presence of a suitcase. Notionally intended to distribute the social and economic impact of asylum-seekers across the country, the policy of dispersal takes away the freedom of applicants to choose where they might settle to live with the consequence of removing the kinship, community and other social support networks crucial to resettlement, and contributing to experiences of marginalisation and social exclusion (see Bloch and Schuster 2005). First staged at Glasgow's Òran Mór and revived by Leeds Studio as a co-production with the West Yorkshire Playhouse for a national tour, the original idea for the play came about when Nyoni encountered a friend she had known in Leeds on a trip home to Zimbabwe whom she then learnt had been deported. Informed by the work of UK charity City of Sanctuary and Meeting Point, a drop-in session for refugees and asylum-seekers in Armley, Leeds, Nyoni's text depicts the human consequences of a process in which you 'begin as guilty and work your way up to innocence' (Nyoni interviewed in BBC Arts 2015) while also suggesting how a British mythos of hospitality 'to those fleeing from political and religious persecution' (Cohen 1994: 72) may be constrained by Western European preconceptions of sexual identity. In common with *The Bogus Woman*, all the play's eponymous nine parts are performed by a single actor – in the original production, Lladel Bryant – whose cross-gender identifications provide the play's multiple perspectives while also suggesting the suspended relationship to self that is the result of the British asylum process.

Feeling 'strange and distant' from the place that might become familiar but granted only 'temporary accommodation, not home … not leave to remain' in slum-like housing, Ishmael is required to prove his identity as a gay man for the benefit of border services by answering the crudest questions: 'They ask me, what does a penis feel like? Why do I like it?' (Nyoni 2015). Charged with shame and isolated by his sexuality from the possible community of other refugees as 'a citizen of the unwanted being excluded by the excluded' for fear that 'even in our collective misfortune, my brothers and sisters could still shun me' (Nyoni 2015), Ishmael adopts the persona of 'Sam' to form a friendship with Bex, a young single mother. The deception is initially unthinking but quickly takes a life of its own: Sam is funny, studying business at college, likes Tinie Tempah and 'doesn't have a girlfriend, it's a bit complicated' (Nyoni 2015) and – more importantly – allows Ishmael to sit with another person and escape the conditions of suspended non-belonging which mark him as a stranger. Rather than locating (gay) identity in relation to self-affirming disclosure

Figure 10 Lladel Bryant, *Nine Lives* (2016).

and thereby the logic of the closet, Ishmael's orientation on British-born, second-generation Nigerian and multi-award winning-musician (and male model) Tempah invokes – without naming or fixing – a constellation of possible desires, aspirations and identifications.

Impoverished by a minimal allowance from the state, excluded from mainstream welfare benefits and forbidden from working, Ishmael gives up milk and bread until he has enough money to buy time in an Internet café to search for traces of his former lover, David, whose Facebook page has not been updated since an interview with a Zimbabwean radio station led to escalating threats of violence. David eventually replies to Ishmael's answerphone messages but only to refuse any future contact, pleading

> just let me go. Don't ruin this for me. I hope everything works out for you, but I don't want to deal with all that stuff again. I refuse to see another application form. I refuse to answer any more of those questions. I had to explain what I do with men and why I like it. Never again! I've been degraded enough. (Nyoni 2015)

Figure 11 Lladel Bryant, *Nine Lives* (2016).

As in *The Bogus Woman*, the process by which formal recognition has been achieved appears as a potential trauma of its own: an affirmation of identity which is at once injurious to the possibility of identity, and in which the discomforting familiarity of the stranger marks the laboured relationship of that subject to itself within liberalism's logic of formal (i.e. state) recognition. In this instance, recognition made conditional runs perilously close to effacement: shifting to a more poetic register, Ishmael tells the audience that 'Some of us broke our African names / Some of us erased our histories / Some us conjured up secret identities' (Nyoni 2015). Ishmael's speaking position floats between 'us' and his own story, with the authority with which he might speak collectively held in uncertain, suspended tension with the desirability of claiming such a voice.

Though the play's account of the asylum-seeker experience is characterised by forms of recognition which mark the would-be refugee as a stranger in our midst – not least through the socially stigmatising experience of being forced to use the unreliable, cashless 'Azure' card benefit system – there remains the possibility of affirmative self-fashioning. Emma Cox suggests Bryant's performance of Bex (or, rather, of Ishmael-recalling-Bex) involves a form of cross-gender identification in which campness registers as 'part of a performative competence conventionally associated with homosexual men' (Cox 2016). Though potentially stereotypical, the demand to produce 'recognisable versions of refugee-ness' (Luker 2015: 101) is countered by more speculative moments of self-revelation in which a testing out of 'what a British gay identity might look and feel like' brings about

> a theatricalized coding of homosexuality that involves further ghosting of cross-gender performance. Ishmael's experience at a Leeds gay club is recalled in fragments of emotional memory and embodied in terms of liberating personal transgression as he carefully swaps his Everlast trainers for tall, sparkling stilettos. (Cox 2016)

This moment, though, is short-lived as Ishmael returns to his temporary accommodation to find a letter from the Home Office rejecting his claim to remain. In the play's final scene, Sam comes out to Bex as Ishmael 'who can only dream of the life that Sam has' and having 'tasted choice' remains 'waiting to be allowed to live … flickering in and out of existence' (Nyoni 2015).

Alter-egos and queer testimony: *Staying: Dream, Bin, Soft Stud and Other Stories*

The precarious 'deportability' of the LGBT asylum-seeker (see Lewis 2013) also concerns interdisciplinary artist Oreet Ashery's *Staying: Dream, Bin, Soft Stud and Other Stories* (2009), a work created with a group of twelve lesbian refugees that challenges the compulsory forms of testimony detailed within *The Bogus Woman* and *Nine Lives*. Commissioned by the Artangel foundation in collaboration with the UK Lesbian and Gay Immigration Group, the project took the form of six workshops centred on the group development of performative alter-egos that would allow the participants to articulate diverse histories of lesbian migration, and explore and reflect upon the oftentimes traumatic experiences which the asylum process required them to narrate. Most widely known for her portraits and performative interventions in the guise of the orthodox Jew Marcus Fisher, Ashery's practice has repeatedly returned to the relationship between race, outsiderness and practices of self-fashioning – whether in collaboration with Shaheen Merali in *Colored Folks* (2001) to explore the experiences of 'becoming' a white woman and a black man, or in the *Welcome Home* (2004–5) series exploring different forms of contested belonging and (non)return to spaces and places marked as 'home'.

In Ashery's words, *Staying* sought to

> facilitate processes whereby the writing and performing of oneself and one's experiences are freed from the need to 'prove' anything, to be true or accurate, to remember dates and details, to account for over and over again for gaps that might appear in memory and recalling, in which you are interrogated like a suspected criminal. I wanted the participants to be able to tell their stories, something they all seemed very keen to want to share, and perform their identity in a way that allows for gaps, slippages, repetitions and new structures of embodying and imagining the self. (Ashery 2010a)

Oriented on the discovery of means to write the self beyond the closed terms demanded by the British asylum process, this process was facilitated by the involvement of a number of lesbian artists and activists including the film-maker Campbell X, the performance scholar and founder of Split Britches, Lois Weaver, and the poet Cherry Smyth. As a whole, the workshops were intended to allow shared but distinctive experiences of the asylum and deportation system to be shared and witnessed, creating a space for the production 'of alternative narratives of sexual identification in which the erotic autobiographies of lesbian refugees could be articulated as creative works in progress' (Lewis 2013: 187) rather than fixed and already concluded stories.

Though the workshops were not oriented on a public showing or intervention, the texts and images, which were the by-product of the workshops and later published online, can be understood as performance scores or scripts. Ashery has herself drawn conscious parallels between her extensive engagement with 'performances, scripts and constructs of identity, particularly in relation to markers of gender, race, religion, national status, ethnicity and economy' (2010b: 7) and the compulsory 'writing-of-the-self' required to prove one's identity within the asylum process. For Ashery, the opportunity presented by the workshops was not for the participants to create, perform or write fiction but rather 'to express themselves and their authentic experiences in new-to-them and performative ways' (Ashery 2010a). Offered as the manifestation of a process rather than a final product, *Staying*'s characters articulate a heterogeneous range of identities and identity practices, standing as figurative symbols for specific hopes and fears, and different archetypes of female/lesbian identity, while also serving to recount personal experiences of past and ongoing uncertainty within the UK's immigration and asylum system. If, as Rachel Lewis suggests, the group's articulation of queer-deportation stories describes 'how contemporary practices of state violence deprive lesbian refugees and asylum-seekers of crucial emotional resources' (2013: 186), the process of developing of alter-egos also sustained resilience, resistance and critique while equipping its participants with new and alternative means of sustenance.

Bin's text – which Ashery describes as one of the most 'theatrical' in the series – invokes the image of the waste bin as a metaphor to describe the status of a gay person in a homophobic culture: someone who wants to come out and to be recognised but is held down and dominated by a crowd bearing expressions of disgust and anger. The character of the Bin is not merely a representation of victimhood but a position from which an oppressive gaze is returned as a series of questions:

> I feel like trash because society does not recognise me. This is what the Bin says: 'I see you. I recognise you and I hate it. Do I need to say that? And if I do, what would the other bins around me say? How would they feel? I feel the hurt. I can hear her shouting. She told me that they don't want her to be around them. They tell her that she cannot stay. Will she fit in? Is she big enough? Can she face it? Can she cope?' (Ashery 2010b: 26–7)

Framed within but not limited by the UK asylum process, *Staying*'s personae collectively sustain a space for self-narration in which the imagining of a queer future becomes possible, even as past and present trauma are acknowledged: a further character named Farmer describes owning a farmhouse, growing Ugandan fruits and vegetables, keeping livestock and living with her partner. This image is a 'vision' of a life in her home country that might yet exist: a heterotopian – which is to say concrete and located – possibility that resists the narrative of the queer refugee whose happy liberation turns on never 'going back'. The representations which circulate within *Staying* are also not merely oriented on diversifying representations of asylum-seekers and refugees but serve to address the scenes in which refugee-ness and lesbian identity become intelligible. Within this frame, a claim on verifiable identity is displaced for exploratory encounters with multiple versions of a self in which a constellation of potentially contradictory possibilities co-exist. The character House, for example, invokes an image of a life as a building comprised of interlocking public and private spaces, each nested within the other: 'a house with many rooms. Many rooms under one roof. All of them are me' (Ashery 2010b: 36).

The intervention described by *Staying*, then, is one that marks an appropriation of the asylum process to allow for inconsistencies, pluralities and fictions in the production of a self: a continual production of Deleuzian lines of flight which free up 'the fixed relations which contain a body all the while exposing it to new organisations' (Parr 2010: 69). This approach may resonate with the logic of theatre-maker Rajni Shah's durational performance *Mr Quiver* (2005–8) – the first in a trilogy of works concerning empire and cultural identity encompassing *Dinner With America* (2008) and *Glorious* (2009) – in which Shah slowly inhabits and abandons two figures, a British queen and an Indian bride, to discover an in-between place in which she embodies neither. At the same time, a process of improvisation involving costume, sound and light with co-performing designers Cis O'Boyle and Lucille Acevedo-Jones frees up Shah's performing self to the possibility of new associations and resemblances. In *Dinner With America*, Shah similarly occupies a sequence of identifiable female icons – the bride, the starlet, the model – only to dissolve the illusions which sustain them by singing the chorus to *Amazing Grace* over and over until her voice is hoarse before pulling away a mask that has turned her brown skin pale and discarding a wig to reveal her own close-shaved head. In this process, Shah's adoption and estrangement of figurative persona elaborates her body as a space of cultural projection and fantasy while clearing a space for alternatives; in the final sequence of the work, Shah steps out of the performance as the audience is invited in to share a feast of food and conversation in the space left by her absence.

The nature of this dynamic may be clearer when *Staying* is located within the broader trajectory of Ashery's practice from its early emphasis on autobiography – when 'all I felt qualified to talk about was my own experience' (quoted in Kartsaki 2014: 230) – towards more recent performances in which Ashery 'vacates the role of performer' to facilitate open-ended alter-ego experiments within collective encounters (Austin 2010: 17). In her early work in the guise of Marcus Fisher – expressed variously in photographic portraiture, live art events and public interventions – the occupation of an alter-ego allowed Ashery to re-articulate elements of her experience as an outsider as a child in Israel and, later, as an immigrant to the UK to explore a sense of 'belonging through the experience of not belonging' (Mock 2009). In later work – and particularly in her exploration of the seventeenth-century messianic figure Shabbtai Zvi in the works *Here He Comes* (2008) and *The Saint/s of Whitstable* (2008) – Ashery's adoption of an alter-ego is less about an exploration of her personal identity than a tactic for interrogating strange(r)ness in contested circumstances. In *The Saint/s of Whitstable*, a two-week interactive performance/installation residency commissioned as part of the Whitstable Biennale, Ashery re-enacted or reworked a number of Zvi's 'Strange Acts' (actions and incidents which seemingly followed bouts of serious depression but which were claimed as proof of his messianic powers) alongside daily readings of a play,

Shabbtai, Sarah, Nathan – First Reading with a makeshift, changing cast of collaborators and visitors.[2] Framed as a play about a theatre group who are workshopping a performance about Shabbtai Zvi, the text tells stories concerning Zvi's marriage to his wife Sarah and seemingly queer relationship with a faithful follower, Nathan. While animating dense historical information drawn from writings on Zvi's life, repeated 'first' enactments of the play served as the means of a group encounter with outsiderness: a participant audience meeting each other and the historical narrative at the same time through the process of performance (see Kartsaki 2014: 237).

Returning to *Staying* through the logic of *Saint/s*, we might recognise a process in which the role-play of alter-egos does not resemble the performance of a character as by an actor in a play – even though, as in *Saint/s*, that process might engage with consciously performative or theatrical techniques. Instead, the occupation of alter-egos becomes a means of facilitating a kind of 'being in togetherness' in which the demand for singular, attributable and known identity is deferred for the possibility of open-ended discovery and exchange in a heterotopian space marked by the (temporary) suspension of hegemonic conditions. Reading in Ashery's practice a long-standing engagement with Nicolas Bourriaud's concept of relational aesthetics, Julia Austin (2010) proposes that the absence of a final performance as rationale for the project meant that the collaborative, co-operative process of developing alter-egos re-framed autobiographical writing as an intersubjective practice. Austin observes:

> Precariously balanced between personal performance and collective performance, the characters acquire a peculiar ontology: while CameraGunMan does not exist as a separate entity from Patricia, this same character is also not-not the progeny of the other women as they too played a central role in bringing CameraGunMan into being. In this kaleidoscope of refracted egos, the borders between self and other become hazy since the story of one woman's alter-ego or 'other self' is not-not cathected to the imaginaries of all the other women in the group. (2010: 20)

As a response to the asylum system's demand for certainty, *Staying* may even be conceived as a deterritorialistion of the self – not only challenging the Westernised gay subject anticipated by the asylum system, but performing a decolonial gesture that addresses the systems of authority, sexuality, knowledge and 'the general understanding of

---

2 For documentation of the 'Strange Acts', see *The Saint/s of Whitstable* (2008), http://oreetashery.net/work/the-saints-of-whitstable/, accessed 19 January 2018.

being' (Maldonado-Torres 2007: 242) which are the long-term result of European colonialism.[3]

The (un)familiar stranger: *White Rabbit, Red Rabbit*

The terms of investment in the figure of the stranger as a site of communal identification may become more pronounced when the stranger is rendered as an absence rather than merely 'not present' or threatened with removal. This perspective is enabled by both the dramaturgy and critical reception of Iranian playwright Nassim Soleimanpour's widely performed play, *White Rabbit, Red Rabbit* (2011). Written when Soleimanour's abstention from mandatory national service meant that he was refused a passport and therefore unable to leave Iran, the play offers a series of loosely biographical allegorical stories about power, complicity and scapegoating. The play is performed sight-unseen by an unrehearsed actor who is supplied with the script in a sealed envelope at the beginning of the performance. The script remains unpublished, in part so that the events of the play remain unknown to each new audience and performer, and the following section draws on my own experiences of viewing the play during the Edinburgh Festival Fringe in 2014 and 2015. At the heart of the work is an encounter with a stranger – Soleimanpour – whose absent-presence is conveyed through a series of exchanges in which the playwright prompts the audience to consider their collective willingness to comply with his instructions. Originally developed in 2011 by the Canadian companies Volcano and Necessary Angel for presentation at New York's SummerWorks festival, and with Berlin-based Aurora Nova for the Edinburgh Festival Fringe, *Rabbit* has now been translated into more than twenty different languages and staged over a thousand times across the world – most frequently in Europe, Canada and the United States. At time of writing, the show has appeared for six consecutive years at the Edinburgh Fringe, and has completed an extended season at the West Side Theatre, New York, where it featured high-profile stage and

3 For an ongoing series of interviews with queer migrant artists exploring related issues, see Xavier de Sousa's *queeringborders* project, https://performingborders.live/category/queeringborders/, accessed 16 January 2018.

screen actors including Nathan Lane, Whoopi Goldberg, Cynthia Nixon and Alan Cumming.

Though Soleimanpour was able to obtain a passport in 2013 when a medical examination ruled that a problem with his eyesight meant that he was ineligible for military service (see Youngs 2013), the play continues to be performed as originally written with the script referring to the moment of its creation in 2010 when Soleimanpour was unable to leave Iran. Absent from the scene of its enactment, Soleimanpour's role in the work – as playwright and as authorial voice – figures the politics of the stranger on several levels. First, Soleimanpour's absent-presence may figure the stranger's capacity to dispute the distinction between here and elsewhere, with the repeated and always changing acts of surrogacy through which Soleimanpour's voice is heard articulating the stranger's suspension between the familiar and the unfamiliar (an affect that may be heightened by the participation of celebrity performers who may feel well known to us even though we have never met them in person). Second, and though the script details Soleimanpour's physical appearance well enough that an audience might picture him, the possibility of recognition is undercut by uncertainty as the audience is repeatedly prompted to acknowledge a gap of time and space between the act of authorship and the instance of the text's performance. While appealing to the possibility of universal, humanist identification in the capacity of the playwright to know and imagine his audience and they to imagine him in return, *Rabbit* also draws attention to the precarity of that task by stressing the quality of potentially threatening 'not knowing' which permeates the work as a theatrical event.

While the cosmopolitan subject's encounter with difference is oftentimes characterised as 'autonomous, masterful and expansive' (Marotta 2016: 83), *Rabbit*'s dramaturgy turns on the apprehension of stranger danger – and where the boundary line made uncertain is the divide between real world and theatrical action. At the start of the performance, the stage is set with two identical glasses of water and the actor carries a vial of white powder which – as the audience and performer are told in the same moment – is deadly poison. Reading from the script, the actor recruits a volunteer from the audience to mix the powder into one of the glasses, before telling an absurdist, allegorical story about state repression: a rabbit who attends the circus to watch cheetahs performing as ostriches but is obliged to conceal her ears under a hat. Threatened with arrest by the bears in charge of security when her ears are revealed, the rabbit and her pursuers cross the stage and get caught up in the performance: 'Nobody is who they are supposed to be. Nobody really is an ostrich. Nobody really is anybody' (Soleimanpour 2011). Shifting register, the actor directly addresses the audience as the playwright and explains the circumstances of the work: for Soleimanpour, it is 25 April 2010 and he dreams of travel but is unable to leave Iran, so has written this text to travel on his behalf: 'You see, it tastes like freedom to know there are these other people in one's play and it tastes like freedom to be able to travel to other worlds through my words' (Soleimanpour 2011). Through the actor, Soleimanpour recruits an audience member to keep notes during the performance and email this record to him at the end of the show. The note-keeping is necessary, he explains, because 'the police might call you tomorrow and ask how well you know Nassim Soleimanpour, or whether in your opinion he is capable of being involved in a murder' (Soleimanpour 2011). Though the poison placed on stage is most likely a theatrical prop, there remains the chance that it is real poison placed there by accident or introduced by the audience volunteer. Whether the poison exists or not, 'what really matters is possibility. What matters is not knowing' (Soleimanpour 2011).

Trading on the particular liveness of an unrehearsed event and the participation of audience members, *Rabbit*'s dramaturgy can be understood in terms of what Claire Bishop has theorised as practices of 'delegated performance' characterised by 'the act of hiring non-professionals or specialists in other fields to undertake the job of being present and performing at a particular time and a particular place on behalf of the artist, and following his/ her instructions' (2012: 219). In Bishop's analysis, such practice involves forms of surrogacy in which non-professionals serve to signify particular kinds of politicised identity (by dint of their apparent class, race, age or gender), or who are recruited on the basis of their professional identity (e.g. as musicians or policeman) rather than for being representatives of a particular class or race, or who are called upon to 'perform themselves' in staged or scripted scenarios in which the artist assumes a strong editorial role (2012: 220–6). In Soilemanpour's dramaturgy of obligatory participation, both audience and actor are called upon to authenticate the event through a mutual staging of liveness by appearing as themselves (unrehearsed, unprepared and so unable to behave other than as they 'really are') and as representatives of given roles in the theatrical process (as surrogate/performer and audience/witness respectively). At the same time, the stranger encounter at the heart of the text attempts to call these distinctions and the boundaries which they describe into question: 'Who is this actor? Is this actor herself? Is she someone else? Is she acting a role? Is she now a young writer from Iran?' (Soleimanpour 2011).

Nonetheless, critical reception of *Rabbit* has frequently framed the work as an act of personal, authorial creativity that allows Soleimanpour 'to speak us in defiance of the political and geographic boundaries that restrict him physically' (Wicker 2012) in a gesture which illustrates the broader capacity of art to cross borders and challenge oppressive, censorious regimes around the world. That celebration of free expression has involved the imagining of Soleimanpour as a cosmopolitan stranger whose synthesis of nearness and remoteness allows him to relay the experiences of the margin to the centre, with critics across Europe and in North America celebrating *Rabbit* as a work that might give a 'voice to someone who might not otherwise be heard' (American Theatre Wing 2016) and counter prejudicial misconceptions by going 'behind the Persian veil' to articulate Iran's 'sophisticated millennium culture' (Rohter 2011). This affirmative construction of Iran, though, has more frequently been deferred in favour of the description of Soleimanpour's remote authorship in terms of his 'isolation', wherein his absence from the scene of the play's enactment illustrates his exclusion from the (global) public sphere. Echoing the production's promotional material, the *Guardian*'s Safraz Manzoor suggests that 'unable to travel, Soleimanpour has turned his isolation to his own advantage' (Manzoor 2012). In turn, the *Washington Post*'s Nelson Pressley offered that 'In a brilliant paradox, Soleimanpour exerts deliberate and near-total control over an actor and an audience from his own isolation in Tehran' (Pressley 2013), with Peter Crawley's review in the *Irish Times* similarly suggesting that 'Writing in isolation, Soleimanpour uses his imagination as a political tool' (Crawley 2012).

The difficulty with this narrative, though, is the way it invokes a broadly Manichean worldview of 'free' and 'oppressed' cultures that reserves the possibility of cultural expression to Western spaces: in this account, Soleimanpour is only able to 'tell his story' by leaving Iran, even though *Rabbit* has been performed in the country on a number of occasions in Shariz, Mahabad and Tabriz as well as the capital city of Tehran (see Christopherson 2011). While Iranian artists have faced high levels of scrutiny and suppression following the disputed 2009 Iranian presidential elections which returned conservative populist Mahmoud Ahmadinejad to power, this was preceded by a theatre 'boom' under the presidency of reformist Mohammad Khatami after the end of the Iran–Iraq war during which drama schools re-opened and theatre festivals re-appeared (see ARTICLE 19 2006: 28) – a period which was itself preceded by a time of heavy-handed control on arts and culture during Iran's Cultural Revolution (1980–87). An attentiveness to this complex history allows us to follow how the allegorical content of *Rabbit* is not merely a metaphor but an intervention within specific circumstances in which censorship is not only common but expected – 'in the theatre, in Parliament, and even in the Friday Prayer' (Karimi-Hakak 2003: 17) – and in which playwrights have learnt 'how to skirt Islamic law and present their topics symbolically and metaphorically in scripts and on the stage' (Mostafa, Robertson and Aghdami 2011: 53).

While the 'immobility of the detained visitor' (Tyler 2006: 186) may be exemplified in the figure of the asylum-seeker or refugee, Soleimanpour's *Rabbit* invites us to think more broadly about the cultural imaginaries of constraint which characterise the stranger's relation to the social, and to consider how fantasies of an art capable of 'crossing all borders' may reinforce 'the persistent trope of the artist's condition as one of self-exile or estrangement' (Cox 2014: 23) in a manner that retains the stranger as an instructive example of the difference between 'here' (civilised) and 'there' (not). At the least, we might recognise how critical responses to *Rabbit* which locate the problem of Soleimanpour's 'isolation' exclusively in the refusal of the Iranian government to issue him a passport serve to de-emphasise and elide discussion of the stringent border controls which govern the possibility of entry to North American, UK and EU territories. There is no automatic entitlement of an Iranian passport-holder to travel through or reside in those spaces, only limited and time-bound access through tightly regulated visa programmes.

As such, one of the key cultural narratives at stake in the staging and reception of *Rabbit* in Europe and beyond is the way Soleimanpour's absent-presence coheres to the vision of an individuated cosmopolitan subject whose open involvement with otherness is an expression of his own secure, autonomous agency. This subject is attractive because it serves a critique of cultures 'whose intellectual foundations are mono-dimensional, essentialist and binary' (Marotta 2008: 5): that critique, though, is self-congratulatory insofar as it reserves the capacity for pluralism to the mobile citizen subjects of the 'civilised' West. Against this dynamic we might read Soleimanpour's absence as marking a constitutive *lack* of autonomy, and the dramaturgies of uncertainty which structure *Rabbit* as a whole as advertising the constrained and precarious terms on which the apparent choice to 'enjoy' difference is made available. Ulrich Beck uses the phrase 'cosmopolitanization of reality' to signal 'that we are talking also, or even mainly, of a *compulsory* choice or a *side effect* of unconscious decisions. As a rule, the choice to become or remain a "foreigner" is not freely made but is the consequence of poverty and hardship, of flight from persecution or an attempted escape from starvation' (2004: 134). On these terms, Soleimanpour's emphasis on the significance of 'not knowing' whether the water is poisoned or not – and, consequently, whether the audience has a responsibility or not – comes to describe as a mode of becoming cosmopolitan in the sense of making 'one aware of *uncontrollable liabilities*, of something that merely happens to us' (Beck 2004: 135).

Border troubles / troubling borders: Tanja Ostojić

In this context, the work of Yugoslavian-born and Berlin-based artist Tanja Ostojić may provide further illustration of the stranger's potential in critiquing the uneven distribution of such liabilities and their relationship to established hierarchies of gender, class and ethnicity. Grounded in migrant women's experience, Ostojić's works across performance, visual arts and film have offered an extended critique of the EU's border regimes and their differential distribution of power and mobility across the Balkan states, and the EU's 'immediate outside' (that is, geographically contiguous countries perceived as future EU member states). This work engages reflexively with Ostojić's own status as a non-European Union citizen originating from an Eastern European country – Yugoslavia – which no longer exists, and the majority of whose successor states remain outside of the EU.[4] Though less immediately autobiographical than the work of Yugoslavian-born, UK-based artist Natasha Davis who has drawn on her own history as a person denied citizenship because of her mixed Croatian-Serbian heritage to explore how 'the first experience of exile often feels like existing in limbo' (Davis 2013: 30), Ostojić's practice draws on her status as a migrant, as a woman and as a performance artist whose professional status grants her unusual license to cross borders. Straddling artistic production and political activism, this body of work addresses the systems of inclusion and exclusion that split Europeans into first- and second-class citizens while drawing attention to the broader heteronormative and heterosexist conditions of EU citizenship, and the heightened controls on movement which have come to characterise 'Fortress Europe' as a whole.

---

4 Slovenia joined the EU in 2004, followed by Croatia in 2013. Serbia has been negotiating accession since 2014 but has yet to formally join; at the time of writing, Bosnia and Herzegovina, Kosovo, Macedonia and Montenegro remain outside of the EU.

Though Yugoslavian passports were valued as a source of highly desirable and privileged mobility between East and West during the Cold War, social anthropologist Stef Jansen suggests that their non-EU replacements have become a symbol of collective restriction which render their holders 'collectively guilty until proven innocent (their future "crime" being the "threat of mobility")' (2009: 817). In this context, Ostojić's practice has interrogated the status of marriage as a privileged means for women from Eastern European countries to acquire visas and gain (temporary) access to the EU. The primary terms of this critique are evident in Ostojić's *Border Crossings* series as performative interventions 'embodying, with a bit of irony and (black) humor, the situation of dealing with the World while being [a] Yugoslavian passport holder' (Ostojić 2002). In the first action, *Illegal Border Crossing* (2000), Ostojić passed between Slovenia and Austria (and thereby into the European Union) without papers but with the support of Austrian friends who drove her back across the mountains – a route taken by illegal migrants who, Ostojić suggests, are arrested at the rate of eight or nine a day. This action was also born of necessity: Ostojić had applied for the relevant visa but not received it owing to an administrative error, and was due to attend an informal international artists' workshop in Austria.

The second work *Waiting for a Visa* (2000) involved a more public intervention in its staging of a 'six hours queuing action with no result' at the Austrian consulate in Belgrade. Waiting in line between 6 a.m. and midday with hundreds of other people carrying the copious documents and identification papers required to obtain a visa, Ostojić's action anticipated its own futility: 'At noon the embassy closed, so I shared the destiny of failure with more than a hundred others who were "Too late"' (Mignolo and Ostojić 2013). In this scene, the queue is the border: a site of disciplinary interpellation in which the prospective migrant must wait their turn to participate in a privileged category of recognition that might individuate them from a 'mass' of immigrants imagined in tabloid narratives as 'so inhumanely numerous that it does not simply move but "swarms" – threatening not merely attack, but obliteration' (Steuter and Wills 2009: 115). Later that year Ostojić began the series' third work *Looking for a Husband with EU Passport* (2000–5) by creating an advert with the same title in which the artist appeared naked with a shaven head and groin, alongside instructions for prospective suitors to reach her at 'Hottanja@HottMail.com'. Through what Ostojić has herself described as a 'rather concentration camp aesthetic' (Goethe Institut 2012), this image sees the artist take on the appearance of Agamben's *homo sacer* – or, as Suzana Milevska suggests, *homo sacer*'s female version: 'femina sacra …

she who can be killed, she who can be impregnated, and yet who cannot be sacrificed due to her impurity', an emblem of woman as the 'gendered other of the modern state' (2009: 225).

Resembling what Rune Gade examines as 'an amateur snapshot taken with a flash that produces a harsh shadow and reflection on the white wall' (2009: 203), Ostojić's self-portrait confronts the ordinarily implicit narrative of 'dating services' images in which 'soft-erotic visuality [are] always hiding their real intention' (Mignolo and Ostojić 2013) – namely, the trade of sex for access to a particular citizenship status. Rather than presenting herself as a beautiful and sexually available object, smiling for the benefit of the prospective male gaze, Bonnie Zare and Lily Mendoza suggest that Ostojić stares back into the camera as a 'desire-less and undesirable wife-object, thus foiling common expectations of someone marketing herself as a potential wife' (2012: 373). Though initially sent to a circle of acquaintances – 'philosophers, artists, poets, people I expected to react on it as a statement and send their own statements' (Ostojić in Brooklyn Museum 2010) – the advertisement became more widely circulated after appearing in a number of magazines and being published online. Following more than 500 letters from correspondents from around the world – some of whom responded to the advert's image with their own, sometimes idealised, nude self-portraits (see Ostojić and Gržinić 2009: 46–50) – Ostojić received an offer of marriage from the German artist Klemens Golf, who responded to the artistic and political intent of the work and did not want to pursue a romantic or sexual relationship. Following six months of correspondence, Ostojić met Golf for the first time in a publicly staged performance outside of the Museum of Contemporary Art in Belgrade and, shortly after, married him in a registry office ceremony. Drawing on her international marriage certificate, Ostojić then successfully applied for a series of visas allowing her to live in Germany though was eventually refused permanent residency. At this point Ostojić and Golf separated, an event marked by the creation of *Integration Project Office* (2005) installation in Berlin which exhibited her original advert, a selection of emails and photographs sent by male applicants and her marriage certificate alongside footage of their first meeting and an invitation to Ostojić's 'divorce party'.

As a whole, *Looking for a Husband with EU Passport* (2000–5) may be read as a performative intervention which inverts the frame of 'dominant Western man versus helpless foreign woman' (Beck-Gernsheim 2011: 60) through a broadly emancipatory action in which, as Ostojić has emphasised, '*I* chose the husband, *I* chose the method, *I* chose the rules, and *I* financed the project' (quoted in McLaughlin 2016). It is also,

Figure 12 *Looking for Husband With EU Passport* (gallery installation, Berlin, 2005).

though, an artwork which articulates the limit conditions of marriage as a form of citizenship by staging 'a clinical, unsentimental exercise of choice by an otherwise objectified, choice-less subject' (Zare and Mendoza 2012: 374). Recalling the possibilities of complicit critique considered in chapter 4's discussion of the killjoy, we might recognise Ostojić's conscious framing of marriage as a method of 'tricking the law' (Mignolo and Ostojić 2013) as one which proceeds not through a claim on existing rights, available in advance to a full citizen, but works to advertise their absence. As Elisabeth Beck-Gernsheim observes, such a strategy might neatly fit

> the power dynamics between dominant and subordinate groups. It is a kind of action characteristic of minority groups, testing the limits, stretching the borders but also submitting to the rules of the majority while, at the same time, subtly challenging and eroding them. (2011: 63)

As a commentary on the normative '(hetero)sexualised dynamics of entry to the European Union' (Surkis 2009: 197), Ostojić's use of her own life to explore the conditions of depoliticised subjectivity – that is, her adoption/recognition of a migrant woman's identity – places her in proximity to and at distance from the structures that are the object of her critique: near because she is a woman and a migrant seeking to cross borders, and far because her status as an artist grants her a form of agency by which to invoke the law in order to 'trick' it.

These points of possible contact between Ostojić's identity as a migrant and as a performance artist are further suggested in her ongoing international *Misplaced Women? / Missplaced Women?* art project in which participants are invited to traverse spaces associated with transit carrying full suitcases, pausing to pack and re-pack their belongings in a gesture 'that signifies a displacement as common to transients, migrants, war and disaster refugees, as it is to the itinerant artists travelling the world to earn their living' (Ostojić 2009). Taking place in public space, the performative element of *Misplaced Women* enacts a gestus of strange(r) ness that is familiar and, at the same time, marks the performer as one in suspended relation to community and place. It is not a gesture which asserts that the experience of the artist is the same as that of the migrant or refugee, but rather one which opens a space of critical contiguity in which gender calls attention to a structure which allocates recognition differentially. Staged in train stations, shopping centres and on European high streets, the stranger is not somewhere else – confined to the border, or the outside – but made present throughout the EU's internal territories as a recurrent feature of nation states which rely upon migrants and migrant labour even as their governments seek stricter and more punitive controls on movement.

This critique is apparent in in Ostojić's most well-known (and perhaps infamous) work, *O.T. / After Courbet* (2006), a contribution to the *EuroPART* public art project displayed on billboards throughout the city of Vienna and intended to mark Austria's accession to the EU presidency. Ostojić's poster took the form of close-cropped photographic image of her crotch clothed in blue underwear decorated with golden EU stars, styled after Gustave Courbet's *L'origine du Monde* (1866). Appearing on a busy highway roadside amidst ordinary adverts for commercial products, Ostojić's work both blended in – mimicking the commonplace focus of advertising imagery on depersonalised women's bodies – and stood out, being a larger-than-life image of a woman's groin that condensed 'the flag/fetish of the EU, the commodity fetish, and the fetishization of women's bodies' (Fassin and Surkis 2010: 490) into a single image. Though Ostojić does not appear naked in the poster – and shows less of her body than the model in Courbet's original painting – the work was denounced as pornographic in the Austrian tabloid newspaper *Die Krone*, criticised by politicians on the left and right and removed from public display after only two days. Art historian Bojana Videkanić suggests that responses to the poster lay in the poster's implied commentary on the conditionality of access to European citizenship rights, with its larger-than-life presentation of the female body standing as a reminder of women

> who are abducted or tricked into illegally crossing the border between Eastern Europe and Austria to either work in Western European brothels or as servants, earning minimal pay in slave-like conditions. (Videkanić 2009: 103–4)

The problem with Ostojić's depiction, perhaps, was that it was familiar: it offered a rendition of the stranger that was all too readily identifiable in its 'out-of-placeness' as an embarrassing exception to the European ideal of egalitarian citizenship.

Conclusion

In his assessment of 'hierarchies of passage' in post-Yugoslav states, Jansen draws attention to how 'the creation of a borderless Europe was always a doubly constitutive process: removing fences within it, it built higher

fences around' (2009: 819). Ostojić's practice, located in suspended relation to the promise of European citizenship, suggests how that regime
is not constrained to the outer geographical limits of the European project, but is a structural feature of its internal operation. While the phrase
'Fortress Europe' might accurately capture the defensive measures taken
by European states to protect against 'external' threats, it may also serve
to elide how exception's blurring of inside/outside, foreigner/citizen is
endemic to that cultural space. This is not to argue – counter to the works
explored in the first part of this chapter – that such a regime does not
value some lives more than others, but to propose that the regulatory
practices of borders may represent an amplification and intensification
of logics for identity and individuation which more widely characterise
the conditions of neoliberalism. As Ahmed argues, the unassimilable
body of the stranger is not merely rejected or exiled, but retained as a
means of demarcating a 'national body', a way 'of defining borders within
it, rather than just between it and an imagined exterior other' (Ahmed
2000a: 100). If borders operate 'as a confessionary machine for producing
the categories of insider/outsider, citizen/foreigner' (Salter 2008: 373),
they do so in a context wherein recognition preserves misrecognition
and 'unrecognizability' as useful technologies of power. In this manner,
the stranger's purported undecidability – its clouding of 'boundary lines
which ought to be clearly seen' (Bauman 1995: 1) – rationalises regula-
tive scrutiny while also providing a 'blank' space onto which fantasies
of cosmopolitan autonomy might be projected. It is the question of the
marked body – and the demands that it might make on a regime of normative propriety – that I turn to explore next.

6

The misfit: illness, disability and 'improper' subjects

Drawing on the work of disability, queer and performance scholars who have shown how mainstream representations or practices may be spun to 'reveal able-bodied assumptions and exclusionary effects' (Sandahl 2003: 37), this chapter explores how the figure of the misfit – whose name is drawn from the work of disability scholar Rosemarie Garland-Thomson, discussed below – might serve a critique of the neoliberalism's imagining of the subject as 'an "absolute" or "indivisible" self' (Hardes 2014: 16). Returning to Esposito's diagnosis of an 'immunitary crisis' in Western culture in which there is 'nothing that can be effectively isolated, instituted, even immunized, as something apart, something that might be considered proper only to itself' (Bird and Short 2013: 1), I examine how a range of recent works concerning illness, impairment and disability might expose and challenge the constellation of norms and cultural narratives that characterise neoliberalism's preferred singular, detached and self-complete subject. If the relationships between illness, impairment and disability are highly contentious and mark a shifting field of power, knowledge and responsibility – with the definition of all three terms repeatedly deployed to resolve questions of distributive justice (see Stone 1984) – it is because they are integral to a wider political imaginary of 'responsible' citizenship in which individuals are tasked with liberating themselves from whatever circumstances might constrain their participation in the public sphere. It is also the imbrication of illness, impairment and disability – such as that 'illness may cause disability, and disability may cause illness' (Couser 2015: 106) and that disability and illnesses *may or may not* share similar forms of impairment (Wendell 2001: 24) – that characterises and qualifies their availability to neoliberal forms of biopower.

In drawing works from across the field of disability arts to explore these ideas, I do not suggest that the ontology of mental or physical disability, illness and impairment is defined by an intrinsic lack of sovereignty that might be reliably assumed for all other subjects. As Margrit Shildrick argues, 'the implication is not that the corporeality of disabled people is uniquely unstable, vulnerable or interdependent, but rather that the nexus [of disability] signals overtly what is more easily repressed in those whose embodiment satisfies the normative standards of western modernity' (2009: 129). Beyond the truism that we will all experience impairment during our life-course, such thinking involves an attentiveness to the particularity of bodies and minds found exceptional by dint of what Petra Kuppers describes as a 'position of difference from a center' (2013: 5). While conscious of the exercise in power marked by conflating or distinguishing between definitions of illness and disability, or between disability which is the result of illness and that which is not, I chose to explore these terms together precisely because they are already mutually implicated in the production of normative renditions of able-bodied and neurotypical wellness. In this respect, the term misfit – the most immediately prejudicial, pejorative naming in this book – denotes a subject who is materialised by the intersection of such judgements, and whose impropriety might yet challenge their supposed authority.

To theorise the misfit – and experiences of illness, impairment and disability – in terms of propriety is to invoke a dense field of ordered, hierarchical meaning. In the work of Hélène Cixous, the domain of the proper describes

> a political and moral empire that at once includes and excludes, an empire that is semantic, ontological, and sexual: the *proper* is property (*propriéte*), possession, the self (*mon proper*, my own), the generally accepted meaning of a word (*le sens proper*), that which defines or identifies something (the *propre* of a novel e.g. its narration, plot, characterization, etc.) the clean and the orderly … the ethical *propre* and *improper*, and finally … masculine and feminine. (Duren 1981: 39)

In this account, the proper and propriety are both qualities of an object or person, and the characteristics of how objects and persons might relate to each other, describing fixed states and, at once, that which must be maintained through action or adherence to a given code. Though to be proper is to be complete in oneself without external reference, that propriety is negatively defined by what it is not; though propriety may have the appearance of an inherent quality, it is always, already the projection of a claim to an ordering of the sensible that is generative rather than merely descriptive.

Aspects of this epistemology can be traced within Garland-Thomson's development of the critical concept 'misfit' to describe the shifting relationships that work to confer agency and value to the identity and experience of disability. Playing on the ambiguity of fit as in 'proper' or 'conforming to space' and fit as in 'seizure', the term serves to theorise disability as a material arrangement between a body and a space which unfolds temporally and spatially; it is a form of performativity which focuses on the 'disjunctures that occur in the interactive dynamism of becoming' (Garland-Thomson 2011: 594) with the consequence of shaping and delimiting the possibilities for social participation. The conceptual advantage of misfitting, then, is that it describes an 'incongruent relationship' that does not inhere to the qualities of either of the parties in a relationship (say, a body and its environment) but is found 'in their juxtaposition, the awkward attempt to fit them together' (Garland-Thomson 2011: 593). If an effect of the social model of disability's claim that impaired people are disabled by society rather than their bodies may be to 'bracket' bodily difference as a primary grounds of analysis (Shakespeare and Watson 2002: 15–16) and thereby lose the 'real world, real life experiences of disabled people as they go about their everyday lives' (Dewsbury et al. 2004: 152–3), misfitting serves to re-direct our attention to particularity of varying embodiment and experience while avoiding 'a theoretical generic disabled body that can dematerialize if social and architectural barriers no longer disable it' (Garland-Thomson 2011: 592).

As suggested in the previous chapter, the specificity of performance – and of performer's bodies and biographies – may provide the means to extend and elaborate this form of materialist analysis by bringing concrete instances of meaning-making into conversation with the cultural narratives which contour and constrain the kinds of stories that can be told about the individual experience. Perhaps more significantly, and as the work of activists and scholars at the intersection of queer and crip theory have demonstrated, performance signals how knowledge of illness, disability and impairment might be undone through a disruption of propriety's representational and narrative norms. In suggesting how illness and disability might be 'done' differently, such work also brings to light the ways in which normative regimes of embodiment rely upon the orderly distribution of affect – such as that bodily propriety is rendered as taste, courtesy and good manners. If the killjoy illuminates the normative function of happiness as a social imperative, then the misfit might elaborate how care-giving, compassion and charity may similarly serve to maintain unequal distributions of power and agency. This is not to suggest that the misfit is a wholly paranoid figure but rather that it might offer a powerful heuristic for understanding the relationship of liberalism's joint claims to egalitarian, inclusivity and individual agency to what Robert McRuer has theorised as 'compulsory able-bodiedness': a regime which does not merely prize normalcy but functions 'by covering over, with the appearance of choice, a system in which there actually is no choice' (2006: 7–8).

I begin my study of these issues by tracing the development of artist and academic Brian Lobel's trilogy of works concerning his experience of cancer: *BALL* (2003), *Other Funny Stories About Cancer* (2006) and *An Appreciation* (2009). Though these works challenge conventional tropes of heroic, hyper-masculine survivorship surrounding serious illness, they also describe how the articulation of experiences of disabling illness and impairment may be constrained by a sense of proper form. In this respect, Lobel's handling of the 'inappropriate' aspects of his personal cancer narrative – the parts initially judged too queer, too political – and shift from first-person monologue to live art forms suggests how solo performance might navigate the imperatives which surround autobiographical performance. Following that latter thread of argument, I consider Robert Softley's *If These Spasms Could Speak* (2012) to explore how the conventions of verbatim and autobiographical performance may be deployed to pluralise knowledge of disability, and the relationship of disability to sexuality and gender. Reading against verbatim performance's often unmarked conventions of authenticity, I suggest how Softley's staging of his own body may subvert what Petra Kuppers has theorised as the 'hypervisibility' of people with physical impairments, and how performances of bodily impropriety may draw attention to the presumptively able-bodied terms on which agency (and consequently access and social participation) are still commonly conceived.

I then extend this critique of agency and relationality by reading selected performances by Bobby Baker, Katherine Araniello and James Leadbitter (better known as the vacuum cleaner) whose work outside of conventional theatre spaces suggest new ways of thinking about the politics of agency and self-care in their relation to the propriety of the public sphere. In different ways, each artists' work suggests how the demand to comport illness or disability is produced by the intersection of social, medical and administrative logics that might be challenged and made to serve alternative ends. In the third and final section, I turn to the more specific terms of Esposito's biopolitical metaphor of immunity to explore how Martin O'Brien's live art practice – derived from his experience of the chronic and life-limiting illness cystic fibrosis – invokes anxieties about the permeability and contagiousness of unwell bodies to challenge common conceptions of illness. Though centred on O'Brien's body, this work does not invoke 'the autonomy of the singular, detached and self-complete subject' (Shildrick 2009: 35) but serves to elaborate an ethics grounded in the belief that 'we are always already exposed, already immersed in one another, and that in acknowledging our instrinsic openness to the other – all others – lies the best hope of overcoming the insistent hierarchies that strip some bodies of meaning and value' (Shildrick 2009: 35–6).

Performing responsibly

The broader context for the performances discussed in this chapter is one in which the greater recognition of the individual and non-identical qualities of illness, disability and impairment (derived from the spirit of the social model of disability and informed by advances in biomedicine) have become yoked to neoliberalism's preference for self-authoring subjects charged with the management of their health and bodies in a life-long project of 'improvement'. As Brian Brown and Sally Baker argue in *Responsible Citizens* (2012), successive governments in the UK and across Europe have framed 'good citizenship' in terms of agency, autonomy and self-management to produce a discourse of 'responsibilization' in matters of health and social policy heavily characterised by Foucaultian practices of governmentality. Breaking from what Brown and Baker characterise as the policies of collective responsibility which defined the period following the Second World War, a contemporary politics of individualism in healthcare seeks to privatise risk and 'interiorize' the question of health, with the consequence that the difference of disabled bodies is rendered 'rhetorically invisible even while their physical and discursive presence is foregrounded' (Sothern 2007: 147). At the same time, cuts to benefits and welfare in service of austerity economics that have disproportionately impacted disabled people have been accompanied by a narrowing of the administrative definition of both serious illness and disability (see Roulstone 2015).

In the sphere of disability arts, the demand for responsibility contours attempts to challenge negative and reductive cultural tropes for illness and disability. Here, responsibility has been coupled to beliefs in the purpose of representation: most often, that speaking as a member of a given community should also involve speaking to and for them in 'responsible' ways (Lobel 2012a). The circumstances surrounding the staging of Portuguese-British dancer Rita Marcalo's performance *Involuntary Dances* (2009) – a work concerning her own experiences of epilepsy – may exemplify this dynamic. Supported by funding from Arts Council England, the work was conceived as a durational piece intended to explore issues of voyeurism and exposure concerning epilepsy in which Marcalo suspended her usual drug regime and subjected herself to stimuli that she would normally avoid to reduce the risk of fits. Following an interview with local press, the work came under heightened media scrutiny when a public statement from the advocacy group Epilepsy Action expressed concern that a person with epilepsy should stop taking their prescribed medicine and that the performance could influence others to do something similar (Brown 2009). In the event of the performance, the 'uncontrollability and uncertainty of [Marcalo's] condition was emphasized by the fact that she did not, in fact, fit during the work' (Hadley 2014: 119–20) – either because of heavy safety precautions taken to minimise risk, the adrenalin of performing or, simply, because epilepsy is not predictable. Nonetheless, media and online responses preceding and following the performance accused Marcalo's work of being tasteless, dangerous, a waste of public money that might have been spent on 'helping' people and useless for raising awareness about epilepsy (Gotman 2012: 166). This latter claim involved the expectation that Marcalo serve as a representative figure for epilepsy and other epileptics – a demand that may have found particular focus in the form of solo performance itself, such as that 'if one voice is to speak … it should be a voice that adequately represents the community' (Lobel 2012a: 84). Through these responses, we might understand how Marcalo's work challenged norms of propriety in several different ways at once, not only by engaging in 'irresponsible' conduct through the pursuit of 'risky' behaviour but by doing so in public where her actions modelled that behaviour to others as a non-representative figure for those with serious or potentially life-threatening conditions.

Queering cancer: BALL, Other Funny Stories About Cancer and An Appreciation

Developed between 2001 and 2009, Brian Lobel's trilogy of autobiographical shows concerning cancer – *BALL* (2003), *Other Funny Stories About Cancer* (2006) and the live-art cabaret piece *An Appreciation* (2009) – suggests the development of performance strategies that might challenge such a discourse of 'responsible' representation through works that question the kinds of stories which might be told about serious illness.[1] Grounded in the narrative of his diagnosis and treatment for testicular cancer at the age of twenty-one, Lobel's performances deploy 'field notes' from the scene of his illness as a kind of travelogue in which each work marks 'a specific point in my thinking about cancer, my body, and the relationship between my cancer, my body and the world outside of my own experience' (Lobel 2012b: 13). Where Lobel's practice describes a struggle 'with the proper way to be a cancer patient as well as the proper way to be a former cancer patient' (Warren 2008: 185), it operates in relation to what Kimberly Myers (2004) describes as the 'closet of illness' wherein the visible signs of cancer – hair and weight loss, pallor, scarring – are most frequently the result of therapeutic regimes of radiotherapy, chemotherapy and surgery intended to treat it. While Lobel has suggested that solo performance may itself be 'the perfect metaphor for being sick: one body on stage, isolated and vulnerable' (Lobel 2012b: 14), cancer in itself is not readily seen.

In response, Lobel's trilogy traces a critique of the highly selective affirmations which allow a misfit to be seen and, more pointedly, validated as a survivor. While breast cancer's emergence as the highest profile form of cancer (beyond other more prolific killers of women such as lung cancer or heart disease) has involved the relentless 'brightsiding' of the cancer experience and widespread forms of corporatised pinkwashing (Nielsen 2014), the broader cultural narrative of the illness is one in which tacitly masculine, militaristic and heroic metaphors are invoked to describe the need to 'win the battle' and in which being 'tough' against cancer is involved in the maintenance of a myth of agency (Jain 2007: 521). Though works such as Audre Lorde's ground-breaking *Cancer*

---

1 Lobel's trilogy forms part of a larger body of works concerning cancer, including *A Pacifist's Guide to the War on Cancer* (2016), co-written with and directed by Bryony Kimmings. For details, see: www.funwithcancerpatients.com, accessed 1 March 2017.

Journals (1980) and performances as varied as playwright Susan Miller's *My Left Breast* (1994) and stand-up comedian Tig Notaro's *Live* (2013) have challenged the experience of cancer as one of silent, stigmatised suffering best dealt with in isolation, there remains a persistent cultural narrative in which the 'fight' with cancer is a measure of one's personal capacity to meet with adversity (rather than, say, one's access to support networks, medical expertise and complex drug regimens).

Written in the first hours following Lobel's initial cancer diagnosis, *BALL*'s opening monologue describes the queerly camp moment in which he first discovered a 'problematic' lump in his groin while sitting in a hotel bathtub, masturbating, and listening to the day-time TV soap *Family Affairs*. Unnerved by his doctors' repeated reassurances that he will retain 'a NORMAL and healthy sex life' (Lobel 2012b: 23) though Lobel has neither yet to lose, the scene turns on the eye-bulging reaction of the middle-aged woman who performs a scan of his testicle which announces what ultrasound will later confirm. The cancer diagnosis precedes and follows the moment of the telling: we are warned in the first few seconds of the performance that the show is about Lobel's cancer and reassured that he does not die at the end, but then cast backwards to a caesura between diagnosis and treatment when the story seems to have run ahead to a different conclusion: 'And sure enough, my right testicle, lymph nodes in my abdomen and seventeen spots on my lung had cancer' (2012b: 25). As the work proceeds, Lobel's story is interspersed with commentary which interrogates and challenges tropes of cancer survivorship, and the particular impossible standards for recovery from testicular cancer established by champion cyclist Lance Armstrong who won multiple Tour de France competitions and fathered multiple children from sperm banked prior to chemotherapy. At his father's insistence, Lobel visits an infertility clinic where he discovers that his own sperm is 'abnormal in structure. Infrequent in motion', and biological children are suddenly no longer part of his possible future.

'But what do I win?' asks Lobel. If every other cancer survivor 'gets all this wisdom and depth' and if Lobel isn't going to 'become a better person because of all these procedures' then he'd 'sure as hell better win some kind of competition' (2012b: 47). Dressed in tight bicycle shorts and yellow Armstrong bicycle jersey, Lobel becomes his own role model – not on the racetrack but at the Indiana University-Purdue University Indianapolis Stem Cell Transplant Reunion Picnic Hula Hoop Contest, competing against a group of eight-year-old girls. Writing ten years after the work's first performance on news of Armstrong's use of performance-enhancing drugs for much of his professional career, Lobel averred that:

> I have always believed that Lance Armstrong's greatest legacy will be the increase of pressure placed on cancer survivors to be bigger, stronger, more inspiring creatures. (Lobel 2013)

In *BALL*'s finale, the 'odds' are deliberately low-stake as to undermine and refuse this demand: Lobel's display of unmasculine, unathletic prowess which closes the show describes a victory by default when his chief rival – a young girl – is disqualified on a technicality.

Though the detail with which Lobel narrates the progress of his treatment refuses to sanitise the cancer experience – notably in describing life-threatening complications following Retroperitoneal Lymph Node Dissection – its telling is tempered with the consciousness that a measure of misery is required to form 'the requisite dark chapter, the hard stuff' (2012b: 38). First staged in 2006, *Other Funny Stories About Cancer* returns to the scene of Lobel's illness to stage a mild rebuke to the neatness of its original telling and its participation in a canon of cancer stories centred on the enduring and ultimately noble patient who suffers his way back to health. In doing so, the work serves as a corrective to Lobel's erasure of 'trashy stories about faggotry and STDs' from his original account in the apprehension such deviant detail would belie his cancer's 'purity' and distract people 'from my inspiring journey to survival' (Lobel 2012b: 55). Taking a long drag from a cigarette, Lobel opens the show by declaring

> I wish I had AIDS. If I did, though, I'd probably lose all the sympathy I had gained after beating testicular cancer … But think of the story. Cancer survivor turned HIV activist – the solo show nearly writes itself. (2012b: 54)

Cancer is 'a writer and privileged white boy's dream' but, Lobel explains, telling its story with 'all the necessary beautiful parts: diagnosis, sadness, despair, redemption' had led him to excise its queerness – and omit a critique of modern Judaism via an anecdote about his racist rabbi who used the same pulpit to pray for his recovery as 'to dehumanize Arabs and Palestinians' (Lobel 2012b: 55) – as well as his attempt to lose his virginity to a woman.

If including those stories in *BALL* would have made the work 'too complicated and profane' (Lobel 2012b: 56), *Other Funny Stories* is centred on them – and in a manner that transgresses the image of the survivor that Lobel has constructed for himself as well as cancer's assumed narrative form. In place of *BALL*'s teleological ordering of diagnosis, treatment and recovery, *Other Funny Stories* proceeds by juxtaposing three seemingly unconnected stories: a stint as a counsellor at the 'Hands of Abraham' summer camp for Arab and Israeli teenagers where he struggles with the organisers' willingness to tolerate homophobia; repeated attempts to have sex with a number of female friends and, promised at the outset but reserved as dramatic climax, the relief of a wet dream five weeks after the trauma of abdominal surgery. Unlike *BALL*'s linear ordering of event, the chronology of these stories is unclear – Lobel stops at one point to explain he is telling 'the wrong wet dream story … I didn't even work at Hands of Abraham until after my cancer was all over' (2012b: 61) – and the connecting sinew between moments is less the experience of cancer itself than the queer impropriety of the uncertain relationships, responsibilities and relationalities found in its wake.

In this construction, *Other Funny Stories*' queer content may interrupt what Judith Roof (1996) has theorised as heteronarrative, 'a sensemaking pattern in which difference is repressed for the sake of an ultimate synthesis of differences: a pattern that Roof argues is analogous in structure to heterosexual reproduction' (Hanson 2014: 352). Though Lobel demonstrates mastery of his biographical narrative through the act of performance, the form of its telling describes something other than progress towards a secure and uncontested subject whose story is self-authorising. Instead, Lobel's shifts back and forth through the timeline of somatic memory point to ongoing changes in a body's relationship to a self, changes which are experienced, as Jackie Stacey and Mary Bryson have theorised, as a 'warping' of temporality in which cancer survivorship 'undermines our sense of time's sequential flow, of the causative agency of prediction and outcome … and of the narrational flows of personal biography' (Stacey and Bryson 2012: 6). Such warping is apparent in Lobel's more recent *Waiting … for a Cancer Diagnosis* (2013), an audio piece produced by theatre company Fuel for their *While You Wait* series of podcasts, in which a memory of cancer seems suspended between conscious and involuntary recall as to interrupt the linear flow of diagnosis, treatment and recovery.

Autobiographical practices that might allow for new ways of knowing cancer 'in the plural' (Bryson and Stacey 2013) beyond autobiographical mastery are further suggested by the final work of Lobel's trilogy, *An Appreciation*, created eight years after his initial diagnosis. Premiered at the live art event *I'm With You* at the Hayward Gallery, London, the performance re-frames the testimonial format of the first two parts as Lobel invites five volunteers onstage to don latex gloves and 'medically appreciate' his genitals: 'When a doctor or nurse appreciates a lump or a bump, they feel with their hands to recognize the quality, significance or magnitude of a growth – to measure its severity and to gather evidence for further courses of action' (Lobel 2012b: 80). It is, as Lobel notes in his introduction to the collected performance texts, a set-up which could not be further from *BALL*'s anxiety about having his genitals become 'the joke' of the story and one in which a measure of vulnerability is shared on both sides of the encounter. Lobel faces away from the audience and drops his trousers before inviting each participant to 'give them a rub, really work through it all, and think about what you feel' (2012b: 81) before writing a one-word description on a note card. Turning over and reading each card in turn, Lobel meditates on the changes in his relationship towards his body – and his genitals – in the eight years since having his right testicle removed, and the lingering apprehension of threat rather than thrill 'when the pants come off'.

The memory of an encounter with a man who invokes his cancer history to seduce him ('Cancer, huh? So, what does that look like?') is a moment of transport that carries him back into his body – both as it once was, and in its current, changed form. Placing his body in the literal hands of others, Lobel re-encounters the sensorium of his pre-cancer body through its post-cancer state, an embodiment which is not and cannot be wholly 'after' the fact of that experience. Deploying cabaret's appreciation for the live body against its medicalisation, multiple acts of exposure – to judgment, to memory, to touch – describe a knowledge of the body which is not determined by its solitariness. As Heddon concludes in *Autobiography and Performance* (2008), the personal may become more than merely subjective or individual when its relations to its social and historical context are made plain, and we might well understand Lobel's invitation to his audience to 'appreciate' his changed body as the means to such an end.

Crip biographies: *If These Spasms Could Speak*

One constraint on such a claim on pluralism, though, may be Lobel's seeming proximity to norms of autonomous able-bodiedness which the narration of queerness may only temporarily disrupt. An alternative – and perhaps more forceful – strategy may be apparent in Robert Softley's

If These Spasms Could Speak (2012) as a work which deploys biographical material alongside the specificity of physical impairment to ask questions about the lives and experiences of disabled people. First performed in Glasgow at the Arches' Behaviour festival in 2012 before transferring to the Edinburgh Festival Fringe in 2013 as part of the Made in Scotland showcase, *If These Spasms* has toured widely across Scotland and the UK, and appeared in international festivals in Brazil, India, Spain, Ireland and North America. Supported by Creative Scotland's Creative Futures scheme, the work was initially developed through an open survey in which Softley sought stories from disabled people about their bodies on the premise that bodies that are the subject of medical diagnosis and 'usually seen as the impairment to our full participation in society' might also 'carry with them volumes of stories about incidents, scrapes and calamities' (Softley 2011). Through this process, Softley recruited five participants who agreed to be interviewed by him in their own homes and consented have their stories included within the performance. Told in first person, these stories are interwoven with and structured by episodes from Softley's own life to blend verbatim and autobiographical modes of delivery, 'a collage that enables multiple points of view through multiple voices [to be aligned] to a single or central storyline or thematic' (Heddon 2008: 128).[2]

At the outset, Softley enters the performance space by crawling and climbs onto the raised stage area to get the obvious thing out of the way – that he has a speech impediment and that we should raise our hands to stop him if we cannot understand what he is saying. The 'obviousness' of his speech signals and defers the obviousness of his body: Softley has cerebral palsy owing to oxygen deprivation at birth, which means he has difficulties controlling his movements and in straightening his arms and legs. In any case, the way that we see and hear Softley may always be at odds with how he understands himself – as he tells us, 'I don't hear what you hear. In my head, I sound like Laurence Olivier' (Softley 2012), a joke as much about Softley's Scots accent as anything else. In these opening moments, Softley's performance anticipates and generates what Garland-Thomson has described as the 'dynamic of staring, the arrested attentiveness that registers difference on the part of the viewer' (2000: 335). If staring conventionally stigmatises its object and confers agency to the

---

2 The script of *If These Spasms Could Speak* was originally published as a multimedia app for the Apple iOS platform, though updates to that system have rendered it inaccessible. A pre-performance audio description for the show is available at www. ifthesespasmscouldspeak.com/show-info/access/, accessed 1 March 2017.

one who looks, the forms of representation at work in *If These Spasms* re-asserts the capacity of disabled people to shape the terms of their social experience, even as it recognises how participation in the public sphere may involve – as one contributor offers – the choice between heightened scrutiny and being ignored. As Petra Kuppers explores in Mat Fraser's 'freak show' performances as 'Sealo the Sealboy', Softley's appearance as himself and as an actor performing the stories of others establishes his role as 'controlling rather than being controlled, guiding the audience's gaze rather than being the immobile object of its stare' (2013: 37).

Though Softley appears alone on stage, the plural narratives which form the show's text render him as something other than a solitary figure and suggest instead a (counter) public of disability. Behind Softley are projected large, attractive portraits (taken by the Glasgow-based photographer Tommy Ga-Ken Wan) of Softley and, later, his interview subjects: sometimes dressed and sometimes naked. In *If These Spasms*, Softley's body stands in for the bodies of those whose stories he recounts while simultaneously prompting recognition of the particularity of his present – and their absent – embodiment. As records of individual embodiments whose impairments may or may not be visible, the photographs invoke recognition of the specificity of Softley's body and those of the other contributors, and of the pluralising difference(s) that exist within the category of disability. As the show develops, movement between Softley's narration of his own experiences and those of his contributors is suggested by shifts in posture and vocal delivery. There remain, though, transitional moments in which it is unclear whether Softley is recounting his own or another's stories, and in which his performance serves to interrogate that the notion that we are getting unmediated facts 'straight from the mouths of those "involved"' (Bottoms 2006: 59). Rather than standing as an unmediated proof of what disability and disabled bodies are 'really like', Softley's dramaturgy of non-resemblance may shift the audience's attention towards processes of authentication – that is, the social dramaturgies by which authenticity concerning the experience of disability 'is claimed, imposed, or perceived' (Bucholtz and Hall 2004: 498).

In consequence, the cross-identifications involved in recounting the embodied experiences of others serve to unsettle the essentialising assumptions that underpin dominant perceptions of gender, sexuality and disability – and, as the work progresses, the relationships between desire, agency and autonomy. In an early sequence, Softley recounts the story of a young sportsman who sought assisted suicide in Switzerland after an accident left him paralysed, acknowledging a commonplace fear

Figure 13 Robert Softley, *If These Spasms Could Speak* (2012).

Figure 14 Robert Softley, *If These Spasms Could Speak* (2012).

of disability and pondering what sense disabled people make of their own bodies – before shifting tone to declare

> I LOVE my tits! I cannot say this emphatically enough – I just LOVE my tits! … I was at a couple of friends' wedding a few years back – they are two very dashing gay men so it felt more than appropriate to wear a corset that showed off my boobs spectacularly. (Softley 2012)

The moment is charged with the pleasure of the original speech – the assertion of desire and desirability – and, in the sudden change in topic from euthanasia to breast size, a form of queer crip humour that tests the palate of proprietary, heteronormative and able-bodied taste. 'A primary way for crip-queer solo performers to express disability pride', suggests Sandahl, 'is to rearticulate the disabled body as a gendered, sexual being' (2003: 44), precisely because the forms of objectification which constitute disabled bodies frequently find them genderless because they cannot perform conventionally gendered behaviours, and consequently sexless. Here, the narration of living in/with a disabled body refuses disability as unrecoverable – literally unsurvivable – abjection by asserting the possibility of pleasurable spectacle, both in the original scene of the gay wedding and in Softley's re-enactment of the story.

If Softley's performance articulates a practice of 'cripping' which 'spins mainstream representations or practices to reveal able-bodied assumptions and exclusionary effects' (Sandahl 2003: 37), it may also do so by interrupting the relationship between able-bodiedness (hetero) sexuality and reproduction. This effect is achieved through the reframing of Softley's queer body as a site of heterosexual desire and, in one thread of stories, as the mother of a teenage daughter. In another thread, the orientation of desire coincides where a diagnosis of disability does not as Softley voices the story of a man with muscular dystrophy who likes 'having sex with guys – I don't know if I'm gay or bi or whatever but I like messing around with other blokes' but finds the progressive nature of his condition means that sex is increasingly difficult. Though he enjoys the submissive experience of oral sex, he needs to take active control over the scenario and tell his partner how to pull him forward out of his wheelchair headrest because he can't control his head himself. This moment offers a response to McRuer's argument that compulsory heterosexuality and compulsory able-bodiedness work together to produce a system which 'repeatedly demands that people with disabilities embody for others an affirmative answer to the unspoken question, "Yes, but in the end, wouldn't you rather be more like me?"' (2006: 8). Softley's narration leaves no space for that question because it is preoccupied with the negotiation required of all submissives who find themselves breaking character to explain exactly how they need to be dominated. It becomes impossible to answer the question 'wouldn't you rather be straight/able-bodied?' or indeed say anything at all 'once your mouth is full' (Softley 2012).

This claim on queer-crip agency is expressed more explicitly in Softley's recent work *Discourse or Intercourse / Talking & F*cking* (2017) in which one chooses to watch clips from porn films featuring performers with physical disabilities or academics discussing 'why disabled bodies are desexualised' and 'whether pornography is a good measure of social progress' before meeting with Softley as he crawls naked from a shower to talk about his own empowering experiences of making porn. I am conscious, though, of the possible tension between the carefully composed dramaturgies of Softley's performances and the larger context of their development and circulation. Though *If These Spasms* suggests how the intersection of queer and disabled perspectives might invigorate an antinormative politics, mainstream LGBT spaces and communities nonetheless remain frequently inhospitable or inaccessible to people with disabilities and characterised by a form of assimilationist ableism wherein the only difference that a gay person has from a presumptive norm is the non-disqualifying nature of their sexuality.[3] That commercial gay venues remain heavily normative bodily spaces is well illustrated by the circumstances of an incident in 2013 when security staff at the Glasgow gay club/bar Polo Lounge refused entry to Softley and his husband Nathan Gale on the grounds that the venue had 'no facility for wheelchair access to the building' (G1 Group quoted in Reid-Smith 2013), even though they had visited on multiple occasions before. In demonstrating that ramp access was unneeded, Softley pulled himself out of his wheelchair and crawled up the steps to the entrance where he attempted to reason with the door staff – who then called the police to remove him for alleged disorderly and antisocial conduct (Cockburn 2014).

Though media coverage of the incident articulated shock or dismay at Softley's actions by imagining a 'humiliating scene … in front of customers on a busy city center street' (Reid-Smith 2013), Softley's own account of the moment describes crawling as an expression of agency rather than helplessness. Interviewed by Mark Fisher ahead of *If These Spasms'* appearance at the Edinburgh Fringe Festival later that year, Softley explained

---

3 For discussion of the potential oppressions produced by the intersection of LGBTQ and disabled identity, see 'Double the Trouble?' in Shakespeare *et al.* (1996).

Crawling is a very interesting thing – in both circumstances ... For me, I crawl because I can't walk. It's that simple. I get out of bed and crawl to the kitchen. As humans, we react to that quite viscerally. There's something animalistic and infantile about crawling and we can't quite handle that. A lot of the headlines about the incident were about 'Robert crawled up the steps – oh my God!' But actually, why is it such a big deal? (quoted in Fisher 2013)

Softley's assertion of the ordinariness of crawling as a human strategy for movement also recognises its transgressiveness and its value as strategy of non-violent resistance that might make a body hard to 'handle'. While other deployments of crawling as a form of disability activism have turned on the deliberate staging of indignity for a media gaze – as in the 1990 'Capital Crawl' in which sixty protestors left wheelchairs and mobility devices to crawl up the eighty-three stone steps to the US Capitol Building and demand passage of the Americans with Disabilities Act – Softley's impromptu protest suggests something closer to Garland-Thomson's understanding of misfitting as a creative act which draws attention to the incongruent relation of a body to its material circumstances – or, in this instance, the security staff's insistence on such incongruence in the assertion that Softley's body required a wheelchair which, in turn, required an (absent) access ramp.[4]

In *Disability, Public Space Performance and Spectatorship* (2014) Bree Hadley argues for the significance of artists whose work is characterised by interventionist performance practices which 'allow artists with disabilities, and their spectators, to negotiate new ways of relating with self, others and society' (2014: 27). Though such practice is diverse in form, Hadley notes the recurrence of a 'pranksterish' style which deploys deliberately awkward, comic and/or confrontational scenarios for disabled and non-disabled audiences in the street. While Softley's actions on the steps of Polo Lounge were spontaneous rather than planned, we might nonetheless understand them as an intervention which deployed existing prejudices about disabled bodies to force the question of what access and social participation might actually mean. At the least, it is hard not to read the club management's claim of anti-social 'disorderliness' apart from Softley's decision to leave his wheelchair – a frame in which his body might be socially ordered, contained and rendered

4 For further context – and a more literal example of misfitting – see Jess Thom's work as 'Tourettes Hero' and her touring production *Backstage in Biscuit Land* (2014), a body of work prompted by her own experience of being removed from an audience to a sound booth during a trip to the theatre. See www.touretteshero.com, accessed 1 November 2016.

proper. While anxieties about misfit(ting) bodies may take heightened form around visible differences from a perceived norm of able-bodied wellness, Hadley's study makes plain that the critical agency of performance in public spaces is not reducible to the terms of visibility alone but resides in their capacity to unsettle 'ready-made' readings and responses that save spectators 'from having to truly encounter the other, or take responsibility for their relation to the other, in the street or on the stage' (2014: 7).

Public disorder: Bobby Baker and Katherine Araniello

Commissioned as part of *Small Acts at the Millennium* – a series of works marking the personal and political resonances of the millennium 'against a backdrop of global corporate pageantry' (Heathfield 2000) – Bobby Baker's *Pull Yourself Together* (2000) describes a public intervention in which the question of intersubjective responsibility is framed by tropes of personal propriety and charitable togetherness. First known for her autobiographical works exploring domestic expertise, *Cook Dems* (1990), *Kitchen Show* (1991) and *How To Shop* (1993), Baker's practice has increasingly engaged with questions of mental well-being following a diagnosis of borderline personality disorder and then breast cancer in 1996, and publication of *Mental Illness and Me* (2011), a diary of drawings made over a decade of treatment and recovery. Armed with a loudhailer and seated on the back of specially adapted flat-bed truck bearing banners reading 'PULL YOURSELF TOGETHER' along each side and 'IN AID OF MENTAL HEATH ACTION WEEK' along the rear, Baker was driven through central London while calling out unsolicited advice to pedestrians to pull themselves together, 'get a grip' and 'buck up now'. Dressed in the white coat that has become Baker's uniform – a smock simultaneously registering maternal, medical and artistic roles – and wearing 'angry' red boots born of Baker's 'comic / serious obsession with analysing the character of people treating her by their footwear' (Kellaway 2009) – the reception of Baker's hectoring turned on a perception of the scenario's absurdity, with Clare Allan's account of spending the day with Baker recalling the artist's apprehension: 'I just hope they'll get it … I just hope they get the fact that I'm being ironic' (Allan 2000: 131).

Seated above the level of pedestrians on the street and voice amplified by the loudhailer, Baker's jovial commands insisted on the impersonal nature of notionally interpersonal exchanges – the hit-and-run
quality of public admonishments delivered with little warning and
less interest in their impact – while also staging the power differential involved in the policing of emotional conduct, where 'smiling is an
option for people with more power but an *obligation* for those with less
power' (LaFrance 2002: 321). At the same time, the directional quality of
the loudhailer allowed Baker to address individuals – manifesting, perhaps, how the demand to 'pull yourself together' functions as a norm by
singling out misfits whose 'falling apart' describes their improper relationship to a public constituted in effortless cheerfulness. While initially
cautious, Baker describes growing more confident as the day went on
until it became 'delightful to bawl these insults – of which I've been at
the receiving end so much of my life – at crowds of people with such
irreverence' (Baker in Barrett and Baker 2007: 69). Though met with
a range of responses – 'Some people try to ignore [Baker], some shout
back "why?", "how?" and "fuck off", whilst others stop and stare with
expressions ranging from amazement and amusement to confusion and
irritation' (Keidan 2000: 78–9) – Baker and Allan's assessment of the
action at the close of the day judged that what emerged more than anything else was 'an overriding sense of people's warm good will' (Allan
2000: 134).

Baker's ironic performance of hectoring instruction might direct our
attention to the normative field of agency on and through which charitable intervention is imagined, insofar as the possibility of misinterpreting
Baker's intent turns on her apparent fulfilment of a (white, middle-class)
able-bodied norm. The constrained terms of that field may be more
sharply articulated in work of video and live artist Katherine Araniello –
performing as herself, under the guise of SickBitchCrips and with
Aaron Williamson as the satirical arts organisation, the Disabled Avant-
Garde. In *Pity* (2013), performed at the Lock-up Performance Art Fête
in London's Bethnal Green, Araniello staged herself as a living charity
collection doll in the image of collection boxes routinely found outside of
Spastic Society charity shops during the 1970s: a sad child with cerebral
palsy wearing a brace on their leg and pleading for donations. Bringing to
life 'the persona of the intentions of the original collection … downcast
and seeking money' (Araniello 2013), Araniello deploys her appearance
as a small woman who uses a wheelchair to foreground – and disrupt –
the assumed relationship of agency between a donor and a 'charity case'.
As Araniello has noted, the work is intentionally ambiguous in parodying

the ongoing use of emotive imagery by charities to raise funds and, by actively pursuing donations, challenging the assumption that the disabled subject's need for charity is rooted in their helplessness (and that the need for assistance renders them pitiful). Video documentation of the action is accompanied by a parody of the Motown track *Money* popularised by The Beatles, with Araniello singing 'The best things in life are free / pity does not grow on trees / I want your pity / THAT'S WHAT I WANT / I want your pity / THAT'S WHAT I WANT'.

By framing pity as something that might be actively and even aggressively sought, *Pity* forces a consideration of the relationship between the need for assistance, and the assumption that a lack of normative autonomy automatically renders a life less worth living (and therefore deserving of pitiful compensation). This point is made more clearly in Araniello and Williamson's earlier guerrilla street theatre work *Assisted Passage* (2007) where the conceit of a protest against airlines' treatment of disabled people frames an attempt to lure passers-by to sign a petition supporting Araniello's right to buy a flight to attend her assisted suicide in Zurich. The object of the work's critique was not assisted suicide per se but rather 'the idea that people might choose assisted suicide because they have been taught to fear the loss of control over one's own life illness, disease or disability can bring and it is the fear, not the life, that is intolerable' (Hadley 2014: 98). Similar challenges to the logic of mannered, liberal assistance are apparent in Araniello's *Terminal Services* (2008) staged during *Late at Tate Britain* in which she planned to 'approach random members of the public and ask them questions typical of those directed at disabled people, including "Hello, are you okay? Are you looking for someone? Are you lost? Can I help you? Do you want me to see if I can find your friend?"' (Keidan and Mitchell 2012: 168). In these works, Araniello's interventions suggest how the gesture of charitable assistance may work to secure and more deeply imbed the terms on which particular lives are found to be in need of charity in the first place, and do so – paradoxically – through gestures of support notionally intended to 'improve' those lives which proceed by ensuring a power differential remains in place.

That this dynamic might be sustained and even exacerbated through seemingly affirmative, liberal gestures of inclusivity is further signalled by Araniello's series of short films made in response to the 2012 and 2016 Paralympic Games, beginning with *Meet the Superhuman* (2012) – a direct parody of an advertisement by Channel 4 which framed disabled athletes as manifestations of a world where 'possibilities are endless and potential is limitless' (Channel 4 Paralympics 2012) – and since continued in *We're The Superhumans* (2016). In the first, Araniello splices herself into the original broadcast footage, replacing the hypermobile, toned and muscular bodies of professional Paralympians with her own image in team GB training garb enjoying a cigarette and some cake, weightlifting a cotton-bud barbell with her finger and speeding past the camera in her wheelchair. In the second, Araniello lip-syncs to the original advert's version of Sammy Davis Jr.'s *Yes I Can* (1964) while replacing footage of athletes demonstrating singular flexibility, strength and capacity at home and on the track with a montage of tourist imagery of Rio overlaid with her own attempts to compete in ballroom dancing, boxing and other events. In both films, Araniello challenges the valorisation of Paralympian athletes as inspirational examples of positivity and self-discipline for their affirmation of disability on the grounds that it no longer be disabling – having instead been overcome by singular acts of willpower, endurance and, above all, individual human spirit.

Through Araniello's practice we might re-read in Baker's *Pull Yourself Together* a critique which recognises that the rhetorical frame of pulling yourself together 'in aid' of mental health invokes a distribution of power and agency that re-asserts a particular hierarchy. It marks an ordering of social value which proceeds by imagining the capacity of people experiencing mental distress to render support either to themselves or others as turning on their becoming proper – that is, stable and 'together' in themselves in the specific sense of having mastery of their relationships to others, and where dependencies are freely chosen as the expression of an already intact and wilful agency. As I have suggested elsewhere, such claims on autonomy are especially problematic when rendered within the context of neoliberalism's preference – if not demand – for individuals to author their life-course, even as the resources or capacities for doing so remain unevenly distributed or sharply delimited. As Selina Thompson captures within Demi Nandhra's debut solo show concerning severe depression, *Life is No Laughing Matter* (2016), the work of self-care may require one to address 'the line between illness and your personality, the relationship between productivity, capitalism, mental health and medication, and the way in which wellness is packaged and sold to us' (Thompson 2017). Nonetheless, the dynamic relationship between care and self-care may constitute a field of action that is not reducible to the proper distribution of individualised responsibility: that care *may* take the form of a governmentalised demand does not mean that is unable to serve alternative, reparative ends.

Care and self-care: the vacuum cleaner

Such possibilities are apparent in the work of 'art and activism cell of one' James Leadbitter, better known as the vacuum cleaner for his appearance in an anti-globalisation intervention titled *Cleaning Up After Capitalism* (2003). Leadbitter's month-long 'self-initiated anti-section action' *Ship of Fools* (2011) was developed in the spring of 2011 when he became aware of a downturn in his mental health. Wanting to avoid returning to an acute psychiatric ward to which he had been confined during a previous mental health crisis, Leadbitter committed himself for a period of twenty-eight days to his own self-made mental health institution, the Ship of Fools – in actuality, his flat in Hackney, London. Through an online call-out, Leadbitter sought creative residencies from artists and non-artists who would join him in his flat with friend, artist and activist Sophie Nathan while he attempted to continue making work. Though his collaborations with other artists and activists (including Sue Keen and Thom Scullion) took a range of forms, the most significant and recurring feature of that practice was its public orientation – that is, in actions which took place outside of the notional asylum of Leadbitter's flat. On day 5, for example, Leadbitter spray-painted a sign reading 'Paradise Lost' around a letter-box in the hoardings surrounding the site of a former local café demolished by property developers; on day 8, Leadbitter noticed letters missing from a sign outside of his local political station – appearing as METROPOLITAN LICE – and embarked on a later project of rebranding in which he changed the police logo on signs across London; on days 16 through 18, Leadbitter worked with artist Sue Keen to produce a representation of being in bed – where one can spend a lot of time when experiencing depression – that could be installed in a public space.[5]

Inscribed within Leadbitter's practice is the prospect of an ethics of care for others which is simultaneously one of radical self-care. The larger function of the project – described simply by Leadbitter as 'to stop me from killing myself' – was served by Leadbitter's ability to resist institutionalisation (drawing on friends and a mental health solicitor to avoid forcible removal from his own home under mental health law sectioning powers)

---

5 For an alternative framing of the bed in exploring the politics of self-care, see Liz Crow's work *Bedding Out* (2013), www.roaring-girl.com/work/bedding-art-activism-twitter/, accessed 12 February 2018.

and continue making work with others even as he experienced serious mental anguish. Recognising that he would be inviting strangers into his home – and that the success of the project turned on facilitating mutually beneficial relationships between its participants – Leadbitter and Nathan devised guidelines that would frame the residencies as a whole: a series of instructions for care and self-care. Leadbitter's account of the project in his informal performance lecture 'I Went Mental And I All I Got Was This Lousy T-Shirt' given at Nottingham Contemporary in 2013 makes plain these instructions sought mutually binding conditions.[6] A call for 'no restraint' in the first guideline, for example, expressed the desire for no restraint on the imagination, and no restraint in the literal, physical sense of being held down so that treatment might be administered, as experienced during his time on a locked ward. This desire, Leadbitter explained, involved the agreement that he himself was not allowed to put anyone in a situation where they were compelled to restrain him. In turn, Leadbitter described the call for 'no sudden movements' as a way of managing impulsive action in moments of distress that might lead one to hurt oneself or another person – an invitation to 'take the time to stand back from what you're feeling, as much as you can' (Leadbitter 2013).

Evident in this approach are the techniques of mindfulness: an approach to mental well-being oriented on the cultivation of a present-oriented, non-judgemental mind that also provides the dramaturgical logic of Baker's multi-media, self-help lecture *How To Live* (2004) which promised – with tongue-in-cheek – 'a ground-breaking, phenomenal, dialectical cognitive-behavioural set of eleven techniques designed simply to save the world' (Baker 2008). Amongst others, Kristin Barker has problematised mindfulness as a potentially Foucaultian disciplinary practice which 'brings the level of required therapeutic surveillance down to an ever-smaller increment of time: moment to moment or breath to breath' (2014: 172), where being 'healthy' is rendered as a never-ending process of obligatory personal maintenance. Leadbitter's rendition of self-care, though, suggests the tactical rather than compulsory application of mindfulness techniques, and in a manner which imagines a commons of mutual support characterised by its ability to respond and change according to the needs of its participants. Joanna Cook observe that 'an analysis of self-governance as neoliberalism assumes that practices of subjectification are always already in the service of neoliberalism' (2016: 143), a conclusion which serves to secure neoliberalism as a totalising regime in which 'any response to it that entails

6 See Leadbitter (2013).

subjectification tightens its colonization of emotional life' (2016: 152). Here, though, emotional life has its own force and describes its own possibilities for how subjects might relate and respond to each other in difference. What may be distinctive about Leadbitter's exploration of mental health – continued through the autobiographical work *Mental* (2013) and the collaborative *Mad Love* 'designer asylum' project with Hannah Hull (2014–ongoing) – is its deployment of vulnerability as a political affect irreducible to agency's opposite.

Contagion and immunity: Martin O'Brien

To explore this notion – and return to the chapter's invocation of the misfit as a figure who might challenge normative conventions of bodily propriety – the following, final section turns to the work of live artist and performance scholar Martin O'Brien whose performances are drawn from his own experience of the genetic condition cystic fibrosis (CF). Centred on practices of endurance, hardship and pain, O'Brien's practice suggests how the state of 'suffering' from CF is not determined merely by the symptoms of the illness but by the therapeutic interventions required to sustain his life. Informed by the work and mentorship of Ron Athey (see chapter 2) and collaborations with photographer and performance artist Sheree Rose whose sadomasochistic relationship with Bob Flanagan explored his own experiences of CF, O'Brien's work articulates the possibilities of 'sadomedicine' – that is, the rendition of pain and discomfort as a ritual practice of control, pleasure and self-willed endurance (see Kauffmann 1998). In doing so, O'Brien's performances suggest how disciplinary technologies may be made to serve relations other than those imagined by an opposition of the common and proper in which bodies are always held at secure, safe distance. Unlike the individuated risk posed by Marcalo's 'irresponsible' conduct, the threat posed by O'Brien's body of practice – grounded in the performative rendition of disgust – is that of contamination, even though CF is not itself contagious.

O'Brien's earliest and perhaps most well-known solo performance *Mucus Factory* (2011–14) encapsulates many of the recurring concerns of his work to date which 'questions and subverts representations of people with severe illness as icons of bravery or eliciting sympathy' by offering a 'transgressive but more realistic image of what it means to have a severe chronic illness' (O'Brien in Keidan and Mitchell 2012).

Presented as a durational work varying between three and six hours, the performance is structured by a cycle of action through which O'Brien appropriates the techne and apparatus of therapeutic interventions required to maintain his health – or, more accurately, slow the progress of his condition. Originally commissioned by the Live Art Development Agency as part of the *Access All Areas – Live Art and Disability* event in London, 2011, alongside Noemi Lakmaier's *Undress/Redresss*, *Mucus Factory* was staged over two days in a gallery space minimally dressed with medical apparatus: rows of plastic specimen cups, a nebuliser, a treatment table. Presenting his body as medical specimen and art object, O'Brien subjected himself to a repeated score appropriated from physiotherapy techniques intended to loosen excess mucus from the lungs: repeated, rhythmic, percussive 'chest clapping', exercise by bouncing on a small trampoline, and inversion on a sloped treatment table to allow postural drainage. In documentation of the event, the action is monotonous and brutal as he coughs and spits into the specimen cups, over and over. Recalling the progress of Eddie Ladd's self-exhaustion in *The Bobby Sands Memorial Race* (see chapter 2), O'Brien's capacity to perform illness is progressively undermined by his own actions. Watching O'Brien perform an unnamed durational piece naked in the unheated warehouse space of Glasgow's Glue Factory venue during Take Me Somewhere festival in 2017 – his chest marked in pins that trace a silhouette of his lungs – I notice his uncontrolled and uncontrollable shivers become more and more pronounced.

Assisted by Becky Beyts at hourly intervals, O'Brien largely self-administers *Mucus Factory*'s treatment: through this extended action, the scene of biomedical discipline becomes apparent as one which demands the patient's active and prolonged participation. The time of chronic illness seems compressed – the actions of many months condensed into a matter of hours – and extended beyond reasonable measure to mark an 'exhaustive' use of time intended to produce a docile body (Foucault 1995: 149–54). This strategy is also apparent in O'Brien's *Breathe For Me* (2012–16), an endurance work similarly structured by a regime of sufferance in which O'Brien re-embodies illness and therapy by beating, bruising, penetrating, suffocating, examining and exhausting himself, and in which the time and action of chronic illness extends beyond the rationale of self-care or self-improvement. In *Mucus Factory*, though, that regime and its products are aestheticised and eroticised, and made to take on new meaning: O'Brien uses the mucus as 'an adhesive to stick glitter to my body, as hair gel and as lubrication to insert a dildo-shaped mouth-piece from a nebulizer into my anus' (O'Brien 2014: 62).

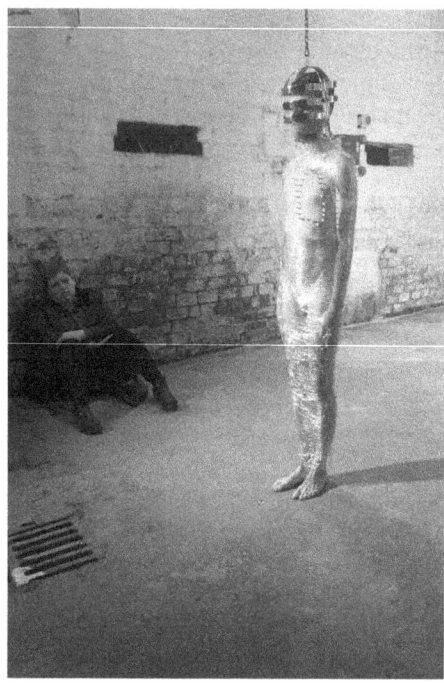

Figure 15 Martin O'Brien. Unnamed durational performance (Take Me Somewhere festival, Glasgow, 2017).

Rather than treating the mucus as hazardous and abject waste, O'Brien reintroduces the matter to his body's surfaces and openings and his chest takes on the purple and red colouration of a bruise which announces the possibility of jouissance: there is a form of masochistic pleasure here. Of O'Brien's more recent work *Taste of Flesh/Bite Me I'm Yours* (2015), Jareh Das suggests that 'a work that is staged by a disabled artist, in so far as the markers for disability to which the work might be attributed are invisible, i.e. the "sick body" looks well, is made explicit through performing the illness' (2016: 267). Here, the signifiers of illness are made to articulate queer identity and desirability; glitter which marks a shift from real body fluids to artifice also advertises the performativity of illness itself and, accordingly, the appropriation of its signs to alternative ends.

In O'Brien's work, the tension between the proper and the common plays out in the relationship between the supposedly autonomous body of the individual subject, and the biomedical regimes which simultan-eously impinge and call upon that body's agency in order to sustain it.

I am also interested, though, in how the specific terms of both O'Brien's practice and his illness might illustrate the flaws of such an oppositional logic. Although CF is not an immune disorder, its symptoms and progression can be understood in terms of an auto-immune crisis, wherein a process intended to protect a host from external danger comes to pose a greater threat – namely, through an over-production of mucus which in 'healthy' bodies serves as a barrier to infection but which in people with CF threatens one's ability to breathe. While the structured repetitions of O'Brien's work analogise the unending endurance required by a biological feedback loop of inflammation, infection and inflammation proper to his condition – 'a chronic and non-resolving activation of the innate immune system' (Rieber *et al.* 2014: 108) – they also hint at the transformation of the body's threat to itself and, in turn, the threat of that body to the body politic. When O'Brien reintroduces his mucus to his chest, the site of its threat to his well-being, the material is disarmed and offered as a surface of contact rather than that which must be refused and rejected.

As such, the ethos of O'Brien's work may be read in terms of an engagement with immunity as a relational filter between inside and outside. Central to that claim is an understanding of the function of disgust in O'Brien's practice as a vector for the social judgements which surround the bodies of the chronically ill and as a dramaturgical strategy which implicates his audience, sensorially, in his staged forbearance. Critics' responses to *Breathe For Me* at In Between Time, for example, noted 'the overwhelming smell of antiseptic' which 'makes you gag' (Papachlimitzou 2013); O'Brien's home-made, apple-green sludge – a surrogate for the paler mucus he beats and coughs from his lungs – was 'disgusting and insidious' (Wagg 2013). At the same performance, artist Mark Leahy observed 'the woman sitting two along [who] hides each time he spits in the jar, that is the bit she can't watch' (Leahy 2013) as well as his own growing nausea. While abjection may describe 'the "unliveable" or "uninhabitable" zones of social life' (Butler 1993: 3), O'Brien's rendition of disgust is firmly entrenched within a social scene where it elaborates culturally normative judgements concerning wellness and, more sharply, the threat of contagion. 'Like fear, disgust induces avoidance', suggest Carolyn Korsmeyer and Barry Smith, 'like hatred, it compels interest' (2004: 20) and so, too, in O'Brien's practice does disgust trace a circuitous path of repulsion and attraction: audiences look away and look back. The bouts of coughing which are a feature of CF are not only the 'voice of illness' (O'Brien and Beyts 2012: 89) presumed to communicate 'a kind of warning. Like a siren or something, like "I'm sick". Get away' (O'Brien and Linsley 2015) but that which serves to call attention close. If 'disgust makes us step back, push away, or otherwise draw a protective line between the self and the threat' (Haidt *et al.* 1997: 127), that line is always porous – a membrane rather than a barrier – and, in the particular slimy and amorphous form of O'Brien's mucus, carrying with it 'the fear of being absorbed into something which has no boundaries of its own' (Grosz 1994: 194).

Conclusion

In this respect, solo performance's treatment of the specificity of the material, lived experiences of illness, impairment and disability might do more than pluralise their representation but address the greater task of challenging and disrupting the normative regimes of propriety which order the duty of a body to compose a self, and – accordingly – contour the relationships that might exist between bodies and selves, whether in desire or pity. Though the works considered in this chapter reflect a range of performance conventions and contexts, they share uses of personal experience which invite us to reconceptualise support and self-care beyond the distribution of power described by proper, individuated responsibility. Such practice challenges the concept of illness and disability as 'a private catastrophe an individual needs to deal with' (Hadley 2014: 10) but without surrendering the detail of specific lived experiences and embodiments: it is work which proposes new and – as O'Brien's work suggests – potentially threatening reconfigurations of the social. That threat derives from the requirement that we abandon or at least loosen our grip on notions of embodied sovereignty enough to acknowledge our bodies' porous borders, the implications of which extend beyond the condition of subjects who are unable or unwilling to fulfil the demands of neurotypical, able-bodiedness. To return to Shildrick,

> The coming together of anomalous and normative embodiment does not erase the encounter of radical and irreducible difference, but lays bare what is at stake in *every* encounter between self and other. (2009: 35, original emphasis)

The terms on which such encounters might unfold, their capacity to serve alternative configurations of the social and – most consequentially – their invocation of vulnerability as a mode of transformative resistance is explored in the following, final chapter's exploration of the optimist.

7

The optimist: alternatives in the here and now

In Lauren Berlant's study *Cruel Optimism* (2011) all attachments appear inherently optimistic, with the desire expressed in attachment taking the form of 'a cluster of promises we want someone or something to make to us and make possible for us' (2011: 23). In this account, optimism describes a relationship to the world and to other people in it that is oriented on the question of what might lie ahead: if we are optimistic about something which already exists, it is because it makes us feel a particular way about the future. That future-feeling is what distinguishes optimism from the desire that a given set of circumstances (our relationship, employment, housing or sex life) will remain the same: optimism is ambitious, moving one out of oneself 'and into the world in order to bring closer the satisfying *something* that you cannot generate on your own but sense in the wake of a person, a way of life, an object, project, concept or scene' (2011: 1–2, original emphasis). Insofar as a promise involves a declaration about the future, optimistic attachments are characterised by uncertainty and vulnerability: attached to potentiality rather than actuality, optimism may engender disappointment when the future fails to bring that which we desire within reach. Indeed, Berlant's primary thesis is that optimism may become cruel when it describes a relationship in which 'something you desire is actually an obstacle to your flourishing' and when the object of your attachment 'actively impedes the aim that brought you to it initially' (2011: 1). Moreover, the experience of optimism may not feel optimistic at all and an optimistic attachment 'might feel any number of ways, from the romantic to the fatalistic to the numb to the nothing' (Berlant 2011: 13). Optimism, most popularly allied with hopefulness, confidence about the future and utopian thinking may feel bad as readily as it feels good, and exist as an affective state which enervates and enables in equal measure. One might even feel cruelly optimistic about optimism itself.

Part of the problem may be that a large proportion of the population experiences an 'optimism bias' (Weinstein 1980). This bias is characterised by the overestimation of the likelihood of good events and the underestimation of the likelihood of bad events (Sharot 2011: 941) – a proclivity which persists despite a lifetime of experience from which we might be imagined to learn and adjust our expectations (Sharot, Korn and Dolan 2011). Though this tendency may lead us to engage in risky and potentially life-threatening behaviour, optimism's wishfulness may have the evolutionary benefit of allowing us to imagine possibilities beyond the world as we currently know it. Recalling Ahmed's critique of happiness as a cultural norm discussed in chapter 4, optimism may also have a normative bent insofar as it serves to orient us on particular futures while rendering others not only undesirable but unimaginable, while operating as part of a neoliberal compulsion to produce ourselves as responsible citizens planning for a future. If the affective structure of optimism takes the form of a binding attachment – a 'sustaining inclination to return to the scene of fantasy that enables you to expect that *this* time, nearness to *this* thing will help you or a world to become different in just the right way' (Berlant 2011: 2) – then its compulsive, repetitive nature describes a habit which is not easily shaken and one about which we may feel deeply conflicted, being constrained by accusations of small-minded pragmatism on one side and head-in-the-clouds idealism on another.

Suspended between involuntary and self-willed action, between the possibility for change and anxiety about what the future holds, the figure of the optimist completes this book's study of solo performance by turning to examine works which figure the vulnerability and potentiality of the here and now. These works offer an alternative to neoliberalism's claim on futurity as a technology of the self – characterised by careful planning and 'smart self-investments' (see Rottenberg 2017) – by presenting uncertainty as a field of action in itself. To that end, I consider two interlocking claims: that optimism in recent solo performance is characterised by a present-tenseness that has a force and significance beyond its promissory content (simply, the idea that optimism is not merely future-stuff) and, in turn, that the figure of the optimist animates the ethical and political potentiality of vulnerability as that which seems 'to follow from our being socially constituted bodies, attached to others, a risk of losing those attachments, exposed to others, at risk of violence by virtue of that exposure' (Butler 2003: 20). In the following, optimism is not presented as a remedy for these experiences but instead marks their availability to reparative change: they describe a way of co-habiting the political in which being dispossessed is not merely a source of anxiety but describes 'a chance "to be moved" – to be affected and prompted to act' (Athanasiou and Butler 2013: 93). This thinking draws on but departs from the accounts of futural utopianism in the work of Jill Dolan and José Esteban Muñoz, explored below, to emphasise the present as a scene of action and emergence. Such a stance does not mean refusing to acknowledge the inimical conditions of the world as we know it but questions a politics which postpones the possibility of change in mistrust of the present as an intractable quagmire.

Utopia, futurity and performance

In *Utopia in Performance* (2005), Jill Dolan theorises utopian performatives as

> small but profound moments in which performance calls the attention of the audience in a way that lifts everyone slightly above the present, into a hopeful feeling of what the world would be like if every moment of our lives were as emotionally voluminous, generous, aesthetically striking, and inter-subjectively intense. (2005: 5)

These experiences are 'voluminous' – richly full of turns, coils and convolutions – because they are collective experiences and because they are not constrained by the terms of reality as we ordinarily experience them and which keep us in our literal and figurative place. Though Dolan suggests these moments might 'critically rehearse' forms of engagement that could be effective in the wider public and political sphere, the efficacy of a utopian performative is grounded in the 'inevitability of its disappearance' (2005: 8). Seemingly more profoundly characterised by loss than by fulfilment, the fleetingness of such experience leaves us 'melancholy but cheered' by the memory of 'what redemption might be like, of what humanism could really mean, of how powerful might be a world in which our commonalities would hail us over our differences' (2005: 8).

Though oriented on the future, the affective structure of Dolan's utopian performative resembles nostalgia as we reach to the future by casting back to something we have lost: 'the possibilities of a process that starts now, in this moment at the theater' (2005: 17) which we are inspired to recover.

In terms that resonate with Dolan's account, José Esteban Muñoz's queer utopianism imagines a future collectivity that refuses prescription, being a 'horizon of possibility, not a fixed schema' which can be understood as 'flux, a temporal disorganisation, as a moment when the here and now is transcended by a then and there that could be and indeed should be' (2006: 9). Echoing Dolan's apprehension that we fall short of our potential humanity in arguing that the 'quagmire of the present' is actively hostile to queers and other non-normative subjects, Muñoz's work turns on a sense of queerness as that which 'lets us feel that this world is not enough, that indeed something is *missing*' (2009: 1, original emphasis). Here, queerness as a utopian formulation involves an economy of desire that is 'always directed at that thing that is not yet here, objects and moments that burn with anticipation and promise' (Muñoz 2009: 26). Though Muñoz maintains that 'the idea is not simply to turn away from the present' but instead to build knowledge of it 'in relation to the alternative and temporal and spatial maps provided by a perception of past and future affective worlds' (2009: 27), that prospect nonetheless turns on the belief that the 'certain surplus' manifest in queer performance work can only promise futurity. While observing how this framing of queerness as 'not quite here' (Muñoz 2009: 7) may contribute to the elision of materialist, class-based critiques, performance scholar Stephen Farrier theorises that such moments of performance in which a 'flash of the utopic' is felt mark 'potential change; and change connotes agency' (2013: 49–50).

In constructing their arguments, Dolan and Muñoz both turn to philosopher Ernst Bloch's account of the 'anticipatory illumination' of art to theorise 'never finished gestures towards a potentially better future' (Dolan 2005: 8) that might help us to 'combat the force of political pessimism' (Muñoz 2009: 4). Variously translated as 'ontological anticipation' and 'pre-appearance', this concept expresses Bloch's belief 'that it is somehow possible to experience a kind of foreglow of future possibilities' (Geoghegan 2008: 37) in a manner which is both objective and open. Bloch's account of hope, in other words, evades the traps of both wishful thinking and leaden pragmatism to figure a realism which is not constrained by what has come before. In elaborating this idea, Muñoz draws on Agamben's extended exploration of potentiality as something which is 'present but not actually existing in the present tense' having instead the quality of 'a trace or potential that exists or lingers after a performance' (Muñoz 2009: 99). For Agamben, potentiality 'conserves' itself even after an event is actualised: it is not 'used up' by any given iteration but extends beyond itself, much as thinking does not exhaust thought (see Cooke 2005: 184). Accordingly, reading for potentiality involves 'scouting for a "not here" or "not now" in the performance that suggests a futurity' (Muñoz 2009: 99) – that is, a willingness to look beyond what is most immediately present in favour of that which signals what might be in the future.

A difficulty with this account is how Muñoz's emphasis on 'not here' and 'not now' and Dolan's insistence on transience as a condition of performative efficacy may serve to constrain recognition of what might be accomplished – and sustained – in the present, while effacing how potentiality's persistent trace may itself constitute the ongoing existence of different worlds beyond hegemonic order. Such an account lends itself to a worldview in which ruling conditions are given to be so overwhelmingly dominant as to make alternatives in the here and now an impossibility. Whatever we might glimpse as 'extra to the everyday transaction of heteronormative capitalism' (Muñoz 2009: 22) cannot be grasped in the everyday without falling into the trap of complacency, reinforcing hegemonic terms for being or investing in neoliberalism's promise of a 'better future' as grounds for privation and sacrifice in the present. This tendency is more sharply articulated in Lee Edelman's *No Future: Queer Theory and the Death Drive* (2004) where the susceptibility of queerness to normalisation through the logic of reproductive futurity becomes an inevitability and in which, as Michael Snediker observes, the ubiquity of 'always' and 'every' in Edelman's argument would seem to make the world 'so irrevocably one thing that response to the world would amount to one thing' (Snediker 2009: 24). Are futurity and the possibilities of the here and now unthinkable except on these narrow terms? Might the potentiality of performance – and the 'certain surplus' that is for Muñoz peculiar to queer performance – indicate something other than or, crucially, *as well as* a vanishing over the horizon?

In response, my readings of performance in this final chapter are informed by what Lloyd Pratt identifies in his analysis of novelist Eudora Welty as a 'condition of radical present-tenseness that subordinates to the future and the past, and which favors a committed attention to what is most clearly *now*' (2011: 200). Grounded in a close reading of the instant as it unfolds, such a stance is 'neither unduly grim and retrospective nor jolly and hopeful without cause' but instead involves 'a form of immanent particularity, which opens onto nothing other than the truth of the present' (Pratt 2011: 200). Beginning with Deborah Pearson's *The Future*

Show, Ivana Müller's *60 Minutes of Opportunism* and Duncan Macmillan's *Every Brilliant Thing* – each of which address the uncertain relationship between past, present and future – I consider how performance might elaborate an understanding of optimism's potentiality as a state of being and not-being, and doing and not-doing. While each work narrates an attachment to the possibility of a future, they also describe how the labour of making oneself present to and for others through performance involves a paradoxical vanishing act wherein optimism registers as an equivocal if not deeply ambivalent attachment to futurity. Structured by attempts to imagine the future in its relation to a persistent present, each of these works elaborates how the figure of the optimist might embody a critique of the conditions in which we find ourselves without reserving the possibility of alternatives to another where and another when.

Such a critique does not privilege hope over hopelessness but draws attention to how the potential of what Robyn Wiegman describes as 'small worlds of sustenance that cultivate a different present and future' (2014: 11) involves the attempt to be present in the present, for the present. In the second part of the chapter I explore three further performances – FK Alexander's *(I Could Go On Singing) Over The Rainbow*, Rosana Cade's *Walking:Holding* and Nando Messias' *The Sissy's Progress* – as works which elaborate how the optimist's insistence on the here and now does not model heroic resilience but instead invokes vulnerability as the means by which an ethics of interpersonal relations might be forged apart from neoliberalism's preference for responsible future-oriented and ultimately paranoid prediction. Such an ethics – centred on our constitutive exposure to one another – is not straightforwardly affirmative, and invites recognition of the contingent qualities of any claim on the future as a remedy to deleterious uncertainty, or social injustice. Characterised by an attentiveness to the possibilities and consequences of life lived beyond its most normative parameters, it articulates a politics which understands that the world as we know it can be different because other worlds already exist.

Optimism as potentiality: *The Future Show*

The strange and even perverse mix of affects which characterise the optimist are apparent in the work of Canadian-born and UK-based theatremaker and founding co-director of Forest Fringe, Deborah Pearson, whose solo works *Music's Been Ruined by Dating* (2008), *Like You Were*

Before (2010 and 2015), *The Future Show* (2011–15) and *History History History* (2016) consider the relationships between time, history and personal identity. Beginning with the final three lines of the show and a prediction of how the audience will clap 'because it's the way we signal an ending' (Pearson 2015b: 17), *The Future Show* describes Pearson's exit from the stage out into the venue and – in slowly decreasing detail – the events of the hours and days which follow until the moment of her imagined death, with each prediction prefaced by the invocation 'I will …'. The monologue is performed by Pearson sitting at a table, reading to the microphone from a folder which contains the script – a composition that resembles a 'very visually paired down version of Spalding Gray's staging for his autobiographical monologues *Swimming to Cambodia* and *Gray's Anatomy*' (Pearson 2015b: 121) that consciously cites a tradition in which 'only dudes sit at desks … We see men sitting and reading at desks and we very rarely see women sitting and reading at desks' (Pearson interviewed by Goode, 2016). Each performance requires Pearson to re-write the script to reflect its particular spatial and temporal context: describing the specific doors and lobbies of the performance venue, the acts scheduled to appear after her own performance, the journey home or back to a hotel room and the anticipated labour of re-writing the script for its next performance.

Figure 16 Deborah Pearson, *The Future Show* (Malta Poznan Festival, Poland, 2015).

The first iteration of the show was presented as a short performance at the Amhurst Republic, London (a pop-up performance space in the studio of artist Souhiel Sleiman) and then developed through work-in-progress showings through 2011–12 with support from Arts Council England, Dublin's MAKE artist development programme and a residency at the Battersea Arts Centre (BAC) where the show premiered in January 2013. In the earliest versions of the show partially documented on the project's website, the work traces a loop in time that extends only a few hours out from the moment of the performance in imagining the journey home by bus and train to conclude with the image of Pearson at home in bed next to her then husband-to-be later that night.[1] By the third performance at the BAC, the script has begun to fold back on itself and even resist the turn towards the future. Pearson predicts the temporal palimpsest of the performance and its text, caught between future and present, writing

> I will look at this script, which is now an old script and needs to be made new. I will begin deleting. I will delete the first line. I will continue reading. I will see that many of the details really should be left the same. (Pearson 2013)

This tension – between writing and re-writing – reflexively advertises the work required to produce and sustain the performance as an intervention in the present. In this, the work of the optimist is figured as present-presence, with the 'weak presence' (Fischer-Lichte 2012: 106) of performer and spectator(s) in the here and now of the performance conjoined to the live, detailed invocation of what is clearly not now.[2]

The issue of reproducibility may also be apparent in the published text of *The Future Show* which contains both three versions of the work staged between April 2013 and November 2014 and a score by which other artists might create their own versions of the performance. This score was derived in part from participation in Andy Field's *Steal This Workshop* Live Art DIY event at the Lancaster Institute for Contemporary Arts in which participants were invited to 'rip off' another artist's work. Pearson's score – 'the skeleton of a house I bring from venue to venue' (2015b: 119) elaborates a conscious attempt to 'manage time' on stage and in the process of (re)writing the script – sometimes day after day – for performance while touring. Across its iterations, the first sections of

---

1 See *The Future Show*, https://thefutureshow.wordpress.com/, accessed 6 July 2017.
2 For similar experiments in performative time, see German performance artist Sylvia Rimat's *Being Here While Not Being Here* (2008/9) in which Rimat tries to retrace her experience of fainting on stage in 2003 and *This Moment Now* (2015) which attempts to accelerate and slow down the audience's perception of time.

The Future Show are clustered around the event of the performance itself after which time begins to elongate and shifts from concrete dates and diary entries to a medium-term future in which the narration 'devolves from precise details to snapshots, little abstract memories that are occasionally out of order' (Pearson 2015b: 135). In describing this structure, Pearson emphasises that the details which describe what she would do in the future are not about the future, but rather the result of looking at 'at your immediate surroundings and thinking about the inevitable and constant passage of time' in a manner that is 'perplexing, intriguing, frightening, or comforting' (Pearson 2015b: 125). Writing the future, in other words, is only made possible by committing oneself to the way one feels in the present moment.

As a kind of self-fulfilling prophecy, Pearson's invocation of the future is what makes the future possible because it safeguards survival in the present by providing 'an antidote to current anxieties, one that makes the next step possible, wherever its tread may fall' (Trueman 2013). At the same time, it also describes how one might experience a relation of cruel optimism to optimism itself in which the antidote to anxiety becomes its present cause. As the performance develops, we learn that Pearson experienced Obsessive Compulsive Disorder as a young adult, that the condition is chronic and that the repeated action of performing the show may be indulging the voice that she ordinarily works hard to ignore.[3] As critic Catherine Love observes, 'in the middle of this meticulously controlled performance, there is the troubling possibility that, by obsessively training her eyes on the future, Pearson may be making her OCD worse' (Love 2013). In this, the practice of futural optimism appears potentially self-destructive as Pearson predicts that she

> will think about how I once showed promise as a writer and I will wonder if this project is my attempt to kill that promise once and for all. To really burn myself out on a project that never ends and that nobody reads and that the audience may even at times find boring. (2015b: 22)

Pearson's narration traces an optimism which is cruel because its attachment to the labour of producing a future threatens her capacity to live in that future: the 'conditions of possibility' (Berlant 2011: 27) which characterise Pearson's attachment to her particular conception of a good life are also those which impede her ability to imagine a future outside of the closed loop of compulsive repetition.

---

3 For an alternative exploration of obsessive compulsive disorder, see Laura Jane Dean's solo *Head Hand Head* (2013).

Yet the performance's following line – 'I will keep typing' – seems deeply ambivalent in that the act which threatens to 'burn her out' also refuses the certainty of that fate. Where Kieran Hurley's *Heads Up* (2016) and Ontroerend Goed's *World Without Us* (2016) both manifest performative mastery in their narration of an imagined apocalypse – with Hurley shifting between four characters' overlapping stories, and Ontroerend Goed's piece turning on the dramaturgical conceit that human perception might persist after humans themselves have departed – Pearson's orientation on whatever may come involves an exercise of will which questions its own surety. It is in doing so that she finds paradoxical grounds for hope. As Pearson wrote on her blog in the initial stages of creating the show:

> How do we come to terms with what hasn't happened yet? And where does that word 'Yet' come from – how do we come to terms with what may or may not happen? We make lists, we make plans, and then we have to abandon ourselves somewhat, to resign ourselves, to do what we can, and then to give ourselves over. (Pearson 2012)

That giving over, I suggest, marks the point at which any projection towards the future folds into the present: it has meaning because it marks the point at which a claim on agency in one's imagined ability to defer the future finds its limit.

(Re)writing the present: *60 Minutes of Opportunism*

The quality of optimism as an unresolved potentiality experienced in the present may be clearer when *The Future Show* is read alongside Croatian artist Ivana Müller's *60 Minutes of Opportunism* (2010) in which the performer appears on stage accompanied by a recording of her own voice.[4] This voice delivers a series of pre-recorded statements in the present tense that describe thoughts, feelings or actions that seem on the verge of taking place, each beginning 'I would like to take this opportunity …'. More tightly focused on the present than Pearson's 'I will' statements, Müller's performative utterances suggest how potentiality is not reducible

4 For documentation of *60 Minutes of Opportunism*, see https://vimeo.com/31035826, accessed 7 July 2017.

to action and being, but also – as Agamben argues, and as Muñoz largely overlooks – constituted in the ability *not* to be something and by 'the potential for inaction' (Cooke 2005: 86). At the least, the conditions of presence rendered by Müller's voice seem at odds with those performed by her physical self on the stage: she smokes a cigarette while the voice explains that this is not really 'her' as she gave up smoking some years before. Best known as a choreographic artist whose group works include *While We Were Holding It Together* (2006), *Working Titles* (2010) and *Playing Ensemble Again and Again* (2008) – the latter occupied with the (re) construction of past and present through the prism of ensemble performance – Müller plays with the aura of her professional reputation: standing still as J. S. Bach's chamber music piece 'Air' plays, she invites the audience to imagine her performing whatever dance we choose.

Philosopher and performance theorist Bojana Kunst – herself a long-term collaborator with Müller – observes how the expectations surrounding Müller as a well-known artist engaged in an agreement with a producer to perform live and alone might constitute a debt or indebtedness. Rather than directly addressing this demand, Kunst suggests that Müller's work creates a series of dramaturgic solutions which allow her to perform on stage while 'delegating' her work elsewhere, through actions 'in which the working conditions have been turned upside down' (Kunst 2015). Despite the terms of her commission, Müller's solo is not strictly a solo: partway through, she is joined by a crowd of silent figures, all shrouded in black 'all equally anonymous … except for me', a group whose inclusion allows her to observe that

> in this performing business, nothing is more annoying than touring a solo. And since this show has quite a number of touring options already, meeting a new group of real people in every city makes the prospect of touring this piece much more joyful. (Müller 2010)

Müller's account of her working conditions is optimistically pragmatic, oriented on the possibility of circumstances that are not in her control wherein taking advantage of them requires recognition of their intractability. In *Finally Together on Time* (2011) – a staged conversation between a live Kunst and a pre-recorded video projection of Müller– this commentary on the terms of artistic labour is made explicit. Knowing that 'you can be late because others, too, expect you to be late' is joined to knowledge that 'being slightly late might confirm our freedom as creative workers to escape dominant patterns of efficiency and the constant delivery of a result' (Kunst and Müller 2012: 131) – a freedom that is paid for by being very badly paid.

One of the central devices of *60 Minutes* is an invitation for the audience to reconsider and imaginatively recreate how they see Müller as live and present in the moment of the performance. Early in the work, Müller's voice speculates

> I guess that when you look at me right now, you might think of someone who is in her mid-30s, [clears her throat] excuse me, who is a contemporary artist, who is not a native speaker and who carries a backpack. When you look at me again, you might think of a suicide-bomber with a bag full of plastic explosives, in a public place, just like this one. Or if you very quickly and superficially look at my gear, you might think of a mountaineer, equipped to climb great heights. (Müller 2010)

Müller's body – or the image which it presents – takes on the quality of an absent presence, not quite fully here (present but yet to be securely indexed within the frame of the performance) and on the verge of transformation. In a later sequence, having covered herself with a black drape in the attempt to become invisible and, not incidentally, coming to resemble a woman in a full-body veil, Müller's dry commentary plays on the uncertain distinction between fear and anticipation by juxtaposing the image of suicide bomber and children's party piñata: 'something that will make children laugh and make adults slightly nervous. Something after it explodes will be very hard to clean up' (Müller 2010).

Across the work, Müller's self-staging frames live performance as a space of projection, with the repeated invocation 'I would like to take this opportunity' opening up and collapsing the space between the phenomenal (that is, physically present) and semiotic registers of her body. In the final sequence of the work – following a live karaoke rendition of The Rolling Stone's *Time is on My Side* (1964) – the temporality of Müller's recorded speech shifts to more closely resemble Pearson's predictions, with speech running ahead of action to warn that the end of the performance is near. But where Pearson's predictions are momentarily secure from falsifiability because the events which she describes have yet to take place, Müller is left to confront the gap between a past effort of writing and the opportunity of the immediate present:

> I can't say whether or not it was a pleasure to be here because I recorded these words some weeks ago when I couldn't possibly know how I would feel at this moment. But I believe it was. (Müller 2010)

Maintaining the deadpan expression she has worn throughout the performance, Müller's temporally displaced optimism remains undecidable – as if to suggest that the more strongly optimism is attached to a future, the less tenable it becomes in the present.

Attempted attachments: *Every Brilliant Thing*

The difficulty of what it might mean to abandon oneself to the present alluded to within *The Future Show* and framed as a condition of artistic labour in *60 Minutes* recurs as a question throughout Duncan MacMillan's *Every Brilliant Thing* (2014), a collaboration with director George Perrin and stand-up Jonny Donahoe that begins in a child's attempt to make sense of their mother's suicidal depression by writing a list 'of everything brilliant about the world. Everything worth living for' (Macmillan 2016: 285). Like *The Future Show*, it is a work which suggests how an optimistic attachment to a future is first an attachment to the present – or, at the least, an attempted attachment. Initially written as a short monologue titled 'Sleeve Notes', the work later evolved to become an installation at the UK arts and music festival Latitude before its first staging at the Ludlow Fringe Festival in 2013, a run at the Roundhouse venue at Summerhall during the 2014 Edinburgh Festival Fringe and a sixteen-week run off-Broadway in New York beginning later that year where it was also adapted for film for US cable and satellite network HBO.[5] In 2017, it returned to Edinburgh for its fourth appearance at the Fringe following tours of Canada, New Zealand and the UK.

The play – and the list – begins following the narrator's mother's first suicide attempt, at first appearing as an attempt to persuade her to remain in the world before unfolding as a biographical device which traces the narrator's own life and mental health. Counter to the glamorising depiction of suicidal artists imagined to experience the world too deeply, this list reflects an understanding of the reality of serious depression as something 'ordinary, domestic, mundane and every day that affects everybody' (Macmillan in Perth International Arts Festival 2015).[6] While a number of Macmillan's other recent plays are concerned with the span of a human life – with the climate change monologue *2071* (2014) and relationship drama *Lungs* (2011) both declaring their concern for the future in their respective opening lines – the text and dramaturgy of *Every Brilliant Thing* emphasise the immediacy of the affective labour required to sustain a liveable life, no matter its length. Though the list's

5 For comedian Ed Byrne's performance reading of *Sleeve Notes* at the Latitude Festival 2009, see www.youtube.com/watch?v=jqfaGMwQnow, accessed 3 March 2017.
6 For an alternative treatment of mental health and suicidal impulses, see artist and comedian Kim Noble's solo show *Kim Noble Must Die* (2009) in which he discussed his plans to throw himself from London's Waterloo Bridge.

entries have no particular order – as 'There was no way of saying that, for example, Danger Mouse was objectively better than Spaghetti Bolognese' (Macmillan 2016: 295) – and range from a child-like pleasure in things with stripes and the colour yellow to the more esoteric particularities of Christopher Walken's voice and Christopher Walken's hair, they describe a patterning of attachments to the here and now insofar as everything on the list has the affective or sensory texture of an immediacy, whether in the form of ice cream, the smell of old books, winning something, or the word 'plinth'. Even 'the prospect of dressing up as a Mexican wrestler … not the action of dressing up as a Mexican wrestler, but the prospect' (Macmillan 2016: 318) describes a pleasurable feeling experienced in the moment of its thinking: a potentiality in the present rather than something in the future.

The list itself – or a section of it – is distributed at the start of the performance to the audience on scraps of paper, who are instructed to shout out the corresponding entry when their number is reached in the script. As the play progresses, audience members are also called upon to play roles in the story: the narrator's seven-year-old self, the narrator's father and the narrator's partner. If, as Catherine Love's review suggests, the audience's involvement in this manner 'becomes both metaphor and demonstration of how we are able to find collective comfort and joy, acting as a necessary counterpoint to the stark realisation that it is not always possible to make those you love happy' (Love 2014), it also comes to articulate the uncontrollable liabilities which constitute our relationships to one another. The narrator tells us that the children of depressed parents have a 'heightened reactivity to stress' and that the real risk is they might act on 'an absolute crystal clear understanding of why someone would no longer want to continue living' (Macmillan 2016: 316). We learn that (frequently ignored) guidelines for reporting suicide exist because suicide is socially contagious: to feel empathy *for* may be to run the risk of overwhelming identification *with*.

When the narrator's mother eventually kills herself after several further failed attempts, we are told directly: 'The list hadn't stopped her. Hadn't saved her. Of course it hadn't' (Macmillan 2016: 327). *Every Brilliant Thing*'s list-making, in other words, is less about 'saving' a future than an ongoing attempt to discover sustaining attachments in and to the present in the hard knowledge that those attachments may be insufficient. The play's 'really simple advice' for anyone contemplating suicide – 'Don't do it. Things get better. They might not always get brilliant. But they get better' (Macmillan 2016: 311) is followed by the invitation to find brilliance in 'the feeling of calm which follows the realization that, although you may be in a regrettable situation, there's nothing you can do about it' (Macmillan 2016: 318), as if to suggest the vertiginous nature of that grasp on the now. Nonetheless, these attachments may bring sustenance to the extent that they extend a form of solidarity grounded in mutual vulnerability in recognition of the difficult truth that 'we're undone by each other. And if we're not, we're missing something … One does not always stay intact' (Butler 2004: 23).

While *Every Brilliant Thing* offers that 'in order to live in the present we have to be able to imagine a future that will be better than the past' (Macmillan 2016: 291), it also articulates what Ann Cvetkovich has explored as 'a vision of hope and possibility that doesn't foreclose despair and exhaustion' (Cvetkovich 2007: 467). If there is a choice to be made, it is not between the supposed political agency of good feelings over bad but between recognition of the force of those affects and their denial. As Macmillan's narrator observes, 'If you live a long life and get to the end of it without ever once having felt crushingly depressed, then you probably haven't been paying attention' (Macmillan 2016: 327). Consequently, if *Every Brilliant Thing* is available to a reparative reading that finds in its list an 'additive and accretive' habit capable of producing 'resources to offer to an inchoate self' (Sedgwick 1997: 27–8), it is not because it simply refuses hopelessness for hope. It is instead because it figures the work of 'paying attention' as something to be achieved in and for the present.

The labour of optimism: *(I Could Go On Singing) Over The Rainbow*

Key to an understanding of the non-futural qualities of this impulse may be an unwillingness to see the optimist as a heroic, resilient and autonomous figure who extends unilateral gestures of care and succour to others, and to prefer instead a reading of optimism which acknowledges its constitutive vulnerability. Such a reading does not romanticise risk and – as I will explore further below in discussion of Rosana Cade's *Walking:Holding* and Nando Messias' *The Sissy's Progress* – is attentive to differential exposure to the possibility of violence and harm. It remains, though, a reading which emphasises the quality of vulnerability as an impasse: to borrow from Berlant, an experience of the 'stretched-out present' (see 2011: 3–4) bringing a heightened awareness of one's relationship to others. The

terms of such attentiveness may be traced within performance artist FK
Alexander's durational work *(I Could Go On Singing) Over The Rainbow*
(2014), a collaboration with the noise music band Okishima Island Tourist
Association (Lea Cummings and Sarah Glass) centred on repeated, one-to-
one performances of Judy Garland's signature song. Originally presented as
a five-hour installation at Into the New festival at the Arches, Glasgow and
since re-staged for festivals around the UK, Europe and the United States,
the performance emerges from a body of work characterised by task-based
rituals of destruction, endurance and renewal, as in the procedural work
DSTRY YR SLF (2013) in which Alexander burnt and destroyed a range
of personal possessions, and the durational seven-day gallery residency *I
Cannot Cope With The Future* (2017).

Referring to both the song made famous by the soundtrack for
Victor Fleming's film *The Wizard of Oz* (1939) and Garland's final film
I Could Go on Singing (1963) which intercuts dramatic scenes with live
concert numbers, the work's title evokes a mix of late-Depression era nostalgia for an agrarian golden age and late twentieth-century sub-cultural
identifications with Garland as an iconic figure of desire and suffering.[7]
In queer cultural studies, the latter involves a form of utopianism which
imagines a magical kingdom, Oz, in which 'difference and deviation
from the norm are the norm' (Benshoff and Griffin 2006: 68) and where
Dorothy's occupation of the masculine narrative role of the questing
hero resists the quotidian and disciplinary world of heterosexuality
(Pugh 2008: 221–5). Alexander's work, though, does not involve a flight
of imaginary transport to another place but instead invokes a committed
attention to what is clearly now: a queerness which is not on the horizon
but immediately in the room, constituted in the act of performance as
unfinished but nonetheless present business.

My own experience of the work came during the Edinburgh Festival
Fringe in August 2016. When I entered the performance space with the
rest of the audience, Alexander was already present and flanked by the
two members of Okishima Island Tourist Association whose abrasively
loud soundtrack had been audible from outside the venue. On entering,
we had exchanged our box office-issued tickets for a smaller, hand-written
stub reading 'admit one'. On the floor a few feet in front of Alexander was a
black 'x' taped to the floor; when this spot was free, we could step forward
and surrender our stubs in exchange for the song. When the first person
stepped forward, Alexander made eye contact and flashed a warm smile

---

7 For discussions of the links between lesbian and gay identity and Judy Garland, see Dyer
(1986) and Pellegrini (2007), alongside Doty (2000).

before turning to a laptop to trigger the track of Garland's performance. As the long orchestral introduction played, Alexander put on a holster and black sequinned jacket before stepping into ruby red slippers. Taking the microphone and coils of cable in one hand, she stepped back towards the audience member and reached out to take their right hand with her left. After a few final bars, and without ever breaking her gaze, Alexander sang along with – over or beneath – Garland's performance. Though it was difficult to make out the full detail of the song under Okishima Island Tourist Association's barrage of sound, it seemed clear that it was not the iconic film version performed by then teenaged Garland – it was, as I later learnt, a recording of Garland's final concert performance of the song, three months before her death from a drugs overdose at the age of forty-seven.

In form *(I Could Go On Singing)* traces a tension between the seeming generosity of the work – its intensely intimate performance(s) of *Somewhere Over the Rainbow* – and the commercial/professional context of its presentation, with the circulation of a one-to-one encounter within the frame of a more conventional audience–performance relationship drawing attention to the ways in which the value of a live event is compounded by the logic of artificial scarcity. Though buying a ticket guaranteed entry to the room, there was not enough time for everyone in the audience to experience Alexander's performance first-hand. In this context, Alexander's ghosting of Garland's 'original' performance – itself a copy of a lifetime of repeated performances – was broadly understood as a commentary on the artistic labour required to sustain the effect of theatrical presence in an economy of voyeuristic consumption. David Pollock's review for *The Scotsman*, for example, prefaced its praise with the disclaimer that the show was 'more a piece of performance art' in which 'the appreciation is not for the way an artist performs, but the way they repeat the performance night after night, riding the same crests of emotion' (Pollock 2016). Conversely, critic Matt Trueman offered that work initially looked 'a lot like love – two people, eyes locked, oblivious to the roar around them' but became increasingly impersonal with each cycle to reveal 'the demands we make on artists … but also the labour of performance and the hollowness of such encounters' (Trueman 2016b).

Suturing these responses is anxiety for how the experience of what feels like 'real' presence – theorised by Erika Fischer-Lichte as 'radical' presence in which one appears and is perceived as 'embodied mind' (2012: 115) – may be the effect of paranoid relations in which one is not truly present at all. Counter to the logic of Dolan's utopian performative which cites performance's ephemerality as the condition of its efficacy, the constitutive lack of performance comes to foreclose the possibility of a generative encounter, less lifting 'slightly above the present' (Dolan 2005: 5) than collapsing into it. From this reading of the present as a quagmire, one might read the rhetorical flourish of *(I Could Go On Singing)* as invoking a queer utopia that can only be encountered in the moment of the song's performance. At the same time, the structure of the work may enact a form of cruel optimism, figuring a repeated attachment to a performance of intense and exhibitionistic intimacy which comes to impede the possibility of a genuine connection which brought the performer (and audience member) to the scene of the action in the first instance. The limitation of these readings, however, is that they misread the performative citation of repetition as something which can only ever be historical (in the sense of a paranoid gesture which cannot enact a change in the present because it cannot change the past).

Though Alexander's gestures are carefully choreographed, the performance does not take the form of a closed loop – if only for the only obvious reason that the encounter changes each time that a new person steps up to take part. While Alexander's voice became noticeably strained from the effort of continued performance as the hour passed, the work of the performance was also not hers alone: while some (including myself) stood silently, experiencing the sheer proximity of Alexander's voice and gaze, many others sang back or with her, amplifying Garland's performance with their own in renewed – if uncertain – acts of optimistic concert. Indeed, the work is cathartic to the extent that it does not ask one to resolve contradictory feelings of grief and hopefulness, but allows both to be occupied simultaneously. At the same time, the double-frame of the work – the 'inner' performance of standing with Alexander and the 'outer' experience of watching someone else in that encounter – complicated what might have otherwise have resembled Dolan's account of utopian performativity as an experience of collectivity born of communal spectatorship and communal affect. What was striking, instead, was the degree to which being together with others was inflected by the feeling of suspended relation to an intimate exchange of which one was not a part but from which one was not wholly excluded.

Optimism as encounter: *Walking:Holding*

The point of the reading offered above is not to suggest that the figure of the optimist is always haunted by a feeling of individuated paranoia in which any feeling of togetherness is underscored by anxiety that one's inclusion within it is temporary, misplaced and the preface to disappointment. It is, rather, to try and recognise how the political potential of optimism necessarily involves a challenge to the terms of community and togetherness as they are already known to us if it is to do more than merely confirm our expectations of how we might relate to each other. The ways in which performance might invoke the frame of a one-to-one encounter in pursuit of an expansive – or, at least, altered – public sphere of sociability as a domain of precarious potentiality is carried throughout performance artist Rosana Cade's *Walking:Holding*, a experiential performance in which one audience member at a time walks through a town or city with a range of different people on a carefully designed route.[8] Originally devised and staged in Glasgow at the Arches in March 2011, the work has been presented at the National Theatre, as part of Spill National Platform and Showcase, at Forest Fringe and Battersea Arts Centre, as well as to venues in Copenhagen, Lisbon, Zurich and Hong Kong. Each performance has involved local participants acting as handholders who are recruited through an open call and chosen to reflect a broad range of genders, sexualities, races, religions, social backgrounds, abilities, appearances and ages, often drawn from local LGBT communities, though the work's form continues to evolve in response to the given contexts of its staging.

Prompted by Cade's own experiences of public hand-holding – comfortable in London but anxiety-inducing in the small Hertfordshire town where she grew up (Cade 2016a) – the work was originally oriented on having audiences understand a sense of dangerous exposure experienced by many in public spaces but developed to become 'a broader experiment into what can be learnt when two strangers share an intimate moment in public' (Cade quoted in Carolin 2013). While informed by real-world experiences of street harassment, *Walking:Holding* also addresses how the anxiety or discomfort which may accompany showing affection to one's same-sex partner in public (or merely being 'different' from a public norm) does not merely arise from the apprehension of a specific threat but involves 'carrying some kind of internalized fear of the threat because we have grown up in a world that presents us with an idea of normality that is different to what we are, so we carry a sense of abnormality and it grows in our flesh as we touch each other' (Cade 2015). To invoke

---

8 Cade's other solo works include *Lady Fingers and Empire Biscuits* (2014) concerning the legacy of Imperial anti-sodomy laws in India, and club performances as the 'glitter-covered vaginal lip syncing sensation' *Disco Derek* (2014–).

Merleau-Ponty's phenomenological account of the social, 'we are our (habit-based) actions … and it is by virtue of those carnal actions that we take up a position in (and thus also sustain) the social world' (Crossley 1996: 101).

In response, *Walking:Holding* stages a negotiation of exposure, risk, vulnerability and care that is both generative and reparative by inviting its participants to 'take up position' in a manner which challenges the idea that certain spaces or ways of being with others in those spaces are irrevocably dangerous. I took part in *Walking:Holding* in May 2015 as part of the Arches' 'Sexology Season', produced in collaboration with The Wellcome Collection, where the performance began on the busy main concourse of Glasgow Central railway station. Positioned with my back to the platforms, I was invited to close my eyes and take three deep breaths: when I opened my eyes, everything that followed would be part of the performance. A few seconds after opening my eyes, I was approached by a middle-aged woman, perhaps ten or fifteen years older than me, who asked if she could hold my hand and walk with me. We could talk if we wanted to, and talk about whatever came to mind, or walk in silence. I took her hand and we began to walk.

If 'one crucial problem with the conventional line on the flâneur is the idea that he roams the streets untouched' seeing 'windows not mirrors' (Munt 1995: 106), the spatial dramaturgy of *Walking:Holding* repeatedly invites its participant to consider their social and self-image, and the relationship of those images to gender norms. After a short distance walking together, my companion stopped us in front of the window display of a clothes shop filled with masculine dummies in formal-wear, suits and kilts. Looking at ourselves dimly reflected in the glass, my partner asked me what I thought other people thought they had seen as we walked hand-in-hand, and what I thought we looked like. The gap between our ages meant that we did not immediately resemble lovers nor parent and adult child, and the gesture of our intimacy, like the reflection, seemed unclear. As we stood, I saw another performer approach to join our reflected image: a tall man with long hair wearing make-up and a dress. He introduced himself and we walked on together, discussing Edinburgh (where he lived and where I had studied as a student), drag and the challenges of walking in heels on cobbled streets. The route took us from a wide, busy shopping street to a narrow alleyway running between two buildings and I recall a flicker of anxiety that a more private space might expose either one of us to harassment. I later learn from the work's audio documentation that Cade has deliberately planned this route to prompt a feeling of claustrophobia and looming threat.

Figure 17 *Walking:Holding* (Glasgow 2008).

Figure 18 Rosana Cade and Laurie Brown, *Walking:Holding* (Glasgow 2008).

I offer my own recollection of the work at length here for several reasons, central to which is a sense of the demand placed by the work on the audience-participant to act as its instigating performer: the work does not exist outside of a first-person, highly subjective encounter. I also do so to recognise the force of my normative social presentation (my white, largely male-masculine and seeming able-bodiedness) as something which both amplified the sense of security afforded by the frame of the performance and drew my attention to the precarity of that seeming assuredness. On the few occasions that I have been subject to street harassment, I have never known what I was 'showing' which singled me out for attention. At the same time, I am rarely subject to homophobic abuse because of how readily I might resemble a cis-gendered heterosexual man. In the act of holding hands, the social invisibility of my gender-conforming masculinity became a lens for thinking about solidarity and responsibility, with hand-holding becoming the site of a mutual exchange of trust and care. If scholarly considerations of walking often carry an implicitly masculinist orthodoxy which 'frames and valorizes walking as individualist, heroic, epic and transgressive' (Heddon and Turner

2012: 224), *Walking:Holding* prompts an understanding of walking as a mode of encounter with difference and potential exposure to change rather than autonomous resilience.[9]

Attuned to the immediacy of the street scene, the mode of optimism figured in *Walking:Holding*'s participant flâneur may also be understood in the terms of a prefigurative politics which proceeds by 'removing the temporal distinction between the struggle in the present and a goal in the future' (Maeckelbergh 2011: 4), as the theatrical frame which emboldens hand-holding is necessarily one of encounter with the normative conditions of the world as it stands. In the work's audio documentation, Cade narrates the experiences of one hand-holder during the staging of *Walking:Holding* in Edinburgh's Leith district whose section of the route took them through a large branch of the supermarket chain Tesco, and who was barred from the premises when security guards decided that his appearance in women's clothing was 'highly suspicious' and threatened to call the police. For the rest of the day, the obstruction became part of the performance, with the hand-holder taking each audience member up to the door of the supermarket, explaining what had happened and then taking them on a different route. This episode is juxtaposed with another story in which Cade describes arriving in Dublin to stage *Walking:Holding* only a week after two gay men had been violently assaulted in the city centre, and discovering a sense of resignation in the gay community that it would never be possible to engage in public displays of affection without harassment. It was, then, transformative for members of that community to take part in the work without experiencing abuse: 'it broke a threshold: they held hands with another man and nothing bad happened' (Cade 2015). Both episodes may be considered optimistic – albeit in different ways – because they involve a present-tenseness which challenges a view of the world as only ever one thing, and point to how the structures which serve to keep the world in place are the result of human choices rather than irrevocable facts.

In framing *Walking:Holding* as an intervention in public space, Cade cites Henri Lefebvre's claim that '(social) space is a (social) product', a tool of thought and action as well as a means of control 'and hence of domination, of power' (Lefebvre 1991: 26), with the consequence that sociability itself becomes a register of action. Though the work may pursue what Cade has more recently described as 'radical softness', a political act constituted by 'being caring and offering yourself, making

9 For further walking works exploring similar dynamics, see Fiona Templeton's *YOU – The City* (1988) and Janet Cardiff's *Her Long Black Hair* (2004).

yourself vulnerable' (quoted in Wyver 2016), it does so in recognition
of the differential forms of agency and exposure to risk that might be
involved. While working with visual artist Kate Shields on *The Safety
Map*, an artistic and community-rooted response to anti-social behaviour faced by LGBTQ people on the streets of Brighton & Hove, Cade
averred the necessity of *Walking:Holding*'s public staging of visible
difference while observing that she spoke from a position of having
experienced verbal abuse but never violent assault, and in consciousness
of the potential long-term effects of homophobic violence extending
long beyond any single event (Cade 2016b). Whatever precautions Cade
might take as the creator and facilitator of the work, participation in
Walking:Holding involves a measure of exposure whose consequences
cannot be fully anticipated in advance.

Yet it is, perhaps paradoxically, the impossibility of knowing which
confirms the work's encounter with and within the public sphere as an
ethical one, insofar as it requires its participants to acknowledge how
their accountability to each other might be the site of their undoing. Such
thinking evokes the terms of Butler's *Giving an Account of Oneself* (2005)
in which she argues that the first condition of subjectivity is dispossess-
sion, as 'the very terms by which we give an account, by which we make
ourselves intelligible to ourselves and to others, are not of our making'
(Butler 2005: 21). The other to whom we address ourselves is similarly
opaque to itself, and the question of ethical relation takes the form of
the encounter between the two in knowledge of this mutual opacity of
self. *Walking:Holding* might elaborate that dynamic in the sense that the
forms of mutual recognition and care that the work might enable are
constituted in a state of dispossession in which holding hands in public
amplifies the surrender of oneself to terms of recognition which are not
properly one's own.

Optimism as vulnerability: *The Sissy's Progress*

One difficulty with this reading, though, may be how it risks conflating
the 'kinds of injury that are socially contingent and avoidable, and
kinds of subordination that are, as it were, the constitutive condition
of the subject' (Butler 1997b: 26). Nonetheless, if there is value in such

a distinction, it involves recognition of how one form of injury relates to and may serve to amplify or – crucially – ameliorate the other. Such potential does not demand self-sacrifice but rather an encounter with the limit conditions of one's self intended to transform those conditions: it is a form of tactical dispossession which acknowledges, paradoxically, that dispossession is not merely a matter of choice. The terms of such a process may be traced within a sequence of works by London-based Brazilian performance artist, choreographer and theatre academic Nando Messias – *Sissy!* (2008), *Walking Failure* (2011), *The Sissy's Progress* (2014) and *Shoot the Sissy* (2016) – begun during their practice-based PhD at the Royal Central School of Speech and Drama, and following a violent transphobic assault near their home in east London in 2005. Drawing on live art, dance and queer movement vocabularies, Messias' work has appeared in venues including the Hayward Gallery, the Royal Vauxhall Tavern and Tate Britain, and internationally at the City of Women Festival in Ljubljana, Slovenia and New York City's Abrons Art Center.

In *The Sissy's Progress*, the performance action is split between a theatre space and the street, beginning with a sequence of stylised movements performed alone on stage,

> a choreography of gestural motifs that are repeated, built upon, exaggerated. Legs extend and return; hands run down the face or the body; the face moves into anguished poses, then recovers; the hairpins are pulled out, and the hair tugged and tormented. The body slumps over and is wrenched up. It is intense, and at moments it is close to painting a picture of self-abuse. (Prior 2016)

Messias performs naked but for underwear and red lipstick – a strategy intended to establish complicity between performer and audience and evidence 'the material vulnerability of my body, which the audience is about to witness for themselves on the streets' (Messias 2016a: 288). Joined by five men in tuxedos, Messias' 'sissy' body is thrown into contrast as they (literally) man-handle the performer into a long ball-gown.

Adorned with a floating train of coloured balloons, Messias then leaves the theatre for the street with the audience following at distance beyond and accompanied by the suited men who form a marching band whose music draws more and more attention to the performer's 'dramatically feminine' (Messias 2016a: 290) comportment. Having found themselves both unable to 'correct' their walk (having experimented with doing so in the rehearsal studio) and unwilling to change their social presentation (as recommended by the police officer who investigated their assault), Messias' self-staging enacts a form of hyper-visibility which proceeds by inverting the logic of 'passing' to demand attention. This action marks the rejection of strategies of concealment which are premised on self-censorship and, in Messias' experience, hardly ever successful: it is a theatricalised, overt rendition of feminine-masculinity which paradoxically belies the voluntariness of gender performance. Though framed by Messias as 'a public act of denunciation against hate crime through the mode of performance … a hyperbolic statement, an artistic protest that needed to be made precisely where the original attack had taken place: on the streets themselves' (Messias 2016b), the form of resistance enacted by *The Sissy's Progress* is not straightforwardly affirmative, and the work closes in a pillorying scene in which Messias is drenched with water – an image explored at length in *Shoot The Sissy* in which audience members are called upon to pelt the sissy 'who feels no pain' with fake snow, glitter-filled eggshells and rather harder tomatoes.

While early performances near the Toynbee studios where Messias had been attacked were marked by incidents of verbal abuse, the theatricality of those moments unsettled their meaning without necessarily evacuating their force: 'As I turned the corner, these three boys saw me and started to shout abuse. Then they saw the musicians behind me and the audience behind them and they were quite taken aback' (Messias quoted in Groves 2016). Following at distance from Messias in the wake of their reception but at remove from its focus, the audience is framed as both passive onlookers and guarantors of the performer's safety – or, more to the point, as potentially both, a juxtaposition which may prompt the disquieting realisation that the conditions of theatrical witness may be highly compatible with the conditions of social alibi. As one reviewer suggested:

> We are witness to staring, gawking, verbal and even physical abuse. We get a fraction of the experience of living in the sissy body. We get sissy by proxy. Sissy adjacent. Well, for those who aren't sissies themselves, anyway. (Tomrley 2016)

If we are sissy or queer ourselves, we may also experience a flash of guilty relief that someone else is bearing the brunt of unwelcome attention; we might also privately reassure ourselves that someone else will intervene if something goes wrong, and that the frame of the theatrical encounter will stop things from becoming too real – all of which is to say that the performative staging of togetherness is not one in which co-presence automatically gives rise to solidarity. It is instead a form of being-with-others characterised by a pluralising instability akin to Esposito's

Figure 19 Nando Messias, *The Sissy's Progress* (London, 2014).

understanding of community as an exposure to a 'risky continguity with the other' (Esposito 2013: 4), here figured in the material vulnerability of the performer and the uncertain cast of responsibilities for that body. It is that uncertainty which provokes a re-examination of the assumed terms of liberal community – imagined as accessible and welcoming to all but characterised by exclusions, exceptions and the persistently uneven distribution of risk for participation in the social.

Common to both *Walking:Holding* and *The Sissy's Progress* is a desire to respond to the social conditions of the real world as they exist in the present moment, in large part because there is no alternative but the present and because a response to violence and the threat of violence cannot be postponed. In their recent chapbook *Before I Step Outside (You Love Me)* (2017), queer performance artist Travis Alabanza describes the ritual of taking a selfie before stepping outside to 'remind myself of how I looked in that moment. To archive my existence before physical danger'. Though to be black, trans and femme is to face a continual assault course of public harassment, Alabanza's text acknowledges the desire for 'something easier' in order to underscore the affirmation that 'before you step outside, that there are others stepping too. That people have stepped before us, with us, and will step after us ... That we have existed before,

and exist in the present, and will exist in the future' (Alabanza 2017).[10]
While the present may not be enough because it is toxic and insolvent, it
is the only available site of political action, and one with which one may
have no choice but to engage. Messias writes:

> Despite the potential for pessimism and fear, I hold onto the notion that
> 'utopia lets us imagine a space outside of heteronormativity' (Muñoz
> 2009: 35). This is the space I must find. I am taking to the streets. (2016a: 288)

That 'outside' is not an unreachable place in time but something to be
found with the literal immediacy of stepping through a door. Here, the
imperative 'must' does not cathect to action through heroic resilience but
instead to a sense of vulnerability which is a necessary and unavoidable
condition of human sociability and, moreover, social change. As Butler
concludes, 'we must recognize that ethics requires us to risk ourselves
precisely at moments of unknowingness, when what forms us diverges
from what lies before us, when our willingness to becomes undone in
relation to others constitutes our chance of becoming human' (Butler
2005: 136). Such an ethics must also acknowledge – though – that such
moments of unknowingness are not simply a matter of choice, and that
the consequences of 'becoming undone' remain inequitable.

Conclusion

I began this chapter by questioning some of the arguments made in relation to ideas of utopia, futurity and performance in concern for the ways
in which such thinking seems to defer what might be possible in the present – either in mistrust of the conditions in which we find ourselves,
or in preference for a promise which cannot be failed because its fulfilment is (constitutively) out of reach. A consequence of this argument
has been to suggest how queerness – here understood as an opening up
of the possibilities for being human – might be experienced in the present tense without such experience totalising what else queerness might
stand for or achieve: rather than resolving that queerness is only ever on
the horizon, we might understand how queerness is here but unfinished.

---

10 Alabanza's solo performance works include the autobiographical *Stories of a Queer
   Brown Muddy Kid* (2015) and the in-development *Burgerz* (2017/18). See http://
   travisalabanza.co.uk/, accessed 26 January 2018.

Doing so involves an acknowledgement of optimism's difficult relationship to agency – such as that the figure of the optimist traces the attempt to occupy the present even as one is pulled towards a future that seems wholly out of one's control. Correspondingly, the figure of the optimist suggests the breadth of reparative practices by which we might embrace 'the surprises brought by the unknowability of the future (and indeed of the past and the present)' (Stacey 2014: 40) without recourse to a calculus of agency opposed to involuntariness, and do so in a manner that acknowledges how reparation and paranoia may be co-extensive. What the figure of the optimist allows, then, is recognition of a politics which does not accept the difficulty of being in the present as grounds that a project of transformation must be postponed. It is a politics which understands that the conditions of exceptionality are not permanent or all-encompassing, but riven with opportunity for change – not least because the proof of alternatives is already manifest in the present.

Conclusion

In thinking about the relationship between queer politics and aspirational hopes for a good life, Sara Ahmed reads the term 'aspiration' to describe how the struggle for a bearable life is the struggle 'for queers to have space to breathe ... With breath comes imagination. With breath comes possibility' (2010: 120). The breath of aspiration, though, is also something which undeniably unfurls in present time and space: if breathing brings possibility it is because it marks the operation of alternative ways of being, however tenuous, in the here and now. That promise – and its difficulties – are given literal form in theatre-maker Chris Goode's *Keep Breathing* (2011) in which he invited members of the public to contribute a message for the world that could be spoken in the length of a single breath.[1] Commissioned by Drum Theatre Plymouth and later staged at Stoke Newington International Airport arts venue as part of London Word Festival and UK tour, the show offers a mix of intimately personal and sometimes strongly political detail that makes 'a quiet, unagitated case for activism, especially in relation to local issues' (Goode 2015: 214). At the heart of the work is a conceit drawn from the work of

---

1 Goode's solo shows as performer include *Hippo World Guest Book* (2007), *The Adventures of Wound Man and Shirley* (2009) and the Fringe First-winning *Men in the Cities* (2014). For a recording of *Keep Breathing* at Drum Theatre, Plymouth, in November 2011, see https://vimeo.com/channels/295101/35954313, accessed 6 May 2016.

the American astronomer Harlow Shapley concerning the unavoidable interconnectedness of the act of breathing: though the element of argon forms less than 1 per cent of the atmosphere, trace amounts of the gas contained in a single exhaled breath will become dispersed around the world to all breathable air within a single year. A breath taken a year after the first will still carry a minute trace – at least fifteen atoms – of that original breath. Goode explains:

> You've breathed argon atoms that were in the first little gasp of every baby born on earth a year ago. Your next breath will contain more than 400,000 atoms breathed by Ghandi – that's the example [Shapley] uses, but whoever … seriously, anyone. So who do you miss right now? If you check? Take a breath. As you breathe it in, argon that person once breathed is entering your body. Once it was in them, now it's inside you. Tomorrow it'll be inside someone you've never met in a place you've never been. (Goode 2011)

The show is optimistic – telling stories of resistance, hope, encounter and collective action – but also riven with loss, as if to know the possibility of aspiration is to understand how we are undone by each other, by chance, by time and by the habit that we look no further than our own interests despite our best intentions. It is a show in which optimism – recalling the arguments of the previous chapter – does not ask us to choose between good feelings and bad, but to decide how we might sit with those affects and through them find the grounds, the will and the means for change.

In this book, I have sought to describe how contemporary solo performance's engagement with the demands and conditions of neo-liberalism illuminate a range of possibilities for resistance and critique. That ambition has been served by a figural logic, such as that it has become possible to better understand the ecology of contemporary arts festivals (for example) by focusing on the figure of the entrepreneurial artist whose appetite for singular reward rationalises a deeply uneven distribution of risk. That same figure allows us to better understand the implications of pursuing alternative, experimental and co-operative forms of artistic production – both for creators and for their audiences. In turning to the martyr, pariah, killjoy, stranger and misfit, I have offered readings in which performance intervenes in naturalised configurations of the social to expose selective, exclusionary and precarious distributions of sub-jectivity and personhood – in plainer language, how some are accorded inherent value while others are required to fulfil certain conditions in order to qualify (and must then live in the knowledge that such tenuous recognition may be withdrawn without notice). The final move to con-sider the optimist has involved a slightly different kind of critique – one less consciously paranoid in its analysis of hidden structures of power that instead attends to alternatives which already exist in the here and now. In each case, it is the gap between the figure – marking the nexus of an array of desires, expectations and norms – and the specificity of individual artists' practices which has allowed me to follow where regulatory logics proper to neoliberalism fall short, are disputed, or have already been contested.

Seeing that gap has required a willingness to view neoliberalism as a dominant rather than totalising framework, and as one which requires our participation to function and sustain itself. Reflecting the most optimistic aspects of Agamben's work, this analysis may contribute to the argument that we might only need to 'subtract' ourselves from existing apparatuses of sovereignty and governmentality: a logic of radical transformation 'that draws its resources solely from the condition it denounces, the condition in which we have nothing to lose' (Prozorov 2010: 1060). Nonetheless, the performances explored here clearly indicate how the forms of agency which render any such 'subtraction' imaginable are carefully reserved and how the consequences of risk are unevenly distributed: some are already more exposed than others to the threats of privation and violence. Though we might take seriously Foucault's observation that 'there is no binary and all-encompassing opposition between rulers and ruled at the root of power relations, and serving as a general matrix' (1978: 94), the solo performances encountered here provide an account of the still persistent hierarchies of value that contour the possible recognition of difference, and signal how such ordering is the intended outcome (rather than unfortunate side-effect) of neoliberal economies oriented on the production of difference as a technology of power and commercial value.

While frequently committed to addressing and voicing the experiences and perspectives of marginalised lives, the works explored in this book also describe a renewed negotiation of the relationships that might exist between the personal and the political. One of the recurrent concerns of the body of performance described here is for how singular individuality may take the form of a duty in which possibilities for self-definition and self-recognition become yoked to neoliberalism's preference – if not demand – for autonomous individuals making 'free' and 'responsible' choices regardless of the structural or biographical conditions which might constrain their ability to act. In this context, the possibility of recognition – the goal of so much second and third wave liberal activism – takes on a deeply ambivalent quality, wherein misrecognition may be the deliberate outcome of punitive, regulatory frameworks and simultaneously contain radical, alternative possibilities for being seen and heard. Solo performance brings these tensions to light and subjects them to ethical scrutiny – whether in resistance of the demand for sociable happiness as in discussion of the killjoy, to present oneself as the right kind of proto-European subject as in discussion of the stranger, or to comport oneself as a properly contained body as in discussion of the misfit. Crucially, these interventions do not abandon a claim on the detail of individual lives and experiences but invite us to re-imagine sociability and the social, and the ways in which we may be accountable to and for each other.

Emerging from this study is a queer analytic in which a relationality 'vis-à-vis the normative' – as in David Halperin's often-cited formulation – is not exclusively determined by opposition to whatever is 'the normal, the legitimate, the dominant' (Halperin 1995: 62). It describes instead a relationality characterised by complicity, exchange, contact and – per Esposito – contamination. Uncoupling queerness from opposition – and from what Nikolas Rose describes as the political calculus of domination versus liberation (1999: 95) – is valuable because it might serve to resist a regulatory queerness that insists on transgression as a barometer of individual choice and freedom. Readily compatible with neoliberal priorities, such a vision of queerness is problematic because – as Jasbir Puar observes – it conflates resistance with agency, and because it relies 'on a normative notion of deviance, always defined in relation to normativity, often universalising' (2007: 23). Rather than reinvesting in 'liberal humanism's authorization of the fully self-possessed speaking subject' (Puar 2007: 22), this book's rendition of queer exceptionality has pursued an account of politicised subjects whose questionable agency and precarious personhood allows us to re-examine what resistance might look like, and the forms of intervention that it might engender. Where neoliberalism describes responsibility assigned to proper subjects, a discourse of queer exceptionality finds uncertain and uncontrollable liability: in place of autonomous sovereignty (or the expectation to conduct oneself as though one had the qualities of the same), it finds exposure, vulnerability and the prospect of an undoing of the self which discovers the chance to be moved and to move in return. In place of opposition, it describes forms of complicit antagonism and wounded attachment which do not preclude the possibility of change but advertise more clearly how a better world cannot be imagined outside of our present involvement in the world as it stands.

In his manifesto and polemic *The Forest and the Field* (2015), Goode takes issue with claims that theatre is incapable of changing the world: not only do we not have a 'control' world absent theatre with which to compare this one but 'not all the results are in yet. We haven't made all the theatre yet. We've barely begun to make theatre that knows how to situate itself in relation to the brutal degrading tyrannies of liminoid capitalism' (Goode 2015: 209). The sensation of not knowing how or where to start may be compounded by many theatre and performance institutions whose own priorities rest in sustaining patterns of labour and responsibility for risk in which creative entrepreneurialism engages individuals in the 'free' conduct of protecting the status quo. To return to an observation offered in the Introduction, performance is not inherently radical or transformative and the dominant conditions of performance-making may serve to exacerbate rather than address the dynamics of neoliberalism encountered in this volume. Nonetheless, Goode proposes that

> we can insist that the question of theatre changing the world is in some degree redundant, because we know these two other things to be true: that in theatre – more clearly in theatre that knows it is incorporative – we can act, consequentially; and the world is changing anyway. (Goode 2015: 210)

Nothing is only ever one thing, and neoliberalism – fiercely attached to difference as though to its own immune system – is many things at once, each of which may be open to the possibility of replacement or change.

REFERENCES

Aarhus2017. 2016. Enestående Solo Performance Festival. www.aarhus2017.dk/en/calendar/stand-alone-solo-performance-festival/8304/, accessed 22 March 2017.

Abbing, Hans. 2014. Notes on the Exploitation of Poor Artists, in Jan Sowa and Agnieszka Kurant (eds) *Joy Forever: The Political Economy of Social Creativity*. London: MayFly Books.

Adler, Patricia A. and Peter Adler. 2011. *The Tender Cut: Inside the Hidden World of Self-Injury*. New York: New York University Press.

Adshead, Kay. 2001. *The Bogus Woman*. London: Oberon Books.

Agamben, Giorgio. 1993. *The Coming Community*. Michael Hardt (trans). Minneapolis: University of Minnesota Press.

Agamben, Giorgio. 1998. *Homo Sacer: Sovereign Power and Bare Life*. Daniel Heller-Roazen (trans). Stanford: Stanford University Press.

Agamben, Giorgio. 2005. *State of Exception*. Kevin Attell (trans). Chicago: University of Chicago Press.

Ahmed, Sara. 2000a. *Strange Encounters: Embodied Others in Post-Coloniality*. London and New York: Routledge.

Ahmed, Sara. 2000b. Who Knows? Knowing Strangers and Strangerness. *Australian Feminist Studies* 15: 31, 49–68.

Ahmed, Sara. 2004. *The Cultural Politics of Emotion*. Edinburgh: Edinburgh University Press.

Ahmed, Sara. 2006. *Queer Phenomenology: Orientations, Objects, Others*. Durham, NC: Duke University Press.

Ahmed, Sara. 2010. *The Promise of Happiness*. Durham, NC: Duke University Press.

Ajderian, Jenni. 2015. Free Fringe: Stuart Goldsmith and Caroline Mabey. *The Skinny*. www.theskinny.co.uk/festivals/edinburgh-fringe/comedy/free-fringe-stuart-goldsmith-caroline-mabey, accessed 25 March 2017.

Alabanza, Travis. 2017. *Before I Step Outside (You Love Me)*. London.

Aldarondo, Cecilia. 2012. Loving Franko B. *The New Inquiry*. http://thenewinquiry.com/essays/loving-franko-b/, accessed 19 March 2017.

Allan, Clare. 2000. Pull Yourself Together, in Adrian Heathfield (ed.) *Small Acts: Performance, the Millennium and the Marking of Time*. London: Black Dog.

Aly, Waleed. 2014. Can a Joke about Rape ever be Funny? www.abc.net.au/radionational/ programs/drive/drawing-room/5235606, accessed 7 July 2016.

American Theatre Wing. 2016. Working in the Theatre: White Rabbit Red Rabbit. www. youtube.com/watch?v=SEAH4Vrfb8U, accessed 20 April 2017.

Andrew Lloyd Webber Foundation. 2016. *Centre Stage: The Pipeline of BAME Talent*. http:// andrewlloydwebberfoundation.com/downloads/centre-stage-the-pipeline-of-bame-talent.pdf, accessed 15 May 2017.

Apple, R. W. 1981. Mrs. Thatcher Says Death of Sands Won't Alter London's Ulster Policy. *New York Times*, 6 May.

Araniello, Katherine. 2013. Pity. www.araniello-art.com/PITY, accessed 24 April 2017.

Arendt, Hannah. 1944. The Jew as Pariah: A Hidden Tradition. *Jewish Social Studies* 6: 2, 99–122.

Arendt, Hannah. 1951. *The Origins of Totalitarianism*. New York: Schocken Books.

Arendt, Hannah. 1978. *The Jew as Pariah: Jewish Identity and Politics in the Modern Age*. New York: Grove Press.

ARTICLE 19. 2006. *Unveiled: Art and Censorship in Iran*. www.article19.org/data/files/ pdfs/publications/iran-art-censorship.pdf, accessed 1 May 2016.

ArtsAdmin. 2013. Let's Talk About the Money. www.artsadmin.co.uk/blog/198/let-s-talk-about-the-money-artsfunding, accessed 22 March 2017.

ArtsAdminUK. 2014. Money Talks – Scottee. www.youtube.com/watch?v=GMGgtJERtzI, accessed 19 March 2017.

ArtsProfessional. 2011. Queer Up North Goes South. www.artsprofessional.co.uk/news/ queer-north-goes-south, accessed 25 March 2017.

Arts Council England. 2009. *Theatre Assessment 2009*. London.

Arts Council England. 2016. *Equality, Diversity and the Creative Case, 2015–16*. London.

Ashery, Oreet. 2010a. Making Staying. *Artangel*. www.artangel.org.uk/staying/making-staying/, accessed 17 April 2017.

Ashery, Oreet. 2010b. *Staying: Dream, Bin, Soft Stud and Other Stories*. London: Artangel.

Aston, Elaine. 2003. The 'Bogus Woman': Feminism and Asylum Theatre. *Modern Drama* 46: 1, 5–21.

Aston, Elaine and Geraldine Harris. 2012. *A Good Night Out for the Girls: Popular Feminisms in Contemporary Theatre*. Basingstoke: Palgrave Macmillan.

Athanasiou, Athena and Judith Butler. 2013. *Dispossession: The Performative in the Political*. Cambridge: Polity Press.

Athey, Ron. 2013. Gifts of the Spirit, in Dominic Johnson (ed.) *Pleading in the Blood: The Art and Performances of Ron Athey*. London and Bristol: Live Art Development Agency and Intellect.

Austin, Julia. 2010. Better Than Therapy: Alter Ego Performance and Being-Togetherness, in *Staying: Dream, Bin, Soft Stud and Other Stories*. London: Artangel.

Baker, Bobby. 2008. *How to Live*. DVD. London: Artsadmin.

Baker, Roger. 1994. *Drag: A History of Female Impersonation in the Performing Arts*. New York: New York University Press.

Ballou, Hannah. 2013. Pretty Funny: Manifesting a Normatively Sexy Female Comic Body. *Comedy Studies* 4: 2, 179–86.

Bamford, Kiff. 2012. *Lyotard and the 'Figural' in Performance, Art and Writing*. London: Bloomsbury.

Bankey, Ruth. 2001. La Donna é Mobile: Constructing the Irrational Woman. *Gender, Place & Culture* 8: 1, 37–54.

Bano, Tim. 2015. Iphigenia in Splott. *Exeunt Magazine*. http://exeuntmagazine.com/ reviews/iphigenia-in-splott/, accessed 19 March 2017.

Barker, Kristin K. 2014. Mindfulness Meditation: Do-It-Yourself Medicalization of Every Moment. *Social Science and Medicine* 106, 168–76.

Barrett, Billy. 2014. The Worst of Scottee – More Than a Mirror-Wank. *A Younger Theatre.* www.ayoungertheatre.com/feature-the-worst-of-scottee-more-than-a-mirror-wank/, accessed 19 March 2017.

Barrett, Michèle and Bobby Baker (eds). 2007. *Bobby Baker: Redeeming Features of Daily Life.* London and New York: Routledge.

Bartlett, Neil. 1990. A Vision of Love Revealed in Sleep (Part Three), in Michael Wilcox (ed.) *Gay Plays: Volume Four.* London: Methuen Drama.

Bartlett, Neil. 2005. A Vision of Love Revealed in Sleep (Part One), in *Solo Voices: Monologues 1987–2004.* London: Oberon Books.

Bartlett, Neil. 2012. *Queer Voices.* London: Oberon Books.

Bartlett, Neil. 2016. *Stella.* London: Oberon Books.

Battersea Arts Centre. 2013. The Way We Work with Artists. www.bac.org.uk/resources/0000/0762/The_way_we_work_with_artists.pdf, accessed 27 April 2017.

Bauman, Zygmunt. 1990. Modernity and Ambivalence. *Theory, Culture & Society* 7: 2, 143–69.

Bauman, Zygmunt. 1995. Making and Unmaking of Strangers. *Thesis Eleven* 43: 1, 1–16.

Bauman, Zygmunt. 2001. *The Individualized Society.* Cambridge: Polity Press.

Bauman, Zygmunt. 2005. *Liquid Life.* Cambridge: Polity Press.

Bauman, Zygmunt. 2013. *Liquid Modernity.* Cambridge: Polity Press.

BBC Arts. 2015. Nine Lives: The Horrors of the Asylum Process Laid Bare. www.bbc.co.uk/programmes/articles/1CqjT55ns6KYN8TWF7JqWJZ/nine-lives-the-horrors-of-the-asylum-process-laid-bare, accessed 15 May 2017.

Beck, Ulrich. 2004. Cosmopolitical Realism: On the Distinction between Cosmopolitanism in Philosophy and the Social Sciences. *Global Networks* 4: 2, 131–56.

Beck, Ulrich and Elisabeth Beck-Gernsheim, 2002. *Individualisation: Institutionalized Individualism and Its Social and Political Consequences.* London: SAGE.

Beck-Gernsheim, Elisabeth. 2011. The Marriage Route to Migration: Of Border Artistes, Transnational Matchmaking and Imported Spouses. *Nordic Journal of Migration Research* 1: 2, 60–8.

Bennett, Andy, Jodie Taylor and Ian Woodward (eds). 2014. *The Festivalization of Culture.* London and New York: Routledge.

Benshoff, Harry M. and Sean Griffin. 2006. *Queer Images: A History of Gay and Lesbian Film in America.* Lanham: Rowman & Littlefield.

Berg, Laurie and Jenni Millbank. 2009. Constructing the Personal Narratives of Lesbian, Gay and Bisexual Asylum Claimants. *Journal of Refugee Studies* 22: 2, 195–223.

Berlant, Lauren. 1988. The Female Complaint. *Social Text* 19/20, 237–59.

Berlant, Lauren. 2011. *Cruel Optimism.* Durham, NC and London: Duke University Press.

Bersani, Leo. 1987. Is the Rectum a Grave? *October* 43, 197–222.

Bersani, Leo. 1995. *Homos.* Cambridge, MA: Harvard University Press.

Billington, Michael. 2002. Why I Hate the Fringe. *Guardian.* www.theguardian.com/culture/2002/jul/25/artsfeatures.edinburghfestival20021, accessed 25 March 2017.

Bird, Greg and Jonathan Short. 2013. Community, Immunity and the Proper: An Introduction to the Political Theory of Roberto Esposito. *Angelaki* 18: 3, 1–12.

Bishop, Claire. 2012. *Artificial Hells: Participatory Art and the Politics of Spectatorship.* London and New York: Verso Books.

Bissenbakker Frederiksen, M. M. 2014. How to Bring Your Daughter Up to be a Feminist Killjoy: Shame, Accountability and the Necessity of Paranoid Reading in Lene Kaaberbøl's The Shamer Chronicles. *European Journal of Women's Studies* 25: 1, 102–15.

Blackman, Lisa. 2011. Affect, Performance and Queer Subjectivities. *Cultural Studies* 25: 2, 183–99.

Bloch, Alice and Liza Schuster. 2005. At the Extremes of Exclusion: Deportation, Detention and Dispersal. *Ethnic and Racial Studies* 28: 3, 491–512.

Bockman, Johanna. 2013. Neoliberalism. *Contexts* 12: 3, 14–15.

Bonney, Jo (ed.). 2000. *Extreme Exposure: An Anthology of Solo Performance Texts from the Twentieth Century.* New York: Theatre Communications Group.

Bordo, Susan. 1993. *Unbearable Weight*. Berkeley: University of California Press.

Bottoms, Stephen. 2006. Putting the Document into Documentary: An Unwelcome Corrective? *TDR: The Drama Review* 50: 3, 56–68.

Bouchard, Gianna. 2012. Skin Deep: Female Flesh in UK Live Art since 1999. *Contemporary Theatre Review* 22: 1, 94–105.

Bourdieu, Pierre. 1984. *Distinction: A Social Critique of the Judgement of Taste*. Richard Nice (trans). Cambridge, MA: Harvard University Press.

Boyarin, Daniel, Daniel Itzkovitz and Ann Pellegrini (eds). 2003. *Queer Theory and the Jewish Question*. New York: Columbia University Press.

Brand, Ira. 2016. *Forest Fringe: The First Ten Years*. London: Oberon Books.

Brand, Ira. 2017. To New Directions. *Forest Fringe*. http://forestfringe.co.uk/2017/06/05/to-new-directions/, accessed 15 June 2017.

Braun, Virginia. 2009. 'The women are doing it for themselves': The Rhetoric of Choice and Agency around Female Genital 'Cosmetic Surgery'. *Australian Feminist Studies* 24: 60, 233–49.

Brewis, Becky. 2014. Scottee on Image. *IdeasTap*. www.ideastap.com/IdeasMag/the-knowledge/scottee-on-image-spoken-word, accessed 19 March 2017.

Briggs, Kenneth. 1981. Catholic Church Endeavours To Put Hunger Strikers in Perspective. *New York Times*, 8 June.

Brindley, Michael. 2014. The Worst of Scottee. *Stage Whispers*. www.stagewhispers.com.au/reviews/worst-scottee-0, accessed 19 March 2017.

British Arts Festivals Association. 2008. *Festivals Mean Business 3: A Survey of Arts Festivals in the UK*. London.

Brittain, Jon and Matt Tedford. 2015. *Margaret Thatcher Queen of Soho*. London: Methuen Drama.

Brockes, Emma. 2014. Adrienne Truscott: The Naked Comic. *Guardian*. www.theguardian.com/culture/2014/jan/01/adrienne-truscott-naked-comic-standup, accessed 29 March 2017.

Brooklyn Museum. 2010. Global Feminisms: Tanja Ostojic. www.youtube.com/watch?v=6Z0GvRR36TU, accessed 21 April 2017.

Brouillette, Sarah. 2009. Creative Labor. *Mediations* 24: 2, 140–9.

Brown, Brian J. and Sally Baker. 2012. *Responsible Citizens: Individuals, Health, and Policy Under Neoliberalism*. London and New York: Anthem Press.

Brown, Jonathan. 2009. Artist to Have an Epileptic Fit Live on Stage. *Independent*. www.independent.co.uk/arts-entertainment/art/news/artist-to-have-an-epileptic-fit-live-on-stage-1824122.html, accessed 29 June 2017.

Brown, Wendy. 1995. *States of Injury: Power and Freedom in Late Modernity*. Princeton: Princeton University Press.

Brown, Wendy. 2006. *Regulating Aversion: Tolerance in the Age of Identity and Empire*. Princeton: Princeton University Press.

Bruno, Sean and Luke Dixon. 2015. *Creating Solo Performance*. London and New York: Routledge.

Bryson, Mary K. and Jackie Stacey. 2013. Cancer Knowledge in the Plural: Queering the Biopolitics of Narrative and Affective Mobilities. *Journal of Medical Humanities* 34: 2, 197–212.

Bucholtz, Mary and Kira Hall. 2004. Theorizing Identity in Language and Sexuality Research. *Language in Society* 33, 469–515.

Burt, Ramsay. 2008. Preferring to Laugh. *Parallax* 14: 1, 15–23.

Butler, Judith. 1993. *Bodies That Matter: On the Discursive Limits of 'Sex'*. London and New York: Routledge.

Butler, Judith. 1997a. *The Psychic Life of Power: Theories in Subjection*. Stanford: Stanford University Press.

Butler, Judith. 1997b. *Excitable Speech: A Politics of the Performative*. London and New York: Routledge.

Butler, Judith. 2003. Violence, Mourning, Politics. *Studies in Gender and Sexuality* 4: 1, 9–37.
Butler, Judith. 2004. *Undoing Gender*. London and New York: Routledge.
Butler, Judith. 2005. *Giving an Account of Oneself*. New York: Fordham University Press.
Butler, Judith. 2009. *Frames of War: When is Life Grievable?* London and New York: Verso.
Butt, Gavin. 2007. Just a Camp Laugh? David Hoyle's 'Magazine'. www.tate.org.uk/context-comment/video/identity-and-performativity-study-day-video-recordings#open 260563, accessed 23 April 2017.
Butt, Gavin. 2008. Hoyle's Humility. *Dance Theatre Journal* 23: 1, 30–4.
Butt, Gavin. 2013. Just a Camp Laugh? David Hoyle's Laden Levity, in Irit Rogoff and Gavin Butt (eds) *Visual Cultures as Seriousness*. London: Sternberg Press.
BUZZCUT and LADA. 2016. Pay What You Can. Information leaflet. Glasgow.
Byron, Glennis. 2003. *Dramatic Monologue*. London and New York: Routledge.
Cade, Rosana. 2015. Walking Holding. *SoundCloud*. https://soundcloud.com/rosana-cade/walking-holding, accessed 6 May 2017.
Cade, Rosana. 2016a. The Radical Art of Holding Hands with Strangers. *Guardian*. www.theguardian.com/artanddesign/2016/aug/18/radical-art-of-holding-hands-with-strangers-rosana-cade-walking-holding, accessed 6 May 2017.
Cade, Rosana. 2016b. Safety – Noun. The Safety Map. https://safetymap.wordpress.com/2016/05/11/safety/, accessed 6 May 2017.
Cairns, Jon. 2012. Ambivalent Intimacies: Performance and Domestic Photography in the Work of Adrian Howells. *Contemporary Theatre Review* 22: 3, 355–71.
Campbell, Alyson. 2016. Taking an Affective Approach to 'Doing' Queer Histories in Performance: Queer Dramaturgy as a Reparative Practice of Erotohistoriography, in Alyson Campbell and Stephen Farrier (eds) *Queer Dramaturgies: International Perspectives on Where Performance Leads Queer*. London: Palgrave Macmillan.
Campbell, Patrick and Helen Spackman. 1998. With/out An-aesthetic: The Terrible Beauty of Franko B. *The Drama Review* 42: 4, 56–74.
Campbell-Johnston, Rachel. 2001. No Blood, No Glory. *The Times*, 9 May.
Carlson, Marla. 2010. *Performing Bodies in Pain: Medieval and Post-Modern Martyrs, Mystics, and Artists*. London: Palgrave Macmillan.
Carolin, Louise. 2013. The Art of Holding Hands. *DIVA Magazine*. October.
Carroll, Noel. 1979. Amy Taubin: The Solo Self. *TDR: The Drama Review* 23: 1, 51–8.
Caserio, Robert, Lee Edelman, Judith Halberstam, Jose Esteban Muñoz and Tim Dean. 2006. PMLA Conference Debate: The Antisocial Thesis in Queer Theory. *Modern Language Association Annual Conference* 121: 3, 819–28.
Castelli, Elizabeth. 2006. The Ambivalent Legacy of Violence and Victimhood: Using Early Christian Martyrs to Think With. *Spiritus: A Journal of Christian Spirituality* 6: 1, 1–24.
Causey, Matthew and Fintan Walsh. 2013. Introduction, in *Performance, Identity and the Neo-Political Subject*. London and New York: Routledge.
Ceresoli, Cristian. 2012. *The Shit / La Merda*. London: Oberon Books.
Chamberlain, Franc. 2009. Playing with Post-Secular Performance: Julia Lee Barclay, Ansuman Biswas, Traci Kelly, and Kira O'Reilly in Conversation with Franc Chamberlain. *PAJ: A Journal of Performance and Art* 31: 1, 54–67.
Channel 4 Paralympics. 2012. www.youtube.com/watch?v=tuAPPeRg3Nw, accessed 15 July 2017.
Chortle. 2017. Box Office Boom for Edinburgh's 'Big Four'. www.chortle.co.uk/news/2017/08/28/37745/box_office_boom_for_edinburghs_big_four, accessed 29 August 2017.
Christie, Bridget. 2014. Bridget Christie: 'For now, there's still plenty to be "banging on" about'. *The List*. https://edinburghfestival.list.co.uk/article/62729-bridget-christie-for-now-theres-still-plenty-to-be-banging-on-about/, accessed 7 March 2017.
Christie, Bridget. 2015a. *A Book for Her*. London: Arrow.
Christie, Bridget. 2015b. *Bridget Christie Minds the Gap*. BBC Radio 4. First broadcast 8 January.

Christopherson, Jody. 2011. Performer Soheil Mostajabian and Playwright Nassim Soleimanpour on White Rabbit, Red Rabbit. *New York Theatre Review*. https://newyorktheatrereview.blogspot.co.uk/2011/03/performer-soheil-mostajabian-and.html, accessed 3 March 2017.

Clapp, Susannah. 2000. Child's Play for Adults. *Observer*, 13 August.

Clare, Stephanie D. 2017. 'Finally, She's Accepted Herself!' Coming Out in Neoliberal Times. *Social Text* 35: 2, 17–38.

Clifford, Jo. 2012. (The Gospel According to) Jesus Queen of Heaven: A Personal History of a Controversial Play, in Ian Rivers and Richard Ward (eds) *Out of the Ordinary: Representations of LGBT Lives*. Newcastle upon Tyne: Cambridge Scholars Publishing.

Clifford, Jo and Chris Goode. 2017. *Eve*. London: Oberon Books.

Cockayne, G. E. 1910. *The Complete Peerage of England, Scotland, Ireland, Great Britain and the United Kingdom*, Volume 1. Vicary Gibbs (ed.). Exeter: Sutton Publishing.

Cockburn, Paul F. 2014. Pride Life: Doubly Disadvantaged. www.paulfcockburnjournalist.com/pride-life-doubly-disadvantaged/, accessed 24 April 2017.

Cohen, Robin. 1994. *Frontiers of Identity: The British and the Others*. London: Longman.

Coleman, Brian. 2007. Thatcher the Gay Icon. *New Statesman*. www.newstatesman.com/blogs/brian-coleman/2007/06/lady-thatcher-gay-tory, accessed 31 March 2017.

Cook, Joanna. 2016. Mindful in Westminster: The Politics of Meditation and the Limits of Neoliberal Critique. *HAU: Journal of Ethnographic Theory* 6: 1, 141–61.

Cooke, Alexander. 2005. Resistance, Potentiality and the Law. *Angelaki* 10: 3, 79–89.

Copstick, Kate. 2013. Comedy Review: Adrienne Truscott's Asking For It. *The Scotsman*. www.wow247.co.uk/2013/08/09/comedy-review-adrienne-truscotts-asking-for-it/, accessed 3 March 2017.

Costa, Maddy. 2013. Healing, and Feeling. http://statesofdeliquescence.blogspot.co.uk/2013/11/healing-and-feeling.html, accessed 19 March 2017.

Couser, G. Thomas. 2015. Illness, in Rachel Adams, Benjamin Reiss and David Serlin (eds) *Keywords for Disability Studies*. New York: New York University Press.

Cox, Emma. 2014. *Theatre & Migration*. London: Palgrave Macmillan.

Cox, Emma. 2016. Concealment, Revelation, and Masquerade in Europe's Asylum Apparatus: Intimate Life at the Border. *Lateral* 5: 2.

Crawley, Peter. 2012. White Rabbit, Red Rabbit. *The Irish Times*, 12 September.

Creative Scotland. 2016. *Arts Strategy 2016-7*. www.creativescotland.com/__data/assets/pdf_file/0005/35672/Creative-Scotland-Arts-Strategy-2016-17.pdf, accessed 20 March 2017.

Crimp, Douglas. 2009. Mario Montez, For Shame, in David M. Halperin and Valerie Traub (eds) *Gay Shame*. Chicago: University of Chicago Press.

Crossley, Nick. 1996. Body-Subject/Body-Power: Agency, Inscription and Control in Foucault and Merleau-Ponty. *Body & Society* 2: 2, 99–116.

Crouch, Tim. 2016. The Character of Adrian in The Author, in Deirdre Heddon and Dominic Johnson (eds) *It's All Allowed: The Performances of Adrian Howells*. London: Live Art Development Agency and Intellect.

Cruise, Colin. 2004. Solomon, Simeon (1840–1905), in *Oxford Dictionary of National Biography*. Oxford: Oxford University Press.

Culbertson, Diana. 1993. 'Ain't Nobody Clean': The Liturgy of Violence. *Glory, Religion & Literature* 25: 2, 35–52.

Cvetkovich, Ann. 2007. Public Feelings. *South Atlantic Quarterly* 106: 3, 459–68.

Czajkowski, Elise. 2015. In 'Asking for It,' Adrienne Truscott Reappropriates the Rape Joke. *New York Times*. www.nytimes.com/2015/04/11/arts/in-asking-for-it-adrienne-truscott-reappropriates-the-rape-joke.html, accessed 20 March 2017.

Das, Jareh. 2016. On Curating Pain: The Sick Body in Martin O'Brien's Taste of Flesh/Bite Me I'm Yours. *Leonardo* 49: 3, 266–7.

Dau, Duc. 2017. The Song of Songs for Difficult Queers: Simeon Solomon, Neil Bartlett, and *A Vision of Love Revealed in Sleep*, in Jongwoo Jeremy Kim and Christopher Reed (eds)

Queer Difficulty in Art and Poetry: Rethinking the Sexed Body in Verse and Visual Culture. London and New York: Routledge.

Davies, Seiriol. 2017. *How To Win Against History.* London: Oberon Books.

Davis, Natasha. 2013. Rupture: Things that Throb in our Insides, in Bob Karper, Branislava Kuburovic and Natasha Davis (eds) *Natasha Davis: Performance Film Installation.* London: Natasha Productions.

Dawson, Matt. 2013. *Late Modernity, Individualization and Socialism: An Associational Critique of Neoliberalism.* London: Palgrave Macmillan.

Derrida, Jacques. 2002. *Without Alibi.* Peggy Kamuf (ed. and trans). Stanford: Stanford University Press.

Dessau, Bruce. 2016. Gilded Balloon Responds To Accusation of Venue 'Poaching'. *Beyond The Joke.* www.beyondthejoke.co.uk/content/2490/news-gilded-balloon-responds-accusation-venue-poaching, accessed 25 March 2017.

Dewsbury, Guy, Karen Clarke, Dave Randall, Mark Rouncefield and Ian Sommerville. 2004. The Anti-social Model of Disability. *Disability & Society* 19: 2, 145–58.

Diamond, Elin, Denise Varney and Candice Amich. 2017. *Performance, Feminism and Affect in Neoliberal Times.* London: Palgrave Macmillan.

Dolan, Jill. 2005. *Utopia in Performance: Finding Hope at the Theater.* Ann Arbor: University of Michigan Press.

Dollimore, Jonathan. 1991. *Sexual Dissidence: Augustine to Wilde, Freud to Foucault.* London: Clarendon Press.

Doty, Alexander. 2000. *Flaming Classics: Queering the Film Canon.* London and New York: Routledge.

Douglas, Susan. 1994. *Where the Girls Are: Growing Up Female with the Mass Media.* New York: Random House.

Downey, Anthony. 2009. Zones of Indistinction: Giorgio Agamben's 'Bare Life' and the Politics of Aesthetics. *Third Text* 23: 2, 109–25 .

Doyle, Jennifer. 2013a. The 'Incorruptible Flesh' of Ron Athey. *KCET.* www.kcet.org/shows/artbound/the-incorruptible-flesh-of-ron-athey, accessed 18 March 2017.

Doyle, Jennifer. 2013b. *Hold it Against Me: Difficulty and Emotion in Contemporary Art.* Durham, NC and London: Duke University Press.

Duggan, Patrick. 2009. The Touch and the Cut: An Annotated Dialogue with Kira O'Reilly. *Studies in Theatre and Performance* 29: 3, 307–25.

Dupont, Anthony. 2014. *Preacher of Grace: A Critical Reappraisal of Augustine's Doctrine of Grace in his Sermones ad Populum on Liturgical Feasts and during the Donatist Controversy.* Leiden and Boston: Brill.

Duren, Brian. 1981. Cixous' Exorbitant Texts. *SubStance* 10: 3, 39–51.

Dyer, Richard. 1986. Judy Garland and Gay Men, in *Heavenly Bodies: Film Stars and Society.* New York: St. Martin's.

Easton, Eliza and Evy Cauldwell-French. 2017. *Creative Freelancers.* Creative Industries Federation. www.creativeindustriesfederation.com/publications/creative-freelancers, accessed 18 July 2017.

Edinburgh Festival Fringe Society. 2016a. About the Fringe Society. www.edfringe.com/learn/fringe-society, accessed 25 March 2017.

Edinburgh Festival Fringe Society. 2016b. Fringe Programme Style Guide. Edinburgh. www.edfringe.com/uploads/docs/participants/Fringe_Programme_Style_Guide_2015.pdf, accessed 22 February 2017.

Edinburgh Festival Fringe Society. 2017. The Fringe Guide to Doing a Show. www.edfringe.com/uploads/docs/participants/Fringe_guide_to_doing_a_show_2014.pdf, accessed 22 February 2017.

Edwardes, Jane. 2010. Theatre Reviews – My Stories, Your Emails, Barbican Centre, The Pit, West End. *Time Out*, 11 February.

Ellmeier, Andrea. 2003. Cultural Enterpreneurialism: On the Changing Relationship between the Arts, Culture and Employment. *International Journal of Cultural Policy* 9: 1, 1–15.

Esposito, Roberto. 2008. *Bios: Biopolitics and Philosophy.* Timothy Campbell (trans). Minneapolis: University of Minnesota Press.

Esposito, Roberto. 2010. *Communitas: The Origin and Destiny of Community.* Timothy Campbell (trans). Stanford: Stanford University Press.

Esposito, Roberto. 2011. *Immunitas: The Protection and Negation of Life.* Cambridge: Polity Press.

Esposito, Roberto. 2013. Community, Immunity, Biopolitics. Zakiya Hanafi (trans). *Angelaki* 18: 3, 83–90.

European Festivals Association. 2015. Festivals: the Heart of Europe – Google Arts & Culture. www.google.com/culturalinstitute/beta/exhibit/pgJSMQK6A7LSLg, accessed 22 March 2017.

Evans, Elizabeth. 2015. *The Politics of Third Wave Feminisms: Neoliberalism, Intersectionality, and the State in Britain and the US.* New York: Springer.

Eyres, Harry. 1990. Strange, Sad Choice of Role Model. *The Times,* 8 February.

Farrier, David. 2012. Everyday Exceptions: The Politics of the Quotidian in Asylum Monologues and Asylum Dialogues. *Interventions* 14: 3, 429–42.

Farrier, Stephen. 2013. It's about Time: Queer Utopias and Theater Performance, in Angela Jones (ed.) *A Critical Inquiry into Queer Utopias.* London: Palgrave Macmillan.

Fassin, Didier and Estelle d'Halluin. 2007. Critical Evidence: The Politics of Trauma in French Asylum Policies. *Ethos* 35, 300–29.

Fassin, Éric and Judith Surkis. 2010. Introduction: Transgressing Boundaries. *Public Culture* 22: 3, 487–505.

Ferrari, Roberto C. 2001. From Sodomite to Queer Icon: Simeon Solomon and the Evolution of Gay Studies. *Art Documentation* 20: 1, 11–13.

Ferreday, Debra. 2008. 'Showing the girl': The New Burlesque. *Feminist Theory* 9: 1, 47–65.

Field, Andy. 2012. The Future of Festivals. https://lookingforastronauts.wordpress.com/2012/02/29/the-future-of-festivals/, accessed 25 March 2017.

Field, Andy. 2013. Two Ideas towards Transparency. http://andytfield.co.uk/2013/11/24/transparency/, accessed 22 March 2017.

Field, Andy. 2016. *Forest Fringe: The First Ten Years.* London: Oberon Books.

Finkel, Rebecca. 2009. A Picture of the Contemporary Combined Arts Festival Landscape. *Cultural Trends* 18: 1, 3–21.

Fischer-Lichte, Erika. 2012. Appearing as Embodied Mind: Defining a Weak, a Strong and a Radical Concept of Presence, in Gabriella Giannachi, Nick Kaye and Michael Shanks (eds) *Archaeologies of Presence: Art, Performance and the Persistence of Being.* London and New York: Routledge.

Fisher, Mark. 2012. *The Edinburgh Fringe Survival Guide: How to Make Your Show A Success.* London: Methuen Drama.

Fisher, Mark. 2013. Interview: Robert Softley on Disability and his Fringe Show. *The Scotsman.* www.wow247.co.uk/2013/08/05/interview-robert-softley-on-disability-and-his-fringe-show/, accessed 24 April 2017.

Fitzgerald, Allan and John C. Cavadini (eds). 1999. *Augustine Through the Ages: An Encyclopedia.* Grand Rapids: W. B. Eerdmans.

Fleming, John. 2013. Gay Margaret Thatcher, Queen of Soho, Now Linked To Sight Gags for Perverts. *John Fleming's Blog.* https://thejohnfleming.wordpress.com/2013/12/12/gay-margaret-thatcher-queen-of-soho-now-linked-to-sight-gags-for-perverts/, accessed 31 March 2017.

Florida, Richard L. 2002. *The Rise of the Creative Class: And How It's Transforming Work, Leisure, Community, and Everyday Life.* New York: Basic Books.

Flynn, Paul Philip. 2006. Margaret Thatcher: Gay Icon. *Guardian.* www.theguardian.com/commentisfree/2006/may/16/bypaulflynn, accessed 31 March 2017.

Foley, Helene. 1985. *Ritual Irony: Poetry and Sacrifice in Euripides.* Ithaca: Cornell University Press.

Forest Fringe. 2015. Getting Involved. www.forestfringe.co.uk/about-us/getting-involved/, accessed 25 March 2017.

Forest Fringe. 2016a. Forest Fringe at Somerset House. http://forestfringe.co.uk/new/wp-content/uploads/2016/11/Forest-Fringe-Somerset-House-web.pdf, accessed 25 March 2017.

Forest Fringe. 2016b. Hello Friends. www.facebook.com/ForestFringe/posts/120773186 5930113, accessed 25 March 2017.

Forest Fringe. 2016c. Two Announcements. www.forestfringe.co.uk/2016/11/two-announcements/, accessed 25 March 2017.

Foucault, Michel. 1973. *The Birth of the Clinic: An Archaeology of Medical Perception.* Alan Sheridan (trans). London: Tavistock.

Foucault, Michel. 1978. *The History of Sexuality: Volume I.* Robert Hurley (trans). New York: Vintage Books.

Foucault, Michel. 1988. *Technologies of the Self: A Seminar With Michel Foucault.* Luther H. Martin, Huck Gutman and Patrick H Hutton (eds.). London: Tavistock Publications.

Foucault, Michel. 1995. *Discipline and Punish: The Birth of the Prison.* 2nd edn. Alan Sheridan (trans). New York: Vintage Books.

Fraser, Nancy. 1990. Rethinking the Public Sphere: A Contribution to the Critique of Actually Existing Democracy. *Social Text* 25/26: 56–80.

Free Edinburgh Fringe Festival. 2017. Apply to Perform with Us in 2017. www.freefestival.co.uk/performer_perform_with_us.asp, accessed 25 March 2017.

Freeman, Elizabeth. 2010. *Time Binds: Queer Temporalities, Queer Histories.* Durham, NC: Duke University Press.

Frieden, Ken. 1985. *Genius and Monologue.* Ithaca, NY: Cornell University Press.

Friedman, Sam, Dave O'Brien and Daniel Laurison. 2017. 'Like Skydiving without a Parachute': How Class Origin Shapes Occupational Trajectories in British Acting. *Sociology* 51: 5, 992–1010.

Gade, Rune. 2009. Making Real: Strategies of Performing Performativity in Tanja Ostojić's Looking for a Husband with EU Passport, in Tanja Ostojić and Marina Gržinić (eds) *Integration Impossible? The Politics of Migration in the Artwork of Tanja Ostojić.* Berlin: argobooks.

Gadsby, Hannah. 2017. *Hannah Gadsby – Official Website.* http://hannahgadsby.com.au, accessed 21 February 2018.

Gaillard, Julie. 2013. Figuring Performance. *Cultural Politics* 9: 2, 233–7.

Galetto, Manuela, Chiara Lasala, Sveva Magaraggia, Chiara Martucci, Elisabetta Onori and Charlotte Ross. 2009. Feminist Activism and Practice: Asserting Autonomy and Resisting Precarity, in Daniele Albertazzi, Clodagh Brook, Nina Ross and Charlotte Rothenberg (eds) *Resisting the Tide: Cultures of Opposition Under Berlusconi* (2001–6). London: Bloomsbury.

Gardner, Lyn. 2008. Free for all at the Fringe. *Guardian.* www.theguardian.com/culture/2008/aug/07/edinburghfestival.forestfringe, accessed 25 March 2017.

Gardner, Lyn. 2010. My Stories, Your Emails. *Guardian.* www.theguardian.com/stage/2010/feb/03/my-stories-your-emails-review, accessed 10 April 2017.

Gardner, Lyn. 2014a. Edinburgh Festival 2014: Female Jesus Teaches a Lesson in Tolerance. *Guardian.* www.theguardian.com/stage/theatreblog/2014/aug/07/edinburgh-festival-2014-gospel-according-to-jesus-domino-effect, accessed 24 March 2017.

Gardner, Lyn. 2014b. La Merda Review: Extraordinary, Terrifying and Hard to Ignore. *Guardian.* www.theguardian.com/stage/2014/apr/21/la-merda-review-silvia-gallerano, accessed 10 April 2017.

Gardner, Lyn. 2016. Iphigenia in Splott Review: A Raucous, Brawling Call for Revolution. *Guardian.* www.theguardian.com/culture/2016/jan/31/iphigenia-in-splott-review-national-theatre-london-sherman-cymru-gary-owen-sophie-melville, accessed 11 April 2017.

Gardner, Viv. 2008. Dancing with the Dead. *Dance Theatre Journal* 22: 4, 25–31.

Garland-Thomson, Rosemarie. 2000. Staring Back: Self-Representations of Disabled Performance Artists. *American Quarterly* 52: 2, 334–8.

Garland-Thomson, Rosemarie. 2011. Misfits: A Feminist Materialist Disability Concept. *Hypatia* 26: 3, 591–609.

Geis, Deborah. 1993. *Postmodern Theatric(k)s: Monologue in Contemporary American Drama*. Ann Arbor: University of Michigan Press.

Genz, Stéphanie and Benjamin Brabon. 2009. *Postfeminism: Cultural Texts and Theories*. Edinburgh: Edinburgh University Press.

Geoghegan, Vincent. 2008. *Ernst Bloch*. London and New York: Routledge.

Gibson, Sarah. 2012. Testimony in a Culture of Disbelief: Asylum Hearings and the Impossibility of Bearing Witness. *Journal for Cultural Research* 17: 1, 1–20.

Giorgi, Gabriel and Karen Pinkus. 2008. Zones of Exception: Biopolitical Territories in the Neoliberal Era. *diacritics* 36: 2, 99–108.

Girard, René. 2004. Violence and Religion: Cause or Effect? *The Hedgehog Review* 6: 1.

Goethe Institut. 2012. Tanja Ostojić, Looking for a Husband with EU-Passport. www.youtube.com/watch?v=hPYJqIZ47WQ, accessed 21 April 2017.

Gonzalez Rice, Karen. 2016. *Long Suffering: American Endurance Art as Prophetic Witness*. Ann Arbor: University of Michigan Press.

Goode, Chris. 2011. *Keep Breathing*. https://vimeo.com/channels/295101/35954313, accessed 6 May 2016.

Goode, Chris. 2015. *The Forest and the Field: Changing Theatre in a Changing World*. London: Oberon Books.

Goode, Chris. 2016. *Thompson's Live*. 17 January. https://chrisgoodeandco.podbean.com/e/thompson's-live-s3-ep02–17th-january-2016-deborah-pearson/, accessed 3 March 2017.

Gorman, Sarah. 2013. Feminist Disavowal or Return to Immanence? The Problem of Poststructuralism and the Naked Female Form in Nic Green's Trilogy and Ursula Martinez' My Stories, Your Emails. *Feminist Review* 105: 1, 48–64.

Gotman, Kelina. 2012. Epilepsy, Chorea, and Involuntary Movements Onstage: The Politics and Aesthetics of Alterkinetic Dance. *About Performance* 11, 159–83.

Gray, Amanda and Alexandra McDowall. 2013. LGBT Refugee Protection in the UK: From Discretion to Belief? *Forced Migration Review* 42, 22.

Gray, Louise. 1996. David Versus Goliath. *Guardian*, 29 November.

Greenall, Jessica. 2016. Featured Artist: Franko B. Artinliverpool.com. www.artinliverpool.com/featured-artist-franko-b/, accessed 23 March 2017.

Greer, Stephen. 2012. *Contemporary British Queer Performance*. Basingstoke: Palgrave Macmillan.

Greer, Stephen. 2016. What Money Can't Buy: The Economies of Adrian Howells, in Deirdre Heddon and Dominic Johnson (eds) *It's All Allowed: The Performances of Adrian Howells*. London and Bristol: Live Art Development Agency and Intellect.

Grosz, Elizabeth. 1994. *Volatile Bodies: Towards a Corporeal Feminism*. Bloomington: Indiana University Press.

Groves, Nancy. 2016. A Sissy's Progress: The Dangerous Power of an Effeminate Man. *Guardian*. www.theguardian.com/artanddesign/2016/mar/16/nando-messias-on-a-sissys-progress-london-toynbee, accessed 6 May 2017.

Gundle, Stephen. 2009. Berlusconi, Sex, and the Avoidance of a Media Scandal. *Italian Politics* 25: 59–75.

Guthman, Julie and Melanie Dupuis. 2006. Embodying Neoliberalism: Economy, Culture, and the Politics of Fat. *Environment and Planning D: Society and Space* 24, 427–48.

Gutiérrez-Albilla, Julián Daniel. 2015. Rethinking Spanish Visual Cultural Studies through an 'Untimely' Encounter with the Dance/Performance Art of La Ribot. *Bulletin of Spanish Studies* 92: 3, 361–90.

Gutman, Huck. 1988. Rousseau's Confessions: A Technology of the Self, in Michel Foucault, Luther H. Martin, Huck Gutman and Patrick H. Hutton (eds) *Technologies of the Self: A Seminar with Michel Foucault*. London: Tavistock Publications.

Hadley, Bree. 2014. *Disability, Public Space Performance and Spectatorship: Unconscious Spectators*. London: Palgrave Macmillan.

hadley, jamie lewis. 2014. We Will Outlive The Blood You Bleed. Pacitti Company. https://vimeo.com/110629144, accessed 2 May 2017.

Haidt, Jonathan, Paul Rozin, Clark Mccauley and Sumio Imada. 1997. Body, Psyche, and Culture: The Relationship between Disgust and Morality. *Psychology & Developing Societies* 9: 1, 107–31.

Halberstam, Judith. 1998. *Female Masculinity*. Durham, NC: Duke University Press.

Halberstam, Judith. 2005. *In a Queer Time and Place Transgender Bodies, Subcultural Lives*. New York: New York University Press.

Halperin, David M. 1995. *Saint Foucault: Towards a Gay Hagiography*. Oxford: Oxford University Press.

Halperin, David. 2012. *How To Be Gay*. Cambridge, MA: Belknap Press of University of Harvard Press.

Hammer, Dean. 1997. Hannah Arendt, Identity and the Politics of Visibility. *Contemporary Politics* 3: 4, 321–39.

Hanson, Elizabeth Hanna. 2014. Toward an Asexual Narrative Structure, in Cerankowski Karli June and Milks Megan (eds) *Asexualities: Feminist and Queer Perspectives*. London and New York: Routledge.

Hardes, Jennifer. 2014. Biopolitics and the Enemy: On Law, Rights and Proper Subjects. *Law, Culture and the Humanities*, 1–21.

Hardt, Michael and Antonio Negri. 2009. *Commonwealth*. Cambridge, MA: Harvard University Press.

Harris, Anita and Amy Shields Dobson. 2015. Theorizing Agency in Post-Girlpower Times. *Continuum* 29: 2, 145–56.

Harvey, David. 2005. *A Brief History of Neoliberalism*. Oxford: Oxford University Press.

Harvey, Mark. 2013. Promises Promises. *Performance Research* 18: 4, 83–90.

Harvie, Jen. 2013. *Fair Play: Art, Performance and Neoliberalism*. London: Palgrave Macmillan.

Heathfield, Adrian. 2000. Small Acts. www.adrianheathfield.net/project/small-acts/, accessed 3 May 2017.

Heathfield, Adrian. 2006. After the Fall: Dance-Theatre and Dance-Performance, in Joe Kelleher and Nicholas Ridout (eds) *Contemporary Theatres in Europe: A Critical Companion*. London and New York: Routledge.

Heathfield, Adrian. 2013. Illicit Transit, in Dominic Johnson (ed.) *Pleading in the Blood: The Art and Performances of Ron Athey*. London: Intellect.

Heddon, Deirdre. 2008. *Autobiography and Performance*. Basingstoke: Palgrave Macmillan.

Heddon, Deirdre and Dominic Johnson (eds). 2016. *It's All Allowed: The Performances of Adrian Howells*. London: Intellect.

Heddon, Deirdre and Cathy Turner. 2012. Walking Women: Shifting the Tales and Scales of Mobility. *Contemporary Theatre Review* 22: 2, 224–36.

Heddon, Deirdre, Jennie Klein and Nikki Milican. 2010. *The National Review of Live Art 1979–2010: A Personal History (Essays, Anecdotes, Drawings and Images)*. Glasgow: New Moves International.

Heller, Kevin Jon. 1996. Power, Subjectification and Resistance in Foucault. *SubStance* 25: 1, 78–110.

Hill, Leslie and Helen Paris. 2006. Curious Feminists, in Elaine Aston and Geraldine Harris (eds) *Feminist Futures? Theatre, Performance, Theory*. London: Palgrave Macmillan.

Hoetger, Megan. 2014. Incorruptible Flesh: Messianic Remains by Ron Athey. *Performance Research* 19: 3, 60–1.

Holmes, John. 2008. Flash of Inspiration from Franko B. *Metro*. http://metro.co.uk/2008/10/02/flash-of-inspiration-from-franko-b-554972/, accessed 22 March 2017.

hooks, bell. 1992. *Black Looks: Race and Representation*. Boston: South End Press.

Howells, Adrian. 2007. *14 Stations of the Life and History of Adrian Howells*. DVD. Glasgow: University of Glasgow.

Hoyle, David. 2008a. *MAGAZINE the Reprint*. DVD. London: Live Art Development Agency.

Hoyle, David. 2008b. Gender Dysphoria. www.youtube.com/watch?v=dDgvWt792Xc, accessed 31 March 2017.

Hoyle, David. 2009. *Dave's Drop-in Centre*. Royal Vauxhall Tavern, London.

Hoyle, David. 2010. *David Hoyle's Factory: A Sweatshop for the Soul*. Chelsea Theatre, London.

Hughes, Holly and David Román (eds). 1998. *O Solo Homo: The New Queer Performance*. New York: Grove.

Humphreys, Stephen. 2006. Legalizing Lawlessness: On Giorgio Agamben's State of Exception. *The European Journal of International Law* 17: 3, 677–87.

Hutcheon, Linda. 1989. *The Politics of Postmodernism*. London and New York: Routledge.

Hyde, H. Montgomery. 1970. *The Other Love: An Historical and Contemporary Survey of Homosexuality in Britain*. London: Heinemann.

Ibanez, Victor. 2006. Franko B – Don't Leave Me This Way. https://vimeo.com/122114456, accessed 10 July 2017.

Jain, S. Lochlann. 2007. Cancer Butch. *Cultural Anthropology* 22: 4, 501–38.

Janes, Dominic. 2012. 'One of Us': The Queer Afterlife of Margaret Thatcher as a Gay Icon. *International Journal of Media & Cultural Politics* 8: 2, 211–27.

Jankovic, Bojana. 2014a. Light Art. *Exeunt Magazine*. http://exeuntmagazine.com/features/light-art/, accessed 19 March 2017.

Jankovic, Bojana. 2014b. I, Victim. *Exeunt Magazine*. http://exeuntmagazine.com/reviews/i-victim/, accessed 11 May 2017.

Jansen, Stef. 2009. After the Red Passport: Towards an Anthropology of the Everyday Geopolitics of Entrapment in the EU's 'Immediate Outside'. *Journal of the Royal Anthropological Institute* 15: 4, 815–32.

Johnson, Dominic. 2008. Perverse Martyrologies: An Interview with Ron Athey. *Contemporary Theatre Review* 18: 4, 503–13.

Johnson, Dominic (ed.). 2013. *Pleading in the Blood: The Art and Performances of Ron Athey*. London: Intellect.

Johnson, Dominic. 2015. *The Art of Living: An Oral History of Performance Art*. London: Palgrave Macmillan.

Johnson, Dominic and Lois Keidan. 2012. *Frightening the Horses: An Interview with Neil Bartlett*. Contemporary Theatre Review 22: 1, 152–60.

Johnson, Toni A. M. 2011. On Silence, Sexuality and Skeletons: Reconceptualizing Narrative in Asylum Hearings. *Social & Legal Studies* 20: 1, 57–78.

Jones, Amelia. 2009. Performing the Wounded Body: Pain, Affect and the Radical Relationality of Meaning. *Parallax* 15: 4, 45–67.

Jones, Amelia. 2013. How Ron Athey Makes Me Feel: The Political Potential of Upsetting Art, in Dominic Johnson (ed.) *Pleading in the Blood: The Art and Performances of Ron Athey*. London and New York: Live Art Development Agency and Intellect.

Jones, Kathleen B. 2015. Queer(y)ing Hannah Arendt, or what's Hannah Arendt got to do with Intersectionality? *New Political Science* 37: 4, 458–75.

Joy, Jenn. 2014. *The Choreographic*. Cambridge, MA and London: The MIT Press.

Kaplan, Morris. 1995. Refiguring the Jewish Question: Arendt, Proust, and the Politics of Sexuality, in Bonnie Honig (ed.) *Feminist Interpretations of Hannah Arendt*. University Park: The Pennsylvania State University Press.

Karimi-Hakak, Mahmood. 2003. Exiled to Freedom A Memoir of Censorship in Iran. *TDR: The Drama Review* 47: 4, 17–50.

Kartsaki, Eirini. 2014. Mis-appropriation and Re-appropriation: An Interview with Oreet Ashery. *Journal of Adaptation in Film & Performance* 7: 2, 225–40.

Kauffmann, Linda S. 1998. Sadomedicine: Bob Flanagan's 'Visiting Hours' and Last Rites. *Performance Research* 3: 3, 32–40.

Keidan, Lois. 2000. Artland 2000, in Adrian Heathfield (ed.) *Small Acts: Performance, the Millennium and the Making of Time*. London: Black Dog.

Keidan, Lois and Daniel Brine (eds). 2011. *Programme Notes: Case Studies for Locating Experimental Theatre*. London: Live Art Development Agency.

Keidan, Lois and C. J. Mitchell (eds). 2012. *Access All Areas: Live Art and Disability*. London: Live Art Development Agency.

Kellaway, Kate. 2009. The Interview: Bobby Baker. *Observer*, 28 June.

Kelleher, Joe. 2008. How to Act, How to Spectate (Laughing Matter). *Performance Research* 13: 4, 56–63.

Kimmings, Bryony. 2013. You Show Me Yours. http://thebryonykimmings.tumblr.com/post/67660917680/you-show-me-yours, accessed 22 March 2017.

Kingfisher, Catherine and Jeff Maskovsky. 2008. Introduction: The Limits of Neoliberalism. *Critique of Anthropology* 28: 2, 115–26.

Kirby, Michael. 1979. Autoperformance Issue: An Introduction. *TDR: The Drama Review* 23: 1, 2.

Klein, Gabriele and Kunst, Bojana. 2012. Introduction: Labour and Performance. *Performance Research* 17: 6, 1–3.

Korsmeyer, Carolyn and Barry Smith (eds). 2004. Visceral Values: Aurel Kolnai on Disgust, in *On Disgust*. Aurel Kolnai. Chicago: Open Court.

Krakowska, Joanna. 2016. Auto-Theatre in Times of Post-Truth, in *Confrontations Festival Programme*. Lublin.

Krause, Sharon. 2015. *Freedom Beyond Sovereignty: Reconstructing Liberal Individualism*. Chicago: University of Chicago Press.

Kunst, Bojana. 2015. *Artist at Work: Proximity of Art and Capitalism*. Winchester and Washington: Zero Books.

Kunst, Bojana and Ivana Müller. 2012. Finally Together on Time. *Maska Performing Arts Journal* 27: 149–50, 128–33.

Kuppers, Petra. 2013. *Disability and Contemporary Performance: Bodies on the Edge*. London and New York: Routledge.

LaFrance, Marianne. 2002. Smile Boycotts and Other Body Politics. *Feminism & Psychology* 12: 3, 319–23.

Lawrence, Ben. 2016. Iphigenia in Splott, NT Temporary Theatre, Review: 'Tense and Moving'. *Telegraph*. www.telegraph.co.uk/theatre/what-to-see/iphigenia-in-splott-nt-temporary-theatre-review/, accessed 4 May 2016.

Leadbeater, Charles and Kate Oakley. 1999. *The Independents: Britain's New Cultural Entrepreneurs*. London: Demos.

Leadbitter, James. 2013. I Went Mental And All I Got Was This Lousy T-shirt. https://vimeo.com/62788351, accessed 4 May 2017.

Leahy, Mark. 2013. Martin O'Brien – Breathe for Me. a-n The Artists Information Company. www.a-n.co.uk/reviews/martin-obrien-breathe-for-me, accessed 25 April 2017.

Lee, Stewart. 2012. The Slow Death of the Edinburgh Fringe. *Observer*. www.theguardian.com/culture/2012/jul/30/stewart-lee-slow-death-edinburgh-fringe, accessed 24 April 2017.

Lefebvre, Henri. 1991. *The Production of Space*. Donald Nicholson-Smith (trans). Oxford: Blackwell.

Lemm, Vanessa. 2013. Introduction: Biopolitics and Community in Roberto Esposito, in Roberto Esposito, *Terms of the Political: Community, Immunity, Biopolitics*. New York: Fordham University Press.

Lepecki, André. 2006. *Exhausting Dance: Performance and the Politics of Movement*. London and New York: Routledge.

Lewis, Lisa. 2004. Welsh-Language Production/Welsh-Language Performance: The Resistant Body. *Studies in Theatre and Performance* 24: 3, 163–76.

Lewis, Rachel. 2013. Deportable Subjects: Lesbians and Political Asylum. *Feminist Formations* 25: 2, 174–94.

Linton, Anna. 2008. Virgin Sacrifices: Iphigenia and Jephthah's Daughter, in Helen Fronius and Anna Linton (eds) *Women and Death: Representations of Female Victims and Perpetrators in German Culture 1500–2000*. Rochester, NY: Camden House.

Live Art Development Agency. 2005. What is Live Art? www.thisisliveart.co.uk/about/what-is-live-art/, accessed 24 January 2017.

Lobel, Brian. 2012a. Spokeswomen and Posterpeople: Disability, Advocacy and Live Art. *Contemporary Theatre Review* 22: 1, 79–93.

Lobel, Brian. 2012b. *BALL & Other Funny Stories About Cancer*. London: Oberon Books.

Lobel, Brian. 2013. BALL & Other Funny Stories About Cancer. www.blobelwarming.com/ball-other-funny-stories-about-cancer/, accessed 24 April 2017.

Logan, Brian. 2010. The Rise of the Rape Joke. *Guardian*, 10 September.

Logan, Brian. 2014. Adrienne Truscott's Asking for It Review: Sophisticated Confrontationalism. *Guardian*. www.theguardian.com/culture/2014/may/14/adrienne-truscott-asking-for-it-review-comedy, accessed 24 April 2017.

Long, Thomas. 2000. Plague of Pariahs: AIDS 'Zines and the Rhetoric of Transgression. *Journal of Communication Inquiry* 24: 4, 401–11.

Lorey, Isabell. 2009. Governmentality and Self-Precarization: On the Normalization of Cultural Producers, in Gerald Raunig and Gene Ray (eds), *Art and Contemporary Critical Practice: Reinventing Institutional Critique*. London: MayFly Books.

Love, Catherine. 2012. The Shit / La Merda. *Exeunt Magazine*. http://exeuntmagazine.com/reviews/the-shit-la-merda/, accessed 10 April 2017.

Love, Catherine. 2013. The Future Show. *Exeunt Magazine*. http://exeuntmagazine.com/reviews/the-future-show/, accessed 5 May 2017.

Love, Catherine. 2014. Every Brilliant Thing. *Exeunt Magazine*. http://exeuntmagazine.com/reviews/every-brilliant-thing/, accessed 5 May 2017.

Love, Heather. 2007. *Feeling Backward: Loss and the Politics of Queer History*. Cambridge, MA: Harvard University Press.

Love, Heather. 2009. Emotional Rescue, in David Halperin and Valerie Straub (eds) *Gay Shame*. Chicago and London: University of Chicago Press.

Luibhéid, Eithne. 2008. Queer/Migration: An Unruly Body of Scholarship. *GLQ: A Journal of Lesbian and Gay Studies* 14: 3, 169–90.

Luibhéid, Eithne. 2014. Afterword: Troubling Identities and Identifications. *Sexualities* 17: 8, 1035–40.

Luker, Trish. 2015. Performance Anxieties: Interpellation of the Refugee Subject in Law. *Canadian Journal of Law and Society / Revue Canadienne Droit et Société* 30: 1, 91–107.

Lyotard, Jean-François. 2011. *Discourse, Figure*. Antony Hudek and Mary Lydon (trans). Minneapolis: University of Minnesota Press.

Macmillan, Duncan. 2016. *Plays One*. London: Oberon Books.

Maeckelbergh, Marianne. 2011. Doing is Believing: Prefiguration as Strategic Practice in the Alterglobalization Movement. *Social Movement Studies* 10: 1, 1–20.

Maldonado-Torres, Nelson. 2007. On the Coloniality of Being: Contributions to the Development of a Concept. *Cultural Studies* 21: 2–3, 240–70.

Malkki, Liisa. 2007. Commentary: The Politics of Trauma and Asylum: Universals and their Effects. *Ethos* 35: 3, 336–43.

Manzoor, Sarfraz. 2012. White Rabbit, Red Rabbit: The Play that Asks You to Leave Your Phone On. *Guardian*. www.theguardian.com/stage/2012/jun/21/nassim-soleimanpour-play-censorship, accessed 22 May 2016.

Marotta, Vince. 2008. The Hybrid Stranger and Cosmopolitan Self, in *Questioning Cosmopolitanism: Second Biennial Conference of the International Global Ethics Association*. Deakin University, Faculty of Arts & Education.

Marotta, Vince. 2016. *Theories of the Stranger: Debates on Cosmopolitanism, Identity and Cross-Cultural Encounters*. London and New York: Routledge.

Mars, Rachel. 2016. *Our Carnal Hearts*. Unpublished script.

McEvilley, Thomas. 2005. *The Triumph of Anti-Art: Conceptual and Performance Art in the Formation of Postmodernism*. Kingston, NY: McPherson.

McGrath, John Edward. 1995. Trusting in Rubber: Performing Boundaries during the AIDS Epidemic. *TDR (1988-)* 39: 2, 21–38.

McKinney, Kelly. 2007. 'Breaking the Conspiracy of Silence': Testimony, Traumatic Memory, and Psychotherapy with Survivors of Political Violence. *Ethos* 35: 3, 265–99.

McLaughlin, Laurel. 2016. Marriage and Other Migrations. Kulturni Centar Panceva. www.kulturnicentarpanceva.rs/en/17th-art-biennial/texts-and-interviews/tanja-ostojic-inteview, accessed 17 April 2017.

McLemore, S. Dale. 1970. Simmel's 'Stranger': A Critique of the Concept. *The Pacific Sociological Review* 13: 2, 86–94.

McRobbie, Angela. 2004. Post-Feminism and Popular Culture. *Feminist Media Studies* 4: 3, 255–64.

McRobbie, Angela. 2011. 'Everyone is Creative': Artists as Pioneers of the New Economy?, in Marc James Léger (ed.) *Culture and Contestation in the New Century*. London and New York: Intellect.

McRobbie, Angela. 2016. *Be Creative: Making a Living in the New Culture Industries*. Hoboken: Wiley.

McRuer, Robert. 2006. *Crip Theory: Cultural Signs of Queerness and Disability*. New York and London: New York University Press.

Megarry, Daniel. 2015. Dickie Beau on Adoring Dead Icons and Life as an Anarchist Drag Artist. *Gay Times*. www.gaytimes.co.uk/culture/15011/dickie-beau-adoring-dead-icons-life-anarchist-drag-artist/, accessed 8 June 2017.

Merritt, Stephanie. 2014. Adrienne Truscott's Asking for It. *Observer*. www.theguardian.com/stage/2014/jun/08/adrienne-truscotts-asking-for-it-review-feminist-standup-pants-down, accessed 3 March 2016.

Messias, Nando. 2016a. Sissy That Walk: The Sissy's Progress, in Alyson Campbell and Stephen Farrier (eds) *Queer Dramaturgies: International Perspectives on Where Performance Leads Queer*. London: Palgrave Macmillan.

Messias, Nando. 2016b. On Sissy's Continued Progress. Chisenhale Dance Space. www.chisenhaledancespace.co.uk/on-sissys-continued-progress-nando-messias-staycation-blog/, accessed 6 May 2017.

Mignolo, Walter and Tanja Ostojić. 2013. Crossing Borders / Development of Diverse Artistic Strategies. *Social Text*. https://socialtextjournal.org/periscope_article/crossing-borders-development-of-diverse-artistic-strategies/, accessed 21 April 2017.

Milevska, Suzana. 2009. 'Femina Sacra': Bio-Power and Paradoxes of Humanity in the Art of Tanja Ostojić, in Tanja Ostojić and Marina Gržinić (eds) *Integration Impossible? The Politics of Migration in the Artwork of Tanja Ostojić*. Berlin: argobooks.

Millbank, Jenni. 2002. Imagining Otherness: Refugee Claims on the Basis of Sexuality in Canada and Australia. *Melbourne University Law Review* 26: 1, 1–33.

Miller, Paul Allen. 2006. Truth-Telling in Foucault's 'Le gouvernement de soi et des autres'. *Parrhesia* 1: 1, 27–61.

Mills, Sara. 2008. *Language and Sexism*. Cambridge: Cambridge University Press.

MIT Sloan. 2014. Can Crowdfunding Democratize Access to Capital? MIT Sloan Executive Education. http://executive.mit.edu/blog/can-crowdfunding-democratize-access-to-capital, accessed 20 March 2017.

Mock, Roberta. 2009. Oreet Ashery's Site-Specific Corporeal Turns, in *Oreet Ashery: Dancing with Men*. London: Live Art Development Agency.

Morgan, Thaïs E. 1996. Perverse Male Bodies: Simeon Solomon and Algernon Charles Swinburne, in Peter Home and Reina Lewis (eds) *Outlooks: Lesbian and Gay Sexualities and Visual Cultures*. London and New York: Routledge.

Moses, Caro. 2013. Bridget Christie: No Bic for Her. *ThreeWeeks Edinburgh*. www.threeweeks.co.uk/article/bridget-christie-no-bic-for-her/#, accessed 16 June 2017.

Mostafa, Khalaji, Bronwen Robertson and Maryam Aghdami. 2011. *Cultural Censorship in Iran: Iranian Culture in a State of Emergency*. London. https://smallmedia.org.uk/old/pdf/censorship.pdf, accessed 16 July 2016.

Moylan, Stephen. 2012. Link Adelaide Podcast Interview: Neil Watkins, 22 January.

Müller, Ivana. 2010. 60 Minutes Of Opportunism. https://vimeo.com/31035826, accessed 5 May 2017.

Muñoz, José Esteban. 1999. *Disidentifications: Queers of Color and the Performance of Politics*. Minneapolis and London: University of Minnesota Press.

Muñoz, José Esteban. 2006. Queers, Punks and the Utopian Performative, in D. Soyini Madison and Judith Hamera (eds) *The SAGE Handbook of Performance Studies*. Thousand Oaks: SAGE Publications.

Muñoz, José Esteban. 2009. *Cruising Utopia: The Then and There of Queer Futurity.*
New York: New York University Press.

Munt, Sally. 1995. The Lesbian Flâneur, in David Bell and Gill Valentine (eds) *Mapping
Desire: Geographies of Sexualities.* London and New York: Routledge.

Myers, Kimberly R. 2004. Coming Out: Considering the Closet of Illness. *Journal of Medical
Humanities* 25: 4, 255–70.

Nail, Thomas. 2015. *The Figure of the Migrant.* Stanford: Stanford University Press.

Nally, Claire. 2009. Grrrly Hurly Burly: Neo-Burlesque and the Performance of Gender.
Textual Practice 23: 4, 621–43.

Nielsen, Emilia. 2014. Counternarratives of Breast Cancer and Chronic Illness: Performing
Disruption, Patienthood and Narrative Repair. *Performance Research* 19: 4, 97–106.

Nunn, Heather. 2002. *Thatcher, Politics and Fantasy: The Political Culture of Gender and
Nation.* London: Lawrence & Wishart.

Nyoni, Zodwa. 2015. *Nine Lives and Come to Where I'm From.* London: Methuen Drama.

O'Brien, Cormac. 2013. Performing POZ: Irish Theatre, HIV Stigma, and 'Post-AIDS'
Identities. *Irish University Review* 43: 1, 74–85.

O'Brien, Martin. 2014. Performing Chronic: Chronic Illness and Endurance Art.
Performance Research 19: 4, 54–63.

O'Brien, Martin and Becky Beyts. 2012. Abject Clearances: Considering the Cough, Mucus
and Breathing, in Lois Keidan and CJ Mitchell (eds) *Access All Areas: Live Art and
Disability.* London: Live Art Development Agency.

O'Brien, Martin and Johanna Linsley. 2015. Infecting Archives: An Interview with Martin
O'Brien. *Contemporary Theatre Review* 25: 4.

Oliver, Daniel. 2012. Car Crashes, the Social Turn, and Glorious Glitches in David Hoyle's
Performances. *Liminalities: A Journal of Performance Studies* 8: 3, 9–14.

Oliver, Daniel. 2014. You're Funnier When You're Angry. *Performance Research* 19: 2,
109–15.

Ostojić, Tanja. 2002. Mission Statement. www.van.at/see/tanja/not/mission.htm, accessed
27 June 2017.

Ostojić, Tanja. 2009. Misplaced Women? / Missplaced Women? https://misplacedwomen.
wordpress.com/about/, accessed 24 May 2017.

Ostojić, Tanja and Marina Gržinić (eds). 2009. *Integration Impossible? The Politics of
Migration in the Artwork of Tanja Ostojić.* Berlin: argobooks.

Ovalhouse. 2014. Financial Support Document. www.ovalhouse.com/theatre/financial-
support-info, accessed 22 May 2017.

Ovalhouse. 2016. Working with Us. www.ovalhouse.com/theatre/financial-support-info,
accessed 22 May 2017.

Owen, Gary. 2016. *Collected Plays.* London: Oberon Books.

Paget, Derek. 2010. Acts of Commitment: Activist Arts, the Rehearsed Reading, and
Documentary Theatre. *New Theatre Quarterly* 26: 2, 173–93.

Papachlimitzou, Regina. 2013. In Between Time 2013, Bristol. *Aesthetica Magazine.* www.
aestheticamagazine.com/in-between-time-2013-bristol/, accessed 1 January 2017.

Parr, Adrian. 2010. *The Deleuze Dictionary Revised Edition.* Edinburgh: Edinburgh
University Press.

Paterson, Eddie. 2015. *The Contemporary American Monologue: Performance and Politics.*
London: Bloomsbury.

Paterson, Mary. 2007. Kira O'Reilly 'Syncope'. Spill: Overspill. http://spilloverspill.blogspot.
co.uk/2007/04/overspill2007-mary-kira-oreilly-syncope.html, accessed 18 March 2017.

Pavis, Patrice. 2003. *Analyzing Performance: Theater, Dance, and Film.* Ann Arbor: University
of Michigan Press.

Pavis, Patrice. 2013. *Contemporary Mise en Scène: Staging Theatre Today.* Joel Anderson
(trans). London and New York: Routledge.

PBH's Free Fringe. 2016. Participate. http://freefringe.org.uk/participate/, accessed 25
March 2017.

PBH's Free Fringe. 2017. Free Fringe Ethos and Conditions. http://freefringe.org.uk/ethosconditions/, accessed 25 March 2017.

Pearlman, Lazlo. 2015. 'Dissemblage' and 'Truth Traps': Creating Methodologies of Resistance in Queer Autobiographical Theatre. *Theatre Research International* 40: 1, 88–91.

Pearson, Deborah. 2012. The Second Day of the Future. https://thefutureshow.wordpress.com/2012/03/12/the-second-day-of-the-future/, accessed 5 May 2017.

Pearson, Deborah. 2013. The Future I Predicted Yesterday. (The Future I am Living Now, Warm, Sitting in Bed with My Computer, Unsure). The Future Show. https://thefutureshow.wordpress.com/2013/01/11/the-future-on-thursday-january-10th-the-future-i-am-living-now-warm-sitting-in-bed-with-my-computer-unsure/, accessed 5 May 2017.

Pearson, Deborah. 2015a. Curation as a Form of Artistic Practice: Context as a New Work through UK-Based Forest Fringe. *Canadian Theatre Review* 162, 80–1.

Pearson, Deborah. 2015b. *The Future Show*. London: Oberon Books.

Pellegrini, Ann. 2007. Unnatural Affinities: Me and Judy at the Lesbian Bar. *Camera Obscura: Feminism, Culture, and Media Studies* 22: 2, 127–33.

Perth International Arts Festival. 2015. Every Brilliant Thing: Duncan Macmillan. www.youtube.com/watch?v=zKxDFSI-LKA, accessed 5 May 2017.

Peter, Luc. 2003. *La Ribot Distinguida*. Intermezzo Films.

Peters, John Durham. 2008. Witnessing, in Paul Frosh and Amit Pinchevski (eds) *Media Witnessing: Testimony in the Age of Mass Communication*. London: Palgrave Macmillan.

Peterson, Michael. 1997. *Straight White Male: Performance Art Monologues*. Jackson: University Press of Mississippi.

de Peuter, Greig. 2014. Beyond the Model Worker: Surveying a Creative Precariat. *Culture Unbound: Journal of Current Cultural Research* 6: 263–84.

Phelan, Shane. 2000. Queer Liberalism? *The American Political Science Review* 94: 2, 431–42.

Philips, Deborah and Garry Whannel. 2013. *The Trojan Horse: The Growth of Commercial Sponsorship*. London: Bloomsbury.

Plunka, Gene. 1992. *The Rites of Passage of Jean Genet: The Art and Aesthetics of Risk Taking*. Madison: Fairleigh Dickinson University Press.

Pollard, Patrick. 1991. *André Gide: Homosexual Moralist*. New Haven: Yale University Press.

Pollock, David. 2016. Music Review: (I Could Go On Singing) Over The Rainbow. *The Scotsman*. www.scotsman.com/lifestyle/culture/edinburgh-festivals/music-review-i-could-go-on-singing-over-the-rainbow-1-4199450, accessed 15 May 2017.

Pratt, Lloyd. 2011. Close Reading the Present: Eudora Welty's Queer Politics, in Ellen Lee McCallum and Mikko Tuhkanen (eds) *Queer Times, Queer Becomings*. New York: SUNY Press.

Pressley, Nelson. 2013. A Stage Stunt that Makes You Think. *Washington Post*, 6 December.

Prichard, Dan. 2009. Interview with Adrian Howells. Balcony Productions and British Council. https://vimeo.com/18162810, accessed 23 November 2016.

Prior, Dorothy Max. 2016. Nando Messias: The Sissy's Progress. *Total Theatre*. http://totaltheatre.org.uk/nando-messias-the-sissys-progress/, accessed 6 May 2017.

Prozorov, S. 2010. Why Giorgio Agamben is an Optimist. *Philosophy & Social Criticism* 36: 9, 1053–73.

Puar, Jasbir. 2007. *Terrorist Assemblages: Homonationalism in Queer Times*. Durham, NC: Duke University Press.

Puar, Jasbir. 2012. A Virtual Roundtable with Lauren Berlant, Judith Butler, Bojana Cvejić, Isabell Lorey, Jasbir Puar, and Ana Vujanović. *TDR: The Drama Review* 56: 4, 163–77.

Pugh, Tison. 2008. 'There lived in the Land of Oz two queerly made men': Queer Utopianism and Antisocial Eroticism in L. Frank Baum's Oz Series. *Marvels & Tales* 22: 25, 217–39.

Quinn, Bernadette. 2005. Arts Festivals and the City. *Urban Studies* 42: 5–6, 927–43.

Raboin, Thibaut. 2017. Exhortations of Happiness: Liberalism and Nationalism in the Discourses on LGBTI Asylum Rights in the UK. *Sexualities* 20: 5–6, 663–81.

Recla, Matthew. 2014. Homo Profanus: The Christian Martyr and the Violence of Meaning-Making. *Critical Research on Religion* 2: 2, 147–64.

Reid-Smith, Tris. 2013. Disabled Champions 'Humiliated' at Hands of Glasgow Gay Club. *Gay Star News*. www.gaystarnews.com/article/disabled-champions-humiliated-hands-glasgow-gay-club140613/, accessed 24 April 2017.

Richards, Mary. 2003. Ron Athey, AIDS and the Politics of Pain. *Body, Space and Technology* 3: 2. http://people.brunel.ac.uk/bst/3no2/Papers/mary%20richards.htm, accessed 11 May 2017.

Richards, Mary. 2008. Specular Suffering: (Staging) the Bleeding Body. *PAJ: A Journal of Performance and Art* 30: 1, 108–19.

Ricœur, Paul. 2004. *Memory, History, Forgetting*. Kathleen Blamey and David Pellauer (trans). Chicago: University of Chicago Press.

Rieber, Nikolaus, Andreas Hector, Melanie Carevic and Dominik Hartl. 2014. Current Concepts of Immune Dysregulation in Cystic Fibrosis. *The International Journal of Biochemistry & Cell Biology* 52, 108–12.

Ring, Jennifer. 1991. The Pariah as Hero: Hannah Arendt's Political Actor. *Political Theory* 19: 3, 433–52.

RN Breakfast. 2010. Video: Ursula Martinez Reflects on 'Hanky Panky'. ABC Radio National. www.abc.net.au/radionational/programs/breakfast/video-ursula-martinez-reflects-on-hanky-panky/2969052, accessed 11 April 2017.

Rodowick, David. 2001. *Reading the Figural, Or, Philosophy After the New Media*. Durham, NC: Duke University Press.

Rohter, Larry. 2011. Behind the Persian Veil: Theater Illuminating the Iranian Experience. *New York Times*, 3 March.

Roof, Judith. 1996. *Come As You Are: Sexuality and Narrative*. New York: Columbia University Press.

Rose, Anyusha. 2014. Scottee Interview. *Disorder Magazine*. www.disordermagazine.com/fashion/stories/scottee-interview, accessed 19 March 2017.

Rose, Nikolas. 1999. *Powers of Freedom: Reframing Political Thought*. Cambridge: Cambridge University Press.

Roth, Michael S. 1981. Foucault's 'History of the Present'. *History and Theory* 20: 1, 32–46.

Rottenberg, Catherine. 2017. Neoliberal Feminism and the Future of Human Capital. *Signs: Journal of Women in Culture and Society* 42: 2, 329–48.

Roulstone, Alan. 2015. Personal Independence Payments, Welfare Reform and the Shrinking Disability Category. *Disability & Society* 30: 5, 673–88.

Salter, Mark B. 2008. When the Exception Becomes the Rule: Borders, Sovereignty, and Citizenship. *Citizenship Studies* 12: 4, 365–80.

Sandahl, Carrie. 2003. Queering the Crip or Cripping the Queer? Intersections of Queer and Crip Identities in Solo Autobiographical Performance. *GLQ: A Journal of Lesbian and Gay Studies* 9: 1–2, 25–56.

Sands, Bobby. 1997. *Bobby Sands: Writings from Prison*. New York: Roberts Rinehart Publishers.

Sartre, Jean-Paul. 1956. *Being and Nothingness: An Essay on Phenomenological Ontology*. Hazel Barnes (trans). New York: Philosophical Library.

Schechner, Richard. 2014. *Performed Imaginaries*. New York: Routledge.

Schneider, Rebecca. 1997. *The Explicit Body in Performance*. London and New York: Routledge.

Scott, David. 1995. Colonial Governmentality. *Social Text* 43, 191–220.

Scottee. 2013. The Worst of Scottee – Crowd Funding. www.youtube.com/watch?v=UMRQtklm7gM, accessed 19 March 2017.

Sedgwick, Eve Kosofsky. 1997. *Novel Gazing*. Durham, NC: Duke University Press.

Seidman, Steven. 1997. *Difference Troubles: Queering Social Theory and Sexual Politics*. Cambridge: Cambridge University Press.

Seymour, Gayle M. 1997. Simeon Solomon and the Biblical Construction of Marginal Identity in Victorian England. *Journal of Homosex*uality 33: 3–4, 97–119.

Shakespeare, Tom and Nicholas Watson. 2002. The Social Model of Disability: An Outdated Ideology? *Research in Social Science and Disability* 2, 9–28.

Shakespeare, Tom, Kath Gillespie-Sells and Dominic Davies (eds). 1996. *The Sexual Politics of Disability: Untold Desires*. London: Cassell.

Sharot, Tali. 2011. The Optimism Bias. *Current Biology* 21: 23, R941–R945.

Sharot, Tali, Christoph W. Korn and Raymond J. Dolan. 2011. How Unrealistic Optimism is Maintained in the Face of Reality. *Nature Neuroscience* 14: 11, 1475–9.

Shaw, Peggy. 2011. On Being an Independent Solo Artist (No Such Thing), in Jill Dolan and Peggy Shaw (eds) *A Menopausal Gentleman: The Solo Performances of Peggy Shaw*. Ann Arbor: University of Michigan Press.

Shildrick, Margrit. 2009. *Dangerous Discourses of Disability, Subjectivity and Sexuality*. London: Palgrave Macmillan.

Shuttleworth, Ian. 2010. Ursula Martinez: My Stories, Your Emails, The Pit, London. *Financial Times*, 3 February.

Sierz, Aleks. 2001. 'The element that most outrages': Morality, Censorship and Sarah Kane's Blasted, in Edward Malcolm Batley and David Bradby (eds) *Morality and Justice: The Challenge of European Theatre*. Amsterdam: Rodopi.

Sierz, Aleks. 2016. Iphigenia in Splott, National Theatre. www.sierz.co.uk/reviews/iphigenia-in-splott-national-theatre/, accessed 22 April 2017.

Simmel, Georg. 1971. *On Individuality and Social Forms*. Donald Levine (ed.) Chicago and London: University of Chicago Press.

Skeggs, Bev. 2005. The Making of Class and Gender through Visualizing Moral Subject Formation. *Sociology* 39: 5, 965–82.

Smith, Lacey Baldwin. 1999. *Fools, Martyrs, Traitors: The Story of Martyrdom in the Western World*. Evanston: Northwestern University Press.

Smith, Lacey Baldwin. 2008. Can Martyrdom Survive Secularization? *Social Research* 75: 2, 435–60.

Smith, Lise. 2010. Eddie Ladd in Ras Goffa Bobby Sands/ The Bobby Sands Memorial Race at The Place. LondonDance. http://londondance.com/articles/reviews/ras-goffa-bobby-sands-the-bobby-sands-memori-2933/, accessed 19 March 2017.

Snediker, Michael. 2009. *Queer Optimism: Lyric Personhood and Other Felicitous Persuasions*. Minneapolis: University of Minnesota Press.

Softley, Robert. 2011. Your Body Survey. www.surveymonkey.com/r/bodysurvey?sm=59 NU9PpUfy4fAeHHJ51Im5npZMIPMLjgXokGzxQeVJg%3D, accessed 24 April 2017.

Softley, Robert. 2012. If These Spasms Could Speak. www.ifthesespasmscouldspeak.com/, accessed 1 January 2017.

Soleimanpour, Nassim. 2011. *White Rabbit, Red Rabbit*. Unpublished script.

Solomon, Simeon. 1908. A Vision of Love Revealed in Sleep, in Thomas Bird Mosher (ed.) *The Bibelot*. Portland: T. B. Mosher. Available at archive.org/details/bibelot00ferggoog, accessed 22 May 2017.

Sontag, Susan. 1977. *On Photography*. London: Penguin Books.

Sothern, Matthew. 2007. You Could Truly Be Yourself If You Just Weren't You: Sexuality, Disabled Body Space, and the (Neo)Liberal Politics of Self-Help. *Environment and Planning D: Society and Space* 25: 1, 144–59.

Spring, Alexandra. 2015. Adrienne Truscott: Nudity is a Very Inexpensive and Effective Costume. *Guardian*. www.theguardian.com/stage/2015/jan/14/adrienne-truscott-nuditys-a-very-inexpensive-and-effective-costume, accessed 22 May 2017.

Stacey, J. 2014. Wishing Away Ambivalence. *Feminist Theory* 15: 1, 39–49.

Stacey, Jackie and Mary Bryson. 2012. Queering the Temporality of Cancer Survivorship. *Aporia* 4: 1, 5–17.

Stephens, Elizabeth. 2015. Bad Feelings. *Australian Feminist Studies* 30: 85, 273–82.

Stern-Gillet, Suzanne. 1987. The Rhetoric of Suicide. *Philosophy & Rhetoric* 20: 3, 160–70.

Steuter, Erin and Deborah Wills. 2009. Discourses of Dehumanization: Enemy Construction and Canadian Media Complicity in the Framing of the War on Terror. *Global Media Journal* 2: 2, 7–24.

Stone, Deborah. 1984. *The Disabled State*. Philadelphia: Temple University Press.

Surkis, Judith. 2009. Tanja Ostojić's European Border Work, in Tanja Ostojić and Marina Gržinić (eds) *Integration Impossible? The Politics of Migration in the Artwork of Tanja Ostojić*. Berlin: argobooks.

Swain, Margaret Byrne. 2009. The Cosmopolitan Hope of Tourism: Critical Action and Worldmaking Vistas. *Tourism Geographies* 11: 4, 505–25.

Szalwinska, Maxie. 2010. Ursula Martinez: Naked Ambition. *Independent*. www.independent.co.uk/incoming/ursula-martinez-naked-ambition-1879678.html, accessed 10 April 2017.

Terry, David P. 2006. Once Blind, Now Seeing: Problematics of Confessional Performance. *Text and Performance Quarterly* 26: 3, 209–28.

Thomas, Günter. 2009. Witness as a Cultural Form of Communication, in Paul Frosh and Amit Pinchevski (eds) *Media Witnessing: Testimony in the Age of Mass Communication*. London: Palgrave Macmillan.

Thompson, Selina. 2016. Race Cards, in *Forest Fringe: The First Ten Years*. London: Oberon Books.

Thompson, Selina. 2017. *Life is No Laughing Matter*. issuu.com/deminandhra/docs/mental_illness__performance_and_a_d, accessed 9 May 2017.

Tomlinson, Barbara. 2010. *Feminism and Affect at the Scene of Argument: Beyond the Trope of the Angry Feminist*. Philadelphia: Temple University Press.

Tomrley, Corinna. 2016. Shoot The Sissy. *Loverboy Magazine*. www.loverboymagazine.com/shoot-the-sissy/, accessed 6 May 2017.

Trueman, Matt. 2013. Review: The Future Show, Battersea Arts Centre. http://matttrueman.co.uk/2013/01/review-the-future-show-battersea-arts-centre.html, accessed 16 May 2017.

Trueman, Matt. 2016a. Iphigenia in Splott: Gary Owen's Protest Letter to a Hard-Hearted State. *Guardian*. www.theguardian.com/stage/2016/jan/28/iphigenia-in-splott-gary-owen-interview-protest-letter-to-a-hard-hearted-state, accessed 11 April 2017.

Trueman, Matt. 2016b. Edinburgh Review: (I Could Go on Singing) Over the Rainbow (Summerhall). WhatsOnStage.com. www.whatsonstage.com/edinburgh-theatre/reviews/i-could-go-on-singing-festival-fringe-summerhall_41603.html, accessed 6 May 2017.

Tyler, Imogen. 2006. Welcome to Britain: The Cultural Politics of Asylum. *European Journal of Cultural Studies* 9: 2, 185–202.

Tyler, Imogen. 2008. 'Chav Mum Chav Scum'. *Feminist Media Studies* 8: 1, 17–34.

United Solo. 2016. Online Application Form. http://unitedsolo.org/submit/, accessed 22 March 2017.

Videkanić, Bojana. 2009. Postidentity and the Aesthetics of Affect in the Work of Tanja Ostojić. *Kultura* 125, 98–106.

Wacquant, Loïc J. D. 1995. The Pugilistic Point of View: How Boxers Think and Feel about Their Trade. *Theory and Society* 24: 4, 489–535.

Wagg, Rosemary. 2013. Breathe For Me. Dialogue. www.welcometodialogue.com/Breathe-For-Me.html, accessed 25 April 2017.

Wagg, Stephen. 2011. *Because I Tell a Joke or Two: Comedy, Politics, and Social Difference*. London and New York: Routledge.

Waldrep, Shelton. 2004. *The Aesthetics of Self-Invention: Oscar Wilde to David Bowie*. Minneapolis: University of Minnesota Press.

Walsh, Fintan. 2010a. *Male Trouble: Masculinity and the Performance of Crisis*. Basingstoke and New York: Palgrave Macmillan.

Walsh, Fintan (ed.). 2010b. *Queer Notions: New Plays and Performances from Ireland*. Cork: Cork University Press.

Walsh, Fintan. 2012. *Theatre & Therapy*. Basingstoke: Palgrave Macmillan.

Walsh, Fintan. 2016. *Queer Performance and Contemporary Ireland: Dissent and Disorientation*. London: Palgrave Macmillan.

Walters, Ben. 2014. Interview: Ben Walters Dicks Around with Scottee and Talks about The Worst Of… Run Riot. www.run-riot.com/articles/blogs/interview-ben-walters-dicks-around-scottee-and-talks-about-worst-of…, accessed 19 March 2017.

Warr, Tracey. 2005. Dear Body: Endurance and Performance, in *Endurance Festival Catalogue*. Birmingham: VIVID.

Warren, John T. 2008. Performing Trauma: Witnessing *BALL* and the Implications for Autoperformance. *Text and Performance Quarterly* 28: 1–2, 183–7.

Weaver, Abi. 2013. Backpages 23.2. *Contemporary Theatre Review* 23: 2, 249–64.

Weinstein, Neil D. 1980. Unrealistic Optimism about Future Life Events. *Journal of Personality and Social Psychology* 39: 5, 806–20.

Wendell, Susan. 2001. Unhealthy Disabled: Treating Chronic Illnesses as Disabilities. *Hypatia* 16: 4, 17–33.

Werner, Alfred. 1960. The Sad Ballad of Simeon Solomon. *The Kenyon Review* 22: 3, 392–407.

Who, Stewart. 2015. Interview: Franko B. http://stewartwho.com/interview/franko-b/, accessed 23 March 2017.

Wicker, Tom. 2012. White Rabbit, Red Rabbit. *Exeunt Magazine*. http://exeuntmagazine.com/reviews/white-rabbit-red-rabbit/, accessed 3 March 2017.

Wicker, Tom. 2016. How to Get Spotted at Edinburgh, Theatre's Transfer Window. *The Stage*. www.thestage.co.uk/advice/2016/get-spotted-edinburgh-theatres-transfer-window/, accessed 25 March 2017.

Wiegman, R. 2014. The Times We're In: Queer Feminist Criticism and the Reparative 'Turn'. *Feminist Theory* 15: 1, 4–25.

Williamson, Judith. 2003. Sexism with an Alibi. *Guardian*. www.theguardian.com/media/2003/may/31/advertising.comment, accessed 10 April 2017.

Wyver, Kate. 2016. Feature: Walking: Holding – Why We Need Radical Softness Now. *A Younger Theatre*. www.ayoungertheatre.com/feature-walking-holding-why-we-need-radical-softness-now/, accessed 6 May 2017.

Yates, Daniel B. 2013. The Worst of Scottee. *Exeunt Magazine*. http://exeuntmagazine.com/reviews/the-worst-of-scottee/, accessed 19 March 2017.

Young, Jock. 1999. Cannibalism and Bulimia: Patterns of Social Control in Late Modernity. *Theoretical Criminology* 3: 4, 387–407.

Youngs, Ian. 2013. Playwright Nassim Soleimanpour Sees His Own Play. BBC News, 26 February. www.bbc.co.uk/news/entertainment-arts-21577030, accessed 19 March 2017.

Zare, Bonnie and Lily S. Mendoza. 2012. 'Mail-Order Brides' in Popular Culture: Colonialist Representations and Absent Discourse. *International Journal of Cultural Studies* 15: 4, 365–81.

Zerihan, Rachel. 2010. Revisiting Catharsis in Contemporary Live Art Practice: Kira O'Reilly's Evocative Skin Works. *Theatre Research International* 35: 1, 32–42.

Zetter, Roger. 2007. More Labels, Fewer Refugees: Remaking the Refugee Label in an Era of Globalization. *Journal of Refugee Studies* 20: 2, 172–92.

Ziarek, Ewa Płonowska. 2008. Bare Life on Strike: Notes on the Biopolitics of Race and Gender. *South Atlantic Quarterly* 107: 1.

Žižek, Slavoj. 1999. *The Ticklish Subject: The Absent Centre of Political Ontology*. London: Verso.

INDEX

Note: page numbers in *italic* refer to photographs and 'n' after a page number indicates the number of a note on that page.